Empire's Nature

Empire's Nature

Mark Catesby's New World Vision

EDITED BY AMY R. W. MEYERS &

MARGARET BECK PRITCHARD

FOREWORD BY GRAHAM S. HOOD &

EDWARD J. NYGREN

Published by the Omohundro Institute

of Early American History and Culture

& the Colonial Williamsburg Foundation,

Williamsburg, Virginia, by the

University of North Carolina Press,

Chapel Hill and London

The Omohundro Institute of Early American History and Culture is sponsored jointly by the College of William and Mary and the Colonial Williamsburg Foundation.

On November 16, 1996, the Institute adopted the present name in honor of a bequest from Malvern H. Omohundro, Jr.

© 1998
The University of North Carolina Press

Set in Monotype Garamond type
by Keystone Typesetting, Inc.
Manufactured in the
United States of America
The paper in this book meets the guidelines
for permanence and durability of the
Committee on Production Guidelines for
Book Longevity of the Council on Library
Resources.
Library of Congress
Cataloging-in-Publication Data
Empire's nature : Mark Catesby's new world
vision / edited by Amy R.W. Meyers and
Margaret Beck Pritchard.
p.   cm.
Includes bibliographical references (p.   )
and index.
ISBN 0-8078-2459-3 (hardcover : alk. paper).
— ISBN 0-8078-4762-3 (pbk. : alk. paper)
1. Catesby, Mark, 1683–1749.   2. Catesby,
Mark, 1683–1749—Influence.   3. Natural
history—History—18th century.   4. Natural
history illustration—History—18th century.
I. Meyers, Amy R. W.   II. Pritchard,
Margaret Beck.   III. Catesby, Mark, 1683–
1749.   IV. Omohundro Institute of Early
American History & Culture.
QH31.C35E56   1998
508'.09'033—dc21   98-23257
                                          CIP

03   02   01   00   99   5   4   3   2   1

This book would not have been
possible without the generous gifts
of The Hollowell Foundation,
The Chipstone Foundation,
Mr. and Mrs. Richard Vieser,
Mr. Robert Hicklin, and, last but
not least, more than a dozen members
of the Catesby-Cocke family.

To Joseph & Nesta Ewan

Foreword

Completed in 1747, Mark Catesby's *Natural History of Carolina, Florida, and the Bahama Islands* is the foundation on which rests the incredibly rich history of British and American nature illustration of the eighteenth and early nineteenth centuries. Although Catesby was subsequently eclipsed in reputation by naturalist artists such as John James Audubon, his importance to the development of Anglo-American scientific illustration remains considerable. Catesby's close observation and direct representation of plant and animal life during two trips to the southern American colonies in the second and third decades of the eighteenth century were the basis for the 220 etchings that comprise his monumental study, a publication greatly admired by both learned and aristocratic communities when it first appeared and of lasting influence on the field in the two and a half centuries since.

A new opportunity to evaluate Catesby's contributions to the development of art, natural history, and scientific observation was afforded by the decision of The Royal Library, Windsor Castle, to exhibit selections of his original watercolors that have resided there since they were purchased by George III in 1768. Long shielded from destructive light by being bound into volumes, the watercolors have now been removed from their bindings, conserved, and made available for exhibition.

These beautifully fresh watercolors have provided us with new insights into Catesby's subtle and often gentle artistry as well as shown us how he combined forms from individual sheets to create the etchings that he knew would be his final statements, his monuments.

The extended traveling display of more than fifty of Catesby's original watercolors—at The Museum of Fine Arts, Houston, Texas (the American organizer of the exhibition); The Huntington Library and Art Collections, San Marino, California; The DeWitt Wallace Gallery at Colonial Williamsburg, Virginia; The Telfair Museum of Art, Savannah, Georgia; and The Queen's Gallery, London—has also stimulated scholars to study Catesby's work in greater depth than heretofore possible and to place it in that wider context it has long deserved.

Two young scholars, Amy R. W. Meyers, Curator of American Art at The Huntington, and Margaret Beck Pritchard, Curator of Maps, Prints, and Wallpaper at Colonial Williamsburg, conspired to bring their insights and enthusiasms into fruitful collaboration with Fredrika J. Teute, editor of publications at the Omohundro Institute of Early American History and Culture (sponsored by the College of William and Mary and Colonial Williamsburg), to produce both this volume of scholarly essays and a public symposium based on it. To the scholars of art, culture, natural history, and science who eagerly responded to the infectious enthusiasm of these two young curators, we are grateful for the reappraisals of Catesby's work, delicate artistic genius, thoughtful meditations, and curious investigations into the seemingly boundless wealth of natural creations in the New World.

To Her Majesty Queen Elizabeth II and the staff at The Royal Library, Windsor; to Peter C. Marzio and his staff at The Houston Museum of Fine Arts; to the talented staffs at The Huntington, Colonial Williamsburg, and The Telfair; to Ronald Hoffman and his staff at the Institute, we are deeply grateful. Above all, we applaud the dedication and hard work of Amy Meyers, Margaret Pritchard, and Fredrika Teute in bringing this volume with its wealth of insights and information into being.

Edward J. Nygren
Director of Art Collections
The Huntington Library, Art Collections, and Botanical Gardens

Graham S. Hood
Vice President, Retired, Collections and Museums;
Carlisle H. Humelsine Curator
The Colonial Williamsburg Foundation

Acknowledgments

It has been exactly 250 years since Mark Catesby completed his *Natural History of Carolina, Florida, and the Bahama Islands*. Since that time his prints have been well known to scholars and collectors, particularly in the American South. Only a privileged few, however, have been able to view the original works that Catesby executed in preparation for his monumental undertaking. We are consequently deeply grateful to Henrietta McBurney, Deputy Curator of the Print Room at The Royal Library, Windsor Castle, and to her colleague, Theresa-Mary Morton, Curator of Exhibitions, for organizing the traveling exhibition *Mark Catesby's "Natural History" of America: The Watercolors from the Royal Library, Windsor Castle*. Their efforts have allowed a selection of Catesby's original works to be placed on view at four institutions across the United States and one in London and have also provided many scholars with an opportunity to formulate new ideas about Catesby's approach to his scientific studies, including scholars contributing to *Empire's Nature: Mark Catesby's New World Vision*.

There are numerous individuals at each of the three institutions involved with the publication of *Empire's Nature* to whom we are indebted for support and assistance. At the Omohundro Institute of Early American History and Culture we would like to thank Ronald Hoffman, director, for his support for both this collection of essays and the symposium based on it that was held in Williamsburg in February 1998. To Gil Kelly, managing editor, and James Horn, visiting editor of publications, we are extremely grateful.

At The Huntington Library, Art Collections, and Botanical Gardens and at The Colonial Williamsburg Foundation, we appreciate having the opportunity to host The Royal Library's exhibition. For their encouragement and support for the exhibition and for this collection of essays, we are indebted to Edward J. Nygren, Director of the Art Division at The Huntington, and to Graham S. Hood, retired Vice President, Collections, and Carlisle H. Humelsine Curator, at Colonial Williamsburg. At Colonial Williamsburg we would also like to thank Jan Gilliam for compiling the index to this volume, and Hans Lorenz, Craig McDougal, and Tracey Stecklin for their assistance with photography.

This publication would not have been possible without the generous funds provided by The Hollowell Foundation, The Chipstone Foundation, Mr. and Mrs. Richard Vieser, Mr. Robert Hicklin, and numerous members of the Catesby-Cocke family.

Finally, we wish to express our deepest appreciation to Fredrika J. Teute, editor of publications at the Institute, for her thoughtful input and patient perseverance. Her contributions were invaluable, and without her this publication would not have been possible.

Amy R. W. Meyers
Curator, American Art
The Huntington Library, Art Collections, and Botanical Gardens

Margaret Beck Pritchard
Curator of Prints, Maps, and Wallpaper
The Colonial Williamsburg Foundation

Contents

Illustrations

Chronology of Mark Catesby (New Style)

1683
    April 3. Born to John and Elizabeth Jekyll Catesby of Sudbury,
        Suffolk, probably at Castle Hedingham, Essex (Mar. 24, 1682,
        O.S.).
1712
    April 23. Arrives in Virginia, accompanying sister Elizabeth and her
        two children, to stay with Elizabeth's husband, Dr. William Cocke,
        physician and adviser to Lt. Gov. Alexander Spotswood in
        Williamsburg.
    May 21. Stays at Westover, seat of William Byrd, for three weeks.
    September. Returns to Westover; with Byrd, meets Spotswood at
        Pamunkey Indian town.
1714
    Travels to West Indies, primarily Jamaica.
1719
    October. Returns to England.
1720
    May 11. Travels to London to meet English botanist William Sherard.
    October 19. Proposal addressed to Catesby to fund travel to America.
1722
    February. Departs for America.
    May 23. Arrives in South Carolina.
1723
    January 4. At home of Alexander Skene.
    February. At Newington, seat of Joseph Blake.
    March 19. Travels eighty miles on way to Fort Moore
        (near present-day Augusta).
    July–mid-September. Around Fort Moore.
    September. Returns to Charleston for winter.
1724
    Spring and summer. In piedmont region above Fort Moore.
    August. Back in Charleston.
    September 3. Journeys again into the country.
1725
    January. Travels to Bahamas, staying with George Phenney.

1726

Returns to England. Works on *The Natural History,* supplements income by working as horticulturist at Thomas Fairchild's nursery and, after Fairchild's death in 1729, under Stephen Bacon, until 1733. About this time begins tuition in etching under Joseph Goupy.

1729

Issues "Proposals," prospectus to publish *The Natural History,* about this time.

May 22. Invited to meeting of Royal Society; first twenty plates of *Natural History* now completed.

1730

January 8. Attends meeting of Royal Society; perhaps presents second section of *The Natural History.*

March. Likely living in Hoxton (perhaps until mid-decade), certainly in 1731 or 1732, when title page of *The Natural History* printed.

1731

January. Publication of third part of *Natural History* noted in *Gentleman's Magazine.*

December. Indicates in letter that fourth part of *Natural History* is completed.

1732

November 23. Presents fifth section of *Natural History* to Royal Society.

1733

Begins work as horticulturist for Christopher Gray's nursery in Fulham.

February 1. Nominated to become fellow of Royal Society.

April 26. Elected fellow of Royal Society.

1735

January. Sixth section of *The Natural History* presented to Royal Society.

December. Asked by Royal Society to review Linnaeus's *Systema Naturae* but declines.

1735–1736

Meets Georg Dionysius Ehret.

1737

Provides etching for Gray's *Catalogue of American Trees and Shrubs.*

1740

Initiates correspondence with John Bartram.

Circa 1740–1741. Living in Fulham.

1743

May 5, 12. Delivers paper, "State and Conditions of the Indian in America," to Royal Society.

May 19. Delivers paper, "The Manner of Making Tarr and Pitch in Carolina," to Royal Society.

June 23. Delivers paper, on "method used in Carolina for the striking of Sturgeon according to the practice of the Indians," to Royal Society.

December 15. Presents tenth section of *Natural History* to Royal Society.

1744

April 12. Cosponsors George Edwards for membership in Royal Society.

1746

December 6. Brings Dr. John Mitchell to meeting of Royal Society.

1747

March 5. Presents paper, "Of Birds of Passage," to Royal Society.

July 2. Presents completed Appendix of *Natural History* to Royal Society.

October 2. Marries Elizabeth Rowland.

1748

Extract from "Of Birds of Passage" published in *Gentleman's Magazine*.

June 9. Recommends Dr. John Mitchell for membership in Royal Society.

1749

April 6. Recommends James Oglethorpe for membership in Royal Society.

Autumn. Completes work for *Hortus Britanno-Americanus*.

December 23. Dies.

1754

Second edition of *Natural History* revised and published by George Edwards.

1763

Hortus Britanno-Americanus published.

1767

Second edition of *Hortus* published, as *Hortus Europae Americanus.*

1768

Watercolors by Catesby purchased by George III for £120.

1771

Third edition of *Natural History* published.

Empire's Nature

Amy R. W. Meyers & Margaret Beck Pritchard

INTRODUCTION:

TOWARD AN UNDERSTANDING

OF CATESBY

An exceptional array of material survives from the life of the English naturalist Mark Catesby (1682–1749)—from correspondence, drawings, annotated botanical specimens, prints, and publications to the living descendants of plants that he introduced into English and American gardens. When considered collectively, this material attests with extraordinary clarity to the importance of natural science in the formation of the British Empire during the first half of the eighteenth century. Although Catesby's life has been charted and his standing as the author of the first major illustrated natural history of the British colonies in the Americas has long been recognized, the full spectrum of his activities and productions has not been addressed in relation to the broader social, economic, and cultural contexts of which he was a part. It is the purpose of the five essays that constitute *Empire's Nature: Mark Catesby's New World Vision* to examine the naturalist's life and work in terms of the interests of the various, overlapping realms—communities—in which he functioned, particularly as those interests related to the extension of British concerns throughout North America and the Caribbean. The picture of Catesby that emerges, in light of Britain's colonial enterprise, is multifaceted and rich, albeit still fragmented. Let it be a prelude to a more extensive investigation of Catesby's life and work as they illuminate the links between the study of nature and the building of empire.

A Short Biography

Although little evidence survives concerning Catesby's education as a naturalist, enough is known about his youth to sketch the relationships that might have stimulated his "early inclination to search after plants and other productions of nature."[1] As the youngest son and the fourth of five surviving children of John Catesby and Elizabeth Jekyll, Catesby was raised in the town of Sudbury, in Suffolk, East Anglia. His family was of local prominence on both sides; his father was a lawyer who served as mayor of Sudbury several times, and his mother descended from a family of lawyers and well-known antiquaries. Why Catesby did not follow his male kin into the law is unknown—but he clearly fashioned an interest in botany after that of his maternal uncle, Nicholas Jekyll, whom he often visited as a child. Jekyll, like many affluent gentlemen of the period, created a botanic garden on the grounds of his house at Castle Hedingham, and he shared an antiquarian interest in the history of the region with the renowned naturalist John Ray (1627–1705), who lived close by in Black Notley, near Braintree. It was probably Jekyll who introduced the young Catesby to Ray, establishing a relationship that Catesby would later describe to his colleague, George Edwards (1694–1773), as playing a pivotal role in the early development of his interest in the natural world.

Through his uncle, Catesby also came to know the apothecary Samuel Dale (1659–1739), who served as a collector for Ray during the great naturalist's final years.[2] Catesby's collegial relationship with Dale would last many decades and would eventually provide Catesby with an entrée into an important community of botanists, horticulturists, and gardeners in and around London who would offer him his first opportunity to exercise his talents as a naturalist professionally.

In 1712, Catesby took advantage of an opportunity to move beyond his youthful studies of local flora and fauna and observe the natural productions of a region of the globe almost unexamined by European naturalists. In that year he accompanied his sister, Elizabeth, to Williamsburg, the

---

1. Mark Catesby, *The Natural History of Carolina, Florida, and the Bahama Islands: Containing the Figures of Birds, Beasts, Fishes, Serpents, Insects, and Plants: Particularly the Forest-Trees, Shrubs, and Other Plants, Not Hitherto Described, or Very Incorrectly Figured by Authors; Together with Their Descriptions in English and French; to Which, Are Added Observations on the Air, Soil, and Waters: with Remarks upon Agriculture, Grain, Pulse, Roots, etc.; to the Whole Is Prefixed a New and Correct Map of the Countries Treated Of,* 2 vols. (London, 1731–1743 [1729–1747]), I, v. Unless otherwise noted, all factual information regarding Catesby's life and work derives from George Frederick Frick and Raymond Phineas Stearns, *Mark Catesby: The Colonial Audubon* (Urbana, Ill., 1961); and Amy R. W. Meyers, "'The Perfecting of Natural History': Mark Catesby's Drawings of American Flora and Fauna," in Henrietta McBurney, *Mark Catesby's "Natural History" of America: The Watercolors from the Royal Library, Windsor Castle* (London, 1997).

2. Dale, who was a respected botanist in his own right, published his highly regarded *Pharmacologia* in 1693 and contributed frequently to the Royal Society's *Philosophical Transactions*.

capital of the Virginia colony, where her husband, Dr. William Cocke, had established a medical practice. As a supporter of Lieutenant Governor Alexander Spotswood, Cocke was quickly becoming an important force in Virginia politics, and he introduced Catesby to some of the wealthiest and most powerful landowners and merchants of the colony, including William Byrd II (1674–1744), John Custis (1678–1749), and Thomas Jones (1701–1758).[3] Like English gentlemen across the Atlantic, these men developed horticultural interests, testing the possibility of cultivating a wide range of practical and ornamental plants in botanic gardens that they established on their estates.[4]

Catesby's acquaintance with Byrd seems to have played an especially important role in furthering the young naturalist's impulse to study and draw the natural productions of Virginia. Byrd was both an important member of the Council of Virginia and a fellow of the Royal Society. He had inherited an interest in science from his father, who, as one of Virginia's great entrepreneurial landowners of the late-seventeenth century,

3. For a more thorough discussion of the society into which Catesby entered when he came to Virginia, see Frick and Stearns, *Mark Catesby,* 12–16.

4. The history of horticultural experimentation in eighteenth-century English gardens is just beginning to be written. Two works, Mark Laird's *Flowering of the Landscape Garden: English Pleasure Grounds, 1720–1800* (Philadelphia, 1999); and Douglas Chambers, *The Planters of the English Landscape Garden: Botany, Trees, and the Georgics* (New Haven, Conn., 1993), are the most comprehensive works to broach the subject to date. A study focusing specifically on the horticultural concerns of eighteenth-century American gardeners has yet to be published, but helpful information can be found in more general works, such as U. P. Hedrick, *A History of Horticulture in America to 1860* (1950; rpt. Portland, Oreg., 1988); and Stephen A. Spongberg, *A Reunion of Trees: The Discovery of Exotic Plants and Their Introduction into North American and European Landscapes* (Cambridge, Mass., 1990). An invaluable resource, presently in preparation, is the database and publication *Keywords in American Landscape Design,* edited by Therese O'Malley, Elizabeth Kryder-Reid, and Anne Helmreich and sponsored by the Center for Advanced Study in the Visual Arts at the National Gallery of Art, Washington, D.C. Raymond Phineas Stearns, *Science in the British Colonies of America* (Urbana, Ill., 1970), remains an important source of information on early American horticulture, and more specific details concerning Custis, Jones, and Byrd can be found in Frick and Stearns, *Mark Catesby;* E. G. Swem, ed., *Brothers of the Spade: Correspondence of Peter Collinson, of London, and of John Custis, of Williamsburg, Virginia, 1743–1746* (1948; rpt. Worcester, Mass., 1949); and Penelope Hobhouse, *Gardening through the Ages: An Illustrated History of Plants and Their Influence on Garden Styles—from Ancient Egypt to the Present Day* (New York, 1992). William Byrd's horticultural concerns are placed in the context of his broader scientific interests in Margaret Beck Pritchard and Virginia Lascara Sites, *William Byrd II and His Lost History: Engravings of the Americas* (Williamsburg, Va., 1993).

had sought to exploit the colony's natural resources. William Byrd I (1652–1704) had supported the work of the naturalist John Banister (1650–1692), who drew and described Virginia's flora and fauna and hoped to prepare the colony's first natural history. When Banister was accidentally killed on a survey organized by his patron, his books were incorporated into the large library on natural science the elder Byrd was assembling at his country seat, Westover.[5]

William Byrd II hoped to find someone to complete the work that Banister had begun before his unfortunate demise. Byrd was clearly delighted by Catesby's desire to study Virginia's animals and plants, and he entertained the naturalist at Westover, benefiting from his advice on how to put his garden "into a better fashion."[6] In September 1712, Catesby accompanied Byrd on a trip to the Pamunkey Indian town on the Pamunkey River, a venture that allowed the two men to examine the natural productions of the country together. Their shared interest in scientific observation allowed them to establish a lasting friendship that they would continue through correspondence when Catesby returned to England in 1719. When Catesby finally produced his *Natural History,* he referred to Byrd several times in the text and listed Byrd as a subscriber to the publication.[7]

Although Catesby did not formulate a systematic plan to study Virginia

5. Joseph Ewan and Nesta Ewan have outlined the relationship that developed between Byrd and Banister, tracing the fate of Banister's library as it was incorporated into Byrd's; see *John Banister and His Natural History of Virginia, 1678–1692* (Urbana, Ill., 1970), 130–134.

6. William Byrd II, diary entry for June 5, 1712, in Louis B. Wright and Marion Tinling, eds., *The Secret Diary of William Byrd of Westover, 1709–1712* (Richmond, Va., 1941), 540. In 1697 William Byrd II requested that the Royal Society "think of a Fitt person to be sent over to Virginia in order to make observations and Descriptions of all the Naturall productions of those parts and to write the History thereof" (as quoted in Raymond Phineas Stearns, "James Petiver: Promoter of Natural Science, c. 1663–1718," American Antiquarian Society, *Proceedings,* LXII [1952], 304, from Journal-Book, IX, 70, Royal Society, London). Over the course of his life, Byrd would himself contribute toward a picture of the colony's natural history, sending specimens and a series of letters to the Royal Society and authoring several lengthy manuscripts that included his observations.

7. Byrd's admiration for Catesby's illustrated work prompted him, in 1737, to solicit the naturalist to supply pictures of flora and fauna for his own *History of the Dividing Line.* Based on Byrd's experiences with the Virginia Boundary Commission, of which he was appointed head in 1728, this manuscript was circulated among a small circle of Byrd's English friends in 1736. However, the *History* was not printed until after Byrd's death, and it is not known whether Catesby actually executed any drawings for the work. See Frick and Stearns, *Mark Catesby,* 92–93. For a detailed discussion of Catesby's involvement with Byrd's publishing ventures, see Pritchard and Sites, *William Byrd II,* 4, 27, 57, 106, 156, 159, 161, 162, 164, 165.

flora and fauna on his forays across Virginia's tidewater plantations and up the James River, he did refine his techniques of field research and draw animals and plants he considered native to the colony. In addition, he collected live plant materials and specimens for Samuel Dale and the experimental horticulturist Thomas Fairchild (1667–1729), whose nursery at Hoxton, in Shoreditch, on the outskirts of London, would become well known for its stock of American flora.[8] Following the example of the English physician Sir Hans Sloane (1660–1753), who had published the first volume of *A Voyage to the Islands Madera, Barbados, Nieves, St. Christophers, and Jamaica* in 1707, Catesby also traveled to Jamaica, in 1714, to examine the natural productions of the West Indies.

When he returned to England in 1719, Catesby brought with him an extensive knowledge of New World flora and fauna as well as an impressive cache of drawings of animals and plants never before seen by English naturalists. He discussed with Samuel Dale the prospect of returning to America to pursue further study, and Dale, who was struck by his work, introduced him to the celebrated botanist William Sherard (1659–1728) for the purpose of gaining support for the venture. The appeal was made at a propitious moment, since Sherard was then revising Gaspard Bauhin's *Pinax Theatri Botanici* (Basel, 1623), one of the most important and extensive late-Renaissance publications dealing with the taxonomy and classification of the plants of the globe. He was also involved in the development of an extensive collection of exotic flora at his brother James's estate at Eltham, in Kent. Catesby's knowledge of New World plants, along with the possibility of a second American voyage to collect and draw, were consequently of great appeal. In discussing Catesby's planned return to the colonies in a letter to the gardener and horticulturist Dr. Richard Richardson, Sherard revealed his admiration for Catesby's work, remarking, "He designs and paints in water colours to perfection."[9]

8. Fairchild, who, as an experimental botanist, was the first to raise a scientific hybrid (*Dianthus caryophyllus* x *barbatus*), amassed the largest collection of aloes and succulents in England and became the major supplier of American exotics to English gardens (see Chambers, *Planters of the English Landscape Garden,* 141–144).

9. As quoted in Frick and Stearns, *Mark Catesby,* 19, from Richardson Correspondence, c. 4, fol. 23, Radcliffe Trust, Bodleian Library, Oxford University. Unless otherwise noted, information on the life of Sherard has been drawn from Hermia Newman Clokie, *An Account of the Herbaria of the Department of Botany, in the University of Oxford* (London, 1964), 17–30. For a discussion of Bauhin's *Pinax,* see Wilfrid Blunt and Sandra Raphael, *The Illustrated Herbal* (New York, 1994), 162.

Indeed, Sherard would serve as the primary catalyst moving his colleagues to underwrite Catesby's second expedition. In 1720, just as he was becoming acquainted with Catesby's work, Sherard was beginning to collaborate with a group of colleagues with commercial, scientific, and political interests in the Americas to send a naturalist to draw the flora and fauna of that region of the globe. In September of that year, Sherard informed Richardson that Eleazar Albin (fl. 1713–1759), who had just published *A Natural History of English Insects* (London, 1720), had been approached to go "to Carolina to paint there in the summer months, and in the winter to paint in The Carribbe ilands."[10] However, Albin, who had begun his career as a drawing master and who admitted that he produced his first work of natural history because he was drawn to the beauty of butterflies, remained primarily an armchair naturalist and declined the offer. Catesby was then approached, and plans quickly materialized for the venture.[11]

When the Royal Society met on October 19, 1720, Colonel Francis Nicholson (1655–1728), who was departing to serve as first royal governor of South Carolina, offered Catesby a pension of twenty pounds per year "to Observe the Rarities of the Country for the uses and purposes of the Society." Nicholson proposed that he would give Catesby a ten-pound advance at the start of each year and that he would continue to support the naturalist throughout his tenure as governor. Although the Royal Society did not grant monetary support for Catesby's expedition, Nicholson's statement suggests that the institution approved of the venture, lending it the credibility necessary to secure other backers. The tactic proved ef-

10. As quoted in Frick and Stearns, *Mark Catesby,* 18, from Richardson Correspondence, c. 4, fol. 19.

11. In the preface to his *Natural History of English Insects* (London, 1720), Eleazar Albin states that it was specifically the aesthetic appeal of butterflies that initially propelled him to undertake his entomological studies. Albin numbered William Byrd II among his students. During an extended stay in London, which began in 1715, Byrd sought drawing lessons from the naturalist-artist, and he probably commissioned Albin to create illustrations for a projected natural history of North America that was never published. Copper plates, however, seem to have been engraved for the book, presumably based on drawings by Albin. Seven of these plates are now part of the Rawlinson Collection in the Bodleian Library, at Oxford University, and ten prints that relate stylistically to the plates (seven were struck from them) reside at Holkham Hall, in Norfolk, England. Catesby might also have produced drawings that were engraved on these plates, but the postulation is somewhat more speculative. See Pritchard and Sites, *William Byrd II,* for a thorough discussion of the illustrations for this publication.

fective, and Sherard and Nicholson were joined by ten other patrons, including Sir Hans Sloane; Charles Du Bois (1656–1740), treasurer of the East India Company; James Brydges, first duke of Chandos (1673–1744, duke from 1719); and the physician and collector Dr. Richard Mead (1673–1754).[12]

At the beginning of 1721, James Brydges began to press Catesby to travel to Africa in the service of the Royal African Company, but Sherard expressed objections to the change in plans; and Governor Nicholson, who had already advanced his first ten pounds, wished to have his money returned if the venture to America were abandoned. By the turn of the year, Brydges—and Catesby—were evidently swayed, and Catesby embarked for Charleston, South Carolina, in February 1722.[13]

Upon Catesby's arrival, he became acquainted, through the help of Nicholson, with the most affluent and powerful members of Carolina society, including the Moores, Blakes, Bulls, Johnsons, Warings, and Skenes. Many of these planters were invested in western land speculation, which was quickly centralizing control of the high country, and they were eager to learn more about the natural productions that might be extracted for

12. Nicholson as quoted in Frick and Stearns, *Mark Catesby*, 18, from Royal Society, Council Minutes, II, 324, Royal Society, London. Catesby published this list of his primary backers in his "Proposals, for Printing an Essay towards a Natural History of Florida, Carolina, and the Bahama Islands: Containing Figures of Birds, Beasts, Fishes, Serpents, Insects and Plants; Particularly, the Forest-Trees, Shrubs, and other Plants, Not Hitherto Described, Remarkable for Their Rarity, Virtues, etc. . . ." (London, ca. 1729) and in his Preface to *The Natural History*. On the development of the botanical collections by James Brydges at Cannons, see Blanche Henrey, *No Ordinary Gardener: Thomas Knowlton, 1691–1781*, ed. A. O. Chater (London, 1986), 22, 25, 43–45, 112, 190. On Dr. Richard Mead's scientific interests and his activities as a patron of natural history illustration, see *Dictionary of National Biography*, s.v. "Mead, Richard"; Dr. Mattley, "Some Account of the Life and Writings of the Late Dr. Richard Mead," *Gentleman's Magazine, and Historical Chronicle*, XXIV (1754), 510–515; and Gerta Calmann, *Ehret: Flower Painter Extraordinary: An Illustrated Biography*, 1st U.S. ed. (New York, 1977), 65, 68, 128. Support for Catesby's *Natural History* was also given by the Right Honourable Edward Harley, earl of Oxford; the Right Honourable Thomas Parker, earl of Macclesfield; the Right Honourable John Perceval, earl of Egmont; Sir George Markham, bart.; and Sir Henry Goodrick, bart.

13. When Catesby recommitted himself to a North American expedition, Brydges apparently considered Albin for the Royal African Company venture. Hans Sloane seems to have suggested, however, that Albin was not "skill'd enough in the Nature of Drugs, Plants, and Spices" to serve the company's interests, and Brydges asked Sloane to recommend another artist with greater botanical expertise. See James Brydges, first duke of Chandos, to Hans Sloane, Dec. 7, 1721, Sloane MS 4046, fol. 156, British Library, London.

profit from the frontier. Catesby's planned expeditions were consequently of great interest, and the naturalist found himself a welcome ally of the ruling elite. He learned much about the flora and fauna of the lowcountry from investigations on the estates of his friends, and he aided them in the formation of their gardens by supplying them with plants that he discovered on his frontier expeditions as well as European seeds and bulbs that he requested from English colleagues.[14]

In order to observe, draw, and collect the widest range of plants and animals possible, Catesby developed a seasonal program for his expeditions, described in a letter to William Sherard:

> My method is never to be twice at [the same] place in the same season for if in the sp[ring] I am in the low Country [in the Sum]mer I am [at] the hea[ds] of rivers the next Summer in the low countrys, so alternating that in 2 Years [I visit] the two different parts of the Country.[15]

Although he was not always as systematic as he intended, Catesby did manage to survey a large section of the colony. From 1723 to 1725, he made three expeditions to Fort Moore, which he described as "a frontier garrison 140 miles up the Country." Located on the Savannah River, near the future site of Augusta, Georgia, the fort was part of a ring of defenses established to protect British traders and settlers in the Carolina backcountry against attack from Indians loyal to the French, who had gained power over the southern interior. Catesby described the surrounding territory as "one of the Sweetest Countrys I ever saw." He recommended the development of the region, comparing it favorably with Kent—one of the most productive agricultural counties of England of the day.[16] Although the passage containing this recommendation is one of the few landscape descriptions included by Catesby in his correspondence or prepared for *The Natural History,* it shares with almost all of Catesby's prose an emphasis on the beauty and potential productivity of the most remote western reaches of Carolina.

Botany remained the primary focus of Catesby's research, and with an

---

14. Catesby, *Natural History,* I, 31, 35, 43. For a discussion of Catesby's interactions with the most powerful families of lowcountry South Carolina, see Frick and Stearns, *Mark Catesby,* 23.

15. Mark Catesby to William Sherard, Jan. 16, 1723/4, Sherard Letters, CCLIII, 174, Royal Society, London.

16. Ibid., May 10, 1723, Sh. 169, 171; William Page, ed., *The Victoria History of the County of Kent* (London, 1908), I, 457.

eye toward the utilization of natural resources he noted that he "had principally a Regard to Forest-Trees and Shrubs" because of their use "in Building, Joynery, Agriculture . . . Food and Medicine." Catesby justified the attention he next paid to birds on several grounds. He believed these creatures to be the most numerous and beautiful of animals and thought them to have a closer "relation to the Plants on which they feed on and frequent" than any other type of organism.[17] The interdependence of flora and fauna would be of fundamental concern to Catesby in the creation of the etchings for his *Natural History;* but as is revealed by the large group of preparatory drawings for his publication (in the collection of the Royal Library, Windsor Castle), Catesby often executed separate studies of individual organisms in the field, combining them only later as he worked on the final compositions for his published prints.

Knowing he might visit the Bahama Islands later in his trip, Catesby decided to postpone an extensive investigation of marine life until he reached Carolina. And, although he hoped to draw mammals, he concluded that North American species were nearly identical to those of Europe, and so he portrayed only those that had not yet been illustrated or described by other naturalists.[18] He took a particular interest in snakes, attempting to illustrate as many species as possible, but he resisted portraying the numerous insects he encountered for fear that he might be diverted from drawing organisms from his primary categories of concentration.

In the field, Catesby faced the task of collecting and drawing for his patrons as well as for his own purposes. Above all, he seems to have valued his plan to publish a natural history of the regions he was exploring, and he repeatedly complained to his supporters that their demands were imperiling the success of his own publication. Catesby considered purchasing a slave to help him with his work, but he does not seem to have done so.[19] On his trips to the high country he reports, "I employ'd an *Indian* to carry my Box, in which, besides Paper and Materials for Painting,

17. Catesby, *Natural History,* I, ix.

18. Ibid., I, ix–x.

19. Catesby to Sherard, Apr. 6, 1724, Sherard Letters, CCLIII, 176; Catesby to Hans Sloane, Aug. 15, 1724, Sloane MS 4047, fol. 212.

Before beginning his first expedition to Fort Moore in 1722/3, Catesby wrote several times to William Sherard regarding the potential purchase of a "Negro Boy" to aid him with his work. However, he never reported on the slave again. Catesby to Sherard, Dec. 9, 1722, Mar. 19, 1723, Sherard Letters, CCLIII, 165, 169 (for a discussion of this correspondence, see Frick and Stearns, *Mark Catesby,* 24).

I put dry'd Specimens of Plants, Seeds, etc.—as I gather'd them." Catesby continued to feel the need for assistance, and, in planning an expedition with the Charleston physician Thomas Cooper to "the remoter parts of the Continent perticularly Mexico" in 1724, he asked Sherard and Sloane for the help of a painter from London, Paris, or Amsterdam to aid him in assembling "No Mean Collection of Unknown Productions." However, this request went unanswered, and in 1725 Catesby set out on a somewhat less ambitious expedition to the Bahama Islands.[20] As the guest of Governor George Phenney, he explored the island of New Providence, also visiting Eleuthera, Andros, and Abaco. Catesby concentrated his artistic efforts on the portrayal of fishes and crustaceans as well as plants, executing a set of drawings he would later reproduce in *The Natural History*. With this work completed, he then departed for London, where he would begin to produce his publication.

While the production of this ambitious illustrated book would be the primary focus of Catesby's life for the next twenty years, it would not exclude other professional activities associated with the study of the natural world. Indeed, Catesby's expertise as a horticulturist supported him while working on the publication and allowed him continuing access to American plants (and occasional animals) that he wished to illustrate and discuss. First at Thomas Fairchild's nursery, where he worked until 1733, and then at Christopher Gray's nursery in Fulham, he formalized his professional standing as an importer of American flora and was in contact with a community of experimental horticulturists and gardeners with whom he shared observations.[21] His position at the nurseries also allowed

20. Catesby, *Natural History*, I, viii; Catesby to Sherard, Aug. 16, 1724, Sherard Letters, CCLIII, 178; Catesby to Sloane, Aug. 15, 1724, Sloane MS 4047, fol. 212.

As Frick and Stearns note, Catesby's correspondence with his English colleagues appears to end with the set of letters regarding his expedition to the Bahamas (see Frick and Stearns, *Mark Catesby,* 32). However, specimens sent by Catesby from the islands are contained in the Sherardian Herbarium in the Plant Sciences Department at Oxford University, indicating that Catesby might have continued to receive support for his collecting activities from Sherard and others during his stay in the West Indies.

21. Catesby remained at Fairchild's, working for Stephen Bacon, for several years after Fairchild's death in 1729. He then moved to Christopher Gray's nursery, where he probably maintained his own garden. The gardener Thomas Knowlton would write of his colleague's achievement, "The infinity of new Trees, Shrubs, etc. now of late introduced by him into the Garden from North America fill me with the greatest Wonder and Astonishment imaginable" (as quoted in Henrey, *No Ordinary Gardener,* ed. Chater, 209, from Thomas Knowlton to Richard Richardson, July 18, 1749, Richardson Correspondence, c. 11, fols. 57–58).

him to market *The Natural History* to an interested audience with ease, and in 1729 he advertised in the publication's prospectus that potential subscribers might visit him at Fairchild's to examine the preparatory drawings for the plates. Catesby's work as a horticulturist continued throughout his career, and toward the end of his life he authored a manuscript in which he demonstrated his special knowledge of American plants that might be cultivated successfully in English soil. Although *Hortus Britanno-Americanus* was published posthumously, in 1763, the book makes clear Catesby's desire for professional recognition as one of the most important experimental horticulturists of his generation.[22]

Catesby extended his circle of associates with an interest in natural science and furthered his own studies in the field through his involvement with the Royal Society. Contact with society fellows also aided him significantly in the promotion of his *Natural History*.[23] He drew for the society's Register Book and participated in meetings of the fellows, where he occasionally delivered papers on New World flora and fauna. Indeed, at a fellows' meeting on March 5, 1746/7, he delivered the first accurate account of bird migration, in a paper entitled "Of Birds of Passage," subsequently published in the *Philosophical Transactions*.[24]

22. Mark Catesby, *Natural History,* I, ix; Catesby, *Hortus Britanno-Americanus; or, A Curious Collection of Trees and Shrubs, the Produce of the British Colonies in North America; Adapted to the Soil and Climate of England; with Observations on Their Constitution, Growth, and Culture, and Directions How They Are to Be Collected, Packed up, and Secured during Their Passage* (London, 1763). As Frick and Stearns note, the prints in this publication are miniaturized, simplified, and somewhat altered versions of the botanical illustrations that appear in *The Natural History* (*Mark Catesby,* 43, 45, 68–69).

23. According to David Brigham's research, many of the subscribers to Catesby's *Natural History* were members of the Royal Society, including William Bateman, Richard Boyle, William Byrd, Charles Calvert, William Cavendish, Thomas Coke, Peter Collinson, James Douglas, Martin Folkes (vice president, 1722/3; president, 1741–1753), Henry Hare, Thomas Herbert, Charles Lennox, Smart Lethieullier, George Markham (not a subscriber, but a supporter of Catesby's second expedition), Richard Mead (on council 1705, 1707–1754; vice president, 1717), Philip Miller (on council periodically), John Montagu, Cromwell Mortimer (secretary, 1730–1752), Francis Nicholson, Thomas Osborne, Robert James Petre, Isaac Rand, Richard Richardson, Jacob de Castro Sarmento, John Senex, William Sherard (not a subscriber, but a supporter of Catesby's second expedition), Hans Sloane (secretary, 1693–1712; president, 1727–1741), and Thomas Willoughby.

24. Mark Catesby, "Of Birds of Passage," Royal Society, *Philosophical Transactions,* XLIV (1747), 435–444. As Frick and Stearns indicate, on Nov. 10, 1732, at the behest of Cromwell Mortimer, the council of the Royal Society resolved to employ Catesby to provide illustrations for the *Register Book* (*Mark Catesby,* 39, from Royal Society, Council Minutes, III,

The Quaker wholesale linendraper Peter Collinson (1693/4–1768) was often Catesby's host at society meetings, and it was as Collinson's guest on February 1, 1732/3, that Catesby was nominated a fellow. Collinson, who was deeply engaged in the study of the natural world, also worked as a middleman, moving plants and animals gathered by naturalists and collectors across the globe into English gardens, menageries, and cabinets of curiosity.[25] Having received specimens and other materials from Catesby when he was on his Carolina expedition, Collinson helped to support the publication of *The Natural History* by lending Catesby "considerable Sums of Money . . . without Interest." In addition, Collinson introduced Catesby to colonial naturalists and collectors he had not encountered on his own expeditions, who sent him new specimens for inclusion in his work.[26]

---

118). For a detailed discussion of Catesby's involvement with the society and a synopsis of his publications in the *Philosophical Transactions,* see Frick and Stearns, *Mark Catesby,* 37–44, 47, 63, 87.

25. The nomination occurred at approximately the same time that the first volume of *The Natural History* was completed and was undoubtedly made in recognition of the publication's importance.

A substantial historical discussion of Collinson's role in the communities of natural science of Europe and America has yet to be written. His involvement in the world of science can be charted only through historical surveys, such as Stearns, *Science in the British Colonies of America,* and through the biographical accounts of other naturalists, gardeners, and estate builders who became his friends and colleagues (see, for example, Frick and Stearns, *Mark Catesby;* Pritchard and Sites, *William Byrd II;* Gerta Calmann, *Ehret: Flower Painter Extraordinary*). It is through Collinson's voluminous correspondence that the clearest picture can be gained of his important position as an encourager of the study of natural history and as a disseminator of seeds, plants, and specimens throughout English and Continental gardens and scientific cabinets (see, for example, Henrey, *No Ordinary Gardener,* ed. Chater; Swem, ed., *Brothers of the Spade;* Edmund Berkeley and Dorothy Smith Berkeley, eds., *The Correspondence of John Bartram, 1734–1777* [Gainesville, Fla., 1992]).

26. The most important colonial contact Collinson secured for Catesby upon his return was John Bartram (1699–1777), the Pennsylvania farmer and naturalist who, acting through Collinson, became the preeminent supplier of North American seeds to English gardeners in the mid-eighteenth century (see Edmund Berkeley and Dorothy Smith Berkeley, *The Life and Travels of John Bartram: From Lake Ontario to the River St. John* [Tallahassee, Fla., 1982]). In 1740, Catesby proposed to send the parts of his *Natural History* to Bartram in exchange for American plants (William Darlington, *Memorials of John Bartram and Humphry Marshall* [1844; rpt. N.Y., 1967], 319–320). Catesby used plants grown from seeds sent to him and to Collinson by Bartram to create images of new species for *The Natural History* (see Frick and Stearns, *Mark Catesby,* 90; Darlington, *Memorials of Bartram and Marshall,* 136, 141, 166, 255; and Catesby, *Natural History,* II, 56, 71, 72, 73, 98, Appendix, 1, 4, 5, 6, 15, 17).

Catesby presented Collinson with a copy of *The Natural History,* colored beautifully by his

Collinson continued to commission Catesby to draw, and he bound a selection of Catesby's pictures into the second volume of his own copy of *The Natural History*. These drawings were grouped with works by Georg Dionysius Ehret (1710–1770), the most renowned naturalist-artist of the day, who began to help Catesby with his publication in the mid-1730s. Collinson also collected a number of Catesby's smaller studies, which he included in a collection of drawings by a group of Catesby's associates, including Ehret, Albin, George Edwards, and the young Philadelphia naturalist William Bartram (1739–1823), whose father, John, was one of Catesby's most important American correspondents.[27]

Along with Collinson, a number of the formal patrons of Catesby's venture to Carolina helped support the publication of *The Natural History*. Catesby found a particularly powerful ally in Sir Hans Sloane, who served as president of the Royal Society from 1727 to 1741—almost the entire period during which Catesby was at work on his publication. Sloane asked Catesby to contribute to his extensive collection of natural history illustrations, and he allowed Catesby to copy drawings of American animals and plants by other artists for reproduction in *The Natural History*. By virtue of his position at the Royal Society, his standing as a collector, and his patronage of naturalists and naturalist-artists, Sloane's support of Catesby's publication carried special weight, helping Catesby to procure additional subscriptions to his *Natural History*.[28]

---

own hand, in return for Collinson's financial support of the publication. On one of the endpapers, Collinson acknowledged the role he had played in helping to bring the book forth but, with characteristic humility, identified himself, as patron, only as an anonymous "Friend." Collinson's copy of Catesby's publication is now in the collection of the earl of Derby, at Knowsley Hall.

27. This set of drawings, which was bound into an album after 1820, is also in the collection of Lord Derby at Knowsley Hall.

For a discussion of Ehret's involvement with Catesby's publication, see Meyers, " 'The Perfecting of Natural History,' " 23–24, McBurney, section 3, "Plants," 131, and catalog entries 17, 28, 41, 43, 46, 47, 48, 49, 50, 51, 52, in McBurney, *Mark Catesby's "Natural History" of America*.

28. On the value of Sloane's support, see David Brigham, "Mark Catesby and the Patronage of Natural History in the First Half of the Eighteenth Century," below. Drawings by Catesby commissioned by Sloane are now part of the Sloane collections of the British Library and the British Museum. For drawings in the British Library collection, see Add. MSS 5267, 5271. For drawings in the Department of Prints and Drawings at the British Museum, see Add. MS 5283. For a discussion of Catesby's license to copy from Sloane's collection, see Meyers, " 'The Perfecting of Natural History,' " 20–22, 25, McBurney, "Note

The original promoter of the Carolina expedition, William Sherard, also took an interest in the publication that Catesby wished to produce from his venture. Until his death in 1728, the eminent botanist helped Catesby with the Latin designations for the plants to be included in *The Natural History*—designations probably based on specimens and drawings Catesby had sent Sherard from the Americas.[29]

While Catesby was working to establish his place in the scientific community of London and to promote *The Natural History,* he was spending time organizing his drawings and notes to determine the structure and scope of his publication. Although he considered sending his drawings to Amsterdam or Paris to be copied by the finest engravers of the day, he was deterred from doing so by the prohibitive cost. He called, instead, upon the printmaker and drawing master Joseph Goupy (ca. 1698–ca. 1782) to teach him how to etch his own plates. Ultimately, this decision proved advantageous, since it allowed Catesby to maintain complete intellectual and aesthetic control over the printing of his images.[30]

Deciding which drawings to reproduce and the order in which the prints should appear was a complex process that Catesby left somewhat open-ended so that he could incorporate entries on new animals and plants as they came to his attention. Indeed, in his "Proposals, for Printing an Essay towards a Natural History," Catesby did not project a final length for the publication. Although he stated that every four months he would issue a part, consisting of twenty plates with accompanying descriptions, he failed to keep to this schedule. As Catesby wrote the text to accompany his images, he had it translated into French by "a doctor of physic, and a Frenchman born," whose modesty would not permit Catesby to mention his name.[31] This French translation was printed in columns paralleling the

---

on the Natural History Albums of Sir Hans Sloane," 33, section 2, "Fishes," 73, section 3, "Crabs, Turtles, and Corals," 87, section 4, "Snakes, Lizards, and Frogs," 95, section 5, "Mammals," 115, section 6, "Insects," 123, catalog entries 5, 6, 16, 19, 23, 26, 36, 37, 38, 39, in McBurney, *Mark Catesby's "Natural History" of America.*

29. Catesby acknowledged Sherard's help in naming the plants he had depicted in the Preface, *Natural History,* I, xii.

30. Catesby discussed the circumstances that led him to enlist Goupy's aid as an etching teacher (ibid., xi). For an insightful assessment of Goupy's career and his approach to printmaking, see Bruce Robertson, "Joseph Goupy and the Art of the Copy," Cleveland Museum of Art, *Bulletin,* LXXV (1988), 355–382.

31. Catesby, *Natural History,* I, xii. There has been some speculation that Catesby himself was the translator.

English text, allowing a Continental audience unable to read English access to Catesby's narrative.

Catesby decided to sell his book by subscription, offering each part, either uncolored, for one guinea, or hand-colored and printed on imperial stock, for two. This method of publication not only broadened Catesby's potential base of sales, since it allowed subscribers to pay for the book over time; it also gave the naturalist the years he needed to etch his plates and write the accompanying text.[32] Catesby presented each of the eleven parts to the Royal Society as it was printed. He gave parts 1–5, constituting volume I, between 1729 and 1732 (although the title page bears the date 1731). These first one hundred plates portray birds often associated with plants from the same environment (particularly those upon which the birds characteristically feed).

Presuming that Catesby followed standard publication practices of the day, he included the introductory materials to volume I with the last part issued for that volume.[33] These materials included the title page, dedication, list of 155 subscribers, and the "Preface." Catesby chose to dedicate the volume to Queen Caroline (1683–1737), wife of George II, who had reviewed his drawings and agreed to lend royal patronage to his work. Not

32. On prices, see Catesby, "Proposals." On Catesby and subscription publication, see Brigham, "Mark Catesby and the Patronage of Natural History in the First Half of the Eighteenth Century," below.

Although Catesby began to release the parts of *The Natural History* in 1729, the dates of publication, as printed on the title pages of the first and second volumes, are 1731 and 1743, respectively. The Appendix did not appear until 1747.

33. This presumption is based, in part, upon conversations with Thomas V. Lange, associate curator of the Early Printed Book at the Henry E. Huntington Library, Art Collections, and Botanical Gardens. Catesby's contemporaries also provide evidence of the release of the introductory materials that accompanied each volume. On June 28, 1733, Thomas Knowlton reported to Samuel Brewer: "Mr. Catesby has published his fifth part [of *The Natural History*] with a preaface" (as quoted in Henrey, *No Ordinary Gardener,* ed. Chater, 135–136, from Knowlton Correspondence, Botany Library, Natural History Museum, London).

Since "The List of Encouragers" (subscription list) that is bound into most sets before the "Preface" bears the catchword "Preface" at the bottom of the verso and the signature of the "Preface" carries the signature mark "B," both the "List" and the "Preface" must have been issued together with the last set of plates included in this volume. Regarding the map and essay on Carolina that are generally bound into the second volume, Knowlton again wrote to Brewer on Dec. 15, 1741: "Mr. Catesby will very soon publish his Last part to compleat the 2 vollm. wherein youl have a map of Caralina with a Long Disertation [on] Birds of the East and West Indies etc with severall of the most curious plants in America" (quoted in Henrey, *No Ordinary Gardener,* ed. Chater, 199, from Knowlton Correspondence).

only was the queen's name perfectly suited to the subject of Catesby's publication, but her well-known interest in gardening accorded with Catesby's own (and, perhaps more important, with that of most of his subscribers).[34]

Catesby presented the parts that constitute volume II to the Royal Society between 1734/5 and 1743 and the Appendix in 1747. The prints in this volume depict a wide range of fauna, including fishes, crustaceans, reptiles, amphibians, mammals, and insects. Like the birds in volume I, many of these animals are shown with plants from their habitats. A number of botanical illustrations are included as well.

In most bound sets of *The Natural History,* volume II begins with a map of Britain's colonial holdings in the Americas, which Catesby adapted from Henry Popple's *Map of the British Empire in America with the French and Spanish Settlements Adjacent Thereto* (London, 1733).[35] The map is usually followed by Catesby's "Account of Carolina and the Bahama Islands," a detailed description of the climate, soil, and topography of the regions he explored as well as information on animals and plants not illustrated as

34. Queen Caroline was a leading advocate of the naturalistic style of landscape design that was replacing the more formal style that had long been in vogue in English gardens. In the 1720s, she retained Charles Bridgeman to create an important new park at Richmond, and in the early 1730s she had him proceed with alterations to the park at Kensington. She also employed William Kent to design garden structures at Richmond, including a gothic library called Merlin's Cave and a grotto called the Hermitage. As a botanist and nurseryman, Catesby would have been aware of the queen's interest in gardening and for that reason might have wished to honor her by dedicating his *Natural History* to her. (It should be noted that Charles Bridgeman's wife, Sarah, became a subscriber to Catesby's publication.) For more detailed information on the queen's gardening activities, see R. L. Arkell, *Caroline of Ansbach: George the Second's Queen* (London, 1939), 247–249; John Dixon Hunt and Peter Willis, eds., *The Genius of the Place: The English Landscape Garden, 1620–1820* (London, 1975), 26; David Jacques, *Georgian Gardens: The Reign of Nature* (London, 1983), 22, 27, 31; Ronald King, *Royal Kew* (London, 1985), 41–51; Edward Malins, *English Landscaping and Literature, 1660–1840* (London, 1966), 87.

The dedication of Catesby's first volume to Queen Caroline might also have alluded politically to the appropriation by the crown of a significant portion of Carolina through the acquisition of the properties of seven of the eight proprietors of the colony in 1729—the year in which Catesby issued the first part of his publication.

35. Catesby did not identify Popple's map as the source for his own, but, as Frick and Stearns note, the naturalist and cartographer were probably acquainted and might have shared information on the southern colonies. Popple was a subscriber to *The Natural History,* and both men were fellows of the Royal Society. See Frick and Stearns, *Mark Catesby,* 71–72; Brigham, "Mark Catesby and the Patronage of Natural History in the First Half of the Eighteenth Century," below.

separate entries in the main body of *The Natural History*. Catesby also discusses various agricultural practices engaged in by peoples of different cultural backgrounds whom he encountered in Virginia and Carolina. And, based largely on John Lawson's *History of Carolina,* he describes the manners and customs of the peoples native to North America.[36] These prefatory materials helped to create a synthetic picture of the world inhabited by the animals and plants Catesby portrayed in his plates, emphasizing not only the complex relationships between animals and plants and their specific habitats but the human use that could be made of particular resources based on an understanding of these interrelationships.

By the time the last part of the second volume appeared, Queen Caroline had died, and so Catesby dedicated the work to Princess Augusta, wife of Frederick, prince of Wales. Like her mother-in-law, the princess was deeply interested in gardening—an interest she developed with Prince Frederick as they worked with the architect William Kent to plan the grounds of their country retreat, the White House, at Kew. Again Catesby sought the imprimatur of a royal gardener to validate his undertaking.[37]

The Reception of The Natural History *and Its Subsequent Fate*

As the parts of *The Natural History* were issued, the work became increasingly important as a reference for British and Continental naturalists who were attempting to order the natural world according to the ambitious taxonomic systems that characterized mid-eighteenth-century science. Carolus Linnaeus, Johann Friedrich Gronovius, John James Dillenius, and

36. A synopsis of "An Account" and discussion of Catesby's sources can be found in Frick and Stearns, *Mark Catesby,* 71–76. Catesby acknowledged that he based "Of the Indians of Carolina and Florida" on Lawson's work, arguing that, since he had shared many of Lawson's experiences, he could select important passages from his predecessor's account with particular discrimination. See Catesby, "An Account," *Natural History,* II, viii.

37. Even before Augusta's marriage to Frederick in 1736, the prince had become involved with the scientific world of London, which encouraged the introduction of exotic plants from around the globe—and particularly North America—into English gardens (King, *Royal Kew,* 58; John Brooke, *King George III* [London, 1972], 22). The couple began to use the White House in 1737, where they developed a substantial garden designed by William Kent (King, *Royal Kew,* 57). After Frederick's untimely death in 1751, Augusta continued the botanical pursuits that they had embarked on together, building a rich horticultural collection that would lay the groundwork for the Royal Botanic Gardens. See King, *Royal Kew,* 60–74; Miles Hadfield, *A History of British Gardening* (London, 1969), 230–231; John Watkins, *Memoirs of Her Most Excellent Majesty Sophia-Charlotte, Queen of Great Britain, from Authentic Documents* (London, 1819), 234–235.

Phillip Miller all drew extensively upon Catesby's pictures and descriptions of animals and plants to complete their taxonomic identifications of American species; and colonial naturalists, such as William Byrd II, John Clayton, Cadwallader and Jane Colden, and John and William Bartram, utilized Catesby's publication as a guide to their work in the field.[38]

Catesby's *Natural History* was reprinted, translated, and revised many times over the course of the eighteenth century, extending the publication's influence over an ever-widening audience.[39] Indeed, no comparable illustrated natural history of any part of the region that constituted Britain's colonial possessions in the Americas would be undertaken until after the American Revolution, when more specialized publications would begin to appear. Such works would include André Michaux's *Histoire des chênes de l'Amérique* (Paris, 1801), Alexander Wilson's *American Ornithology* (Philadelphia, 1808–1814), Thomas Say's *American Entomology* (Philadelphia, 1824–1828), and John James Audubon's *Birds of America* (Edinburgh and London, 1827–1838). Even these would be written and illustrated against the backdrop of Catesby's *Natural History*, although, by that time, explicit references to his work would be more critical than laudatory.

In fact, the appearance of specialized studies that competed with the drama and beauty of Catesby's work so eclipsed the standing of *The Natural History* that Catesby gained little recognition in the annals of the history of science during the first decades of the nineteenth century. Richard Pulteney's 1790 commemoration of Catesby's publication as "the most splendid of its kind that England ever produced," in *Historical and Biographical Sketches of the Progress of Botany in England,* was followed, over the next twenty years, by only a few brief assessments of Catesby's contributions. After that, his name fades considerably from the historical literature.[40]

No longer thought to be of significant value as a scientific reference work, Catesby's *Natural History,* along with his other publications, manuscripts, drawings, and preserved specimens, rested quietly in private and

---

38. On naturalists who referred to Catesby's *Natural History* for information on American flora and fauna, see Frick and Stearns, *Mark Catesby,* 56, 58, 60–61, 65, 67–68, 76–77, 80–81, 94, 97, 99–108.

39. On the publication history of *The Natural History,* see ibid., 100–103, 109–111.

40. See Richard Pulteney, *Historical and Biographical Sketches of the Progress of Botany in England . . .* (London, 1790), II, 247. See also Emmanuel Mendes da Costa, "Notes on Literati," *Gentleman's Magazine,* I (1812), 206; John Nichols, *Literary Anecdotes of the Eighteenth Century . . .* , 9 vols. (London, 1812–1815), VI, 78; John Nichols, *Illustrations of the Literary History of the Eighteenth Century,* I (London, 1817), 371–372.

institutional collections, treasured by bibliophiles, collectors, and antiquaries as rarities from the early period of colonial American science but neglected as artifacts meriting serious historical appraisal. As Alan Feduccia points out, the first major archival study of Catesby's life was not published until 1937, when Elsa Allen's "New Light on Mark Catesby" appeared in the *Auk*. In 1951, Allen also included an amplified version of the naturalist's biography in "The History of American Ornithology before Audubon," in the *Transactions* of the American Philosophical Society. Reflecting the trend toward specialization that only intensified over the course of one hundred years, Allen's assessments of Catesby's work focused primarily on his treatment of birds rather than the broad spectrum of interests that he had actually pursued. Nonetheless, Allen's research on Catesby's life served as the starting point for George Frederick Frick and Raymond Phineas Stearns as they embarked on a more encompassing, book-length study of the naturalist's career: *Mark Catesby: The Colonial Audubon*. Despite the ornithological emphasis of its title, this book was intended to "rescue Mark Catesby from undeserved oblivion," by making clear his contribution to botany and to various branches of zoology, such as herpetology and ichthyology, in addition to the study of birds.[41] The book treats Catesby's examination of the natural world as if it had been undertaken by the naturalist as an isolated pursuit, apart from other cultural concerns; yet, the authors' extensively researched exploration of Catesby's work was the first to illuminate the wide range of the naturalist's scientific interests, and, in so doing, it moved historians of science to begin to evaluate Catesby's role in the broad practice of natural history in England of the early eighteenth century as well as in colonial America.

In 1970, Stearns himself included Catesby as an important figure in his overarching study, *Science in the British Colonies of America,* and, in 1974, Frick collaborated with Joseph Ewan to reprint on a reduced scale, in black-and-white, all the plates of *The Natural History,* along with Catesby's "Preface" and "Account of Carolina and the Bahama Islands." These publications, which helped to resurrect Catesby's importance as a figure in the history of colonial American science, spurred a series of works examining Catesby's interactions with other naturalists of the day, including Joseph

41. See Alan Feduccia, ed., *Catesby's Birds of Colonial America* (Chapel Hill, N.C., 1985), preface; Elsa G. Allen, "New Light on Mark Catesby," *Auk,* LIV (1937), 349–363; Elsa Guerdrum Allen, "The History of American Ornithology before Audubon," American Philosophical Society, *Transactions,* n.s., XLI (1951), 387–391; Frick and Stearns, *Mark Catesby,* preface.

Kastner's *Species of Eternity,* published in 1977.[42] Kastner's study was the first to stress the importance of the production of visual images to the practice of natural history in America, and in this context his book defined Catesby's *Natural History* as a model for the work of several successive generations of American naturalists.

In the year succeeding the appearance of *A Species of Eternity,* David Scofield Wilson published *In The Presence of Nature,* which contained the first close reading of Catesby's published prints as cultural artifacts.[43] This self-consciously interdisciplinary work was part of a growing literature in American Studies that sought to analyze the concept of nature—and, in particular, the concept of wilderness—as having special meaning for Americans of European descent as they attempted to define their relationship to the continent they sought to inhabit. Whereas earlier studies of this kind mention Catesby only in passing, or not at all, Wilson devotes a third of his book to an appraisal of the naturalist's activities and productions: Catesby serves as the final case study in a group of three, the others being Jonathan Carver and John Bartram.[44] Wilson's close analysis of these men's works helped to elevate them to positions of eminence in the pantheon of intellectual leaders whose ideas were thought to have influenced the ways in which nature was conceived philosophically in colonial America as well as in Britain.

The Revival of Catesby's Reputation

Catesby was served well by Wilson, whose examination of Catesby's visual and textual interpretation of the natural productions in the Amer-

42. See Stearns, *Science in the British Colonies of America,* esp. 286–288, 314–325; Joseph Kastner, *A Species of Eternity* (New York, 1977), esp. 16–19. See also Mark Catesby, *The Natural History of Carolina, Florida, and the Bahama Islands,* ed. George Frick and Joseph Ewan (Savannah, Ga., 1974).

43. See David Scofield Wilson, *In the Presence of Nature* (Amherst, Mass., 1978), esp. 123–185.

44. Of earlier studies, see, for example, Henry Nash Smith, *Virgin Land: The American West as Symbol and Myth* (Cambridge, Mass., 1950); Hans Huth, *Nature and the American: Three Centuries of Changing Attitudes* (Berkeley, Calif., 1957); Leo Marx, *The Machine in the Garden* (Oxford, 1964). The attention that Wilson paid to Catesby should not be interpreted, however, as signaling a general rise in historical consciousness regarding the significance of the naturalist's study in the culture of his own day; thus, Gene Wise, in his introduction to Wilson's book: "Jonathan Carver, John Bartram, Mark Catesby—three rather undistinguished figures of the eighteenth century" (in Wilson, *In the Presence of Nature,* xiv).

icas illuminated, for example, the naturalist's originality as a student of environmental relationships. As we have already noted, Catesby himself spoke in the "Preface" to his *Natural History* of his interest in the association between birds and the plants that they frequent for food and shelter— an interest reported in much of the literature addressing his life, from Elsa Allen's essays to Alan Feduccia's detailed study of each print depicting birds in *The Natural History*. However, none of those earlier discussions equals Wilson's attempt to analyze the compositional structure of Catesby's images as a means the naturalist used to explicate the intricate interconnections that bind the organic world as a closely knit matrix.

In analyzing Catesby as a significant contributor to eighteenth-century thought about the natural world, Wilson introduced the naturalist as a figure worthy of the attention of cultural historians as well as of historians of science. And, although the detailed examination of the rhetorical structure of Catesby's work was not immediately pursued, Catesby did begin to be named as a character of some importance in the history of American exploration and settlement, particularly as written by the western historian William Goetzmann. Arguing for Catesby's place among a group of eighteenth-century naturalist-artists whose depictions of the natural productions on the frontier helped to promote a developmental understanding of the creation, Goetzmann writes:

> These scientific illustrators not only stressed the brilliantly colored and exotic specimens of nature; they also portrayed ecological relationships. Very often these artists were well in advance of more specialized scientists in this area of endeavor. They depicted animals, plants, and people in their "natural surroundings" or "native habitats" in relationship to one another because they, like the mapmakers and geographers, were interested in the interrelationship of all terrestrial phenomena. Thus the artists and mapmakers, in collaboration with the explorer-scientists, helped make the growing, proliferating, changing tree of life the central metaphor of the age.[45]

Although Goetzmann's thesis remains vague, he intimates that there was something unique about the visual process of analysis employed by artist-naturalists to portray the natural productions of the frontier that allowed them to contribute in a special way to the interpretation of nature as a set

45. William H. Goetzmann, *New Lands, New Men: America and the Second Great Age of Discovery* (New York, 1986), 11.

of ever-changing organic and physical relationships, and he identifies Catesby as one of the first in a succession of these early developmental thinkers.[46]

From the mid-1970s through the 1980s, a number of art historians with concerns ranging beyond aesthetic valuation were becoming equally interested in the relationship between the act of visual representation and the examination of the natural world. A series of exhibitions and their accompanying catalogs pointed the way toward a better-developed examination of Catesby's work in terms of the visual rhetoric of science and hailed a broader cultural historical examination of his activities in relation to eighteenth-century attitudes toward the natural world.[47] In so doing, they far surpassed the cursory discussion of Catesby's work to be found in the lavishly illustrated antiquarian publications that, for many years, had served as the only sources of information on the place of pictures in the history of scientific image making.

While art historians interested in Catesby's published etchings were beginning to examine his illustrations in terms of the larger cultural context in which they were produced, garden historians interested in Catesby's activities in the shaping of the English and colonial American landscape were beginning to analyze his work from a similar perspective. Catesby's examination of American flora was already relatively well outlined in publications on the history of English and colonial American botany and horticulture, and from the 1950s on the naturalist's correspondence with other significant contributors (including John Custis, Peter Collinson, John Bartram, and Thomas Knowlton) was published in several important collections of letters. However, the rise of interest in the social and cultural history of the garden in the 1970s and 1980s resulted in a number of publications that began to insist on Catesby's standing as a major supplier of American plants to English gardens and to identify him as a notable influence on the character of colonial American gardens in the early eigh-

---

46. Ibid., 89–90.

47. See Martina R. Norelli, *American Wildlife Painting* (New York, 1975), for the Smithsonian Institution; Ella M. Foshay, *Reflections of Nature: Flowers in American Art* (New York, 1984), for the Whitney Museum of American Art; Edward J. Nygren, *Views and Visions: American Landscape before 1830* (Washington, D.C., 1986), for the Corcoran Gallery of Art. Published in 1990, Madeleine Pinault's *Le peintre et l'histoire naturelle* (Paris, 1990) was a study of the role of visual images in scientific research, based in part upon an exhibition, *Le dessin scientifique*, that Pinault organized at the Louvre in 1984.

teenth century.[48] In *The Pleasure Gardens of Virginia: From Jamestown to Jefferson*, Peter Martin discusses, for example, Catesby's relationship with the planters William Byrd II and John Custis in the creation of their horticultural collections, and he refers to the lasting power Catesby came to exert on the Virginia garden through his *Natural History*. Similarly, in *The Planters of the English Landscape Garden: Botany, Trees, and the Georgics,* Douglas Chambers cites Catesby as the primary source for the American plants cultivated by Archibald Campbell, third duke of Argyll, in his renowned experimental garden at Whitton in the 1720s. Chambers also notes Catesby's role as the provider of most of the American exotics made commercially available in England by the nurseryman Thomas Fairchild during the same period.[49] Yet, despite the emphasis placed on Catesby's importance in the transatlantic garden culture of the eighteenth century, the naturalist remains in these publications essentially a footnote. As in the art historical studies of natural history illustration mentioned above, which note Catesby's influence without fully analyzing his images, these garden histories

48. Important texts include, most extensively, Ann Leighton, *American Gardens in the Eighteenth Century* (Amherst, Mass., 1986); and also Hedrick, *A History of Horticulture in America*, 138, 139, 193; Frick and Stearns, *Mark Catesby,* 64–70, 86–87; Stearns, *Science in the British Colonies of America*, 286–288, 314–327; Alice M. Coats, *The Quest for Plants: A History of the Horticultural Explorers* (London, 1969), 52, 268–271, 273, 277, 332; Blanche Henrey, *British Botanical and Horticultural Literature before 1800 . . .* , 3 vols. (London, 1975), II, 275–277, 336, 348–350, 431; Sandra Raphael, *An Oak Spring Sylva: A Selection of the Rare Books on Trees in the Oak Spring Garden Library* (Upperville, Va., 1989), xxi–xxii, 8, 49, 52–56; Spongberg, *A Reunion of Trees*, 1, 20–27, 52, 129; James L. Reveal, *Gentle Conquest: The Botanical Discovery of North America, with Illustrations from the Library of Congress* (Washington, D.C., 1992), 7, 36–42, 49, 55, 57–58, 60, 75, 82; and Hobhouse, *Gardening through the Ages*, 197, 207, 208, 209, 211, 261, 262, 275, 277.

The publication of Catesby's correspondence with colleagues sharing an interest in horticulture, along with the mention of his name in the correspondence of other gardeners, began in the nineteenth century, with Darlington, ed., *Memorials of Bartram and Marshall,* and continued into this century with collections such as Swem, ed., *Brothers of the Spade,* 39, 48, 67, 70, 120, 154, 163–164, 169, 171, 173, 175–176, 179, 181; Henrey, *No Ordinary Gardener,* ed. Chater, 17, 22, 26–28, 114–142, 168–210, 293; and, extensively, Berkeley and Berkeley, eds., *Correspondence of Bartram.*

49. Peter Martin, *The Pleasure Gardens of Virginia: From Jamestown to Jefferson* (Princeton, N.J., 1991), xvii, 54, 56, 59–60, 66, 178, 195, 201–202, 210; Chambers, *Planters of the English Landscape Garden,* 201, 206. For a detailed discussion of Catesby's relationship to William Byrd II, see Pritchard and Sites, *William Byrd II,* 4, 27, 57, 106, 156, 159, 161–162, 164, 165.

acknowledge the significance of Catesby's activities as an experimental horticulturist without pursuing deep examinations of his work.

New Perspectives on Catesby

Three loosely associated projects, including the volume in hand, have initiated a more thorough, interdisciplinary exploration of Catesby's multifaceted activities as a scientific explorer, naturalist-illustrator, author, printmaker, gardener, and supplier of exotic plants. These projects were conceived in tandem, in the early 1990s, when initial plans were formulated by the Royal Library, at Windsor Castle, for the first exhibition of Catesby's watercolors of American flora and fauna since the 1730s, when Catesby himself displayed his drawings to a London audience of potential subscribers to his *Natural History*. The Royal Library, which houses 263 preparatory drawings by Catesby and his colleagues for *The Natural History*, was aware that few scholars had consulted these drawings in their studies of Catesby's published prints and that even fewer had considered the drawings in pursuing the broader history of scientific illustration. The Royal Library was also concerned about the physical condition of these works, which had been bound into albums shortly after Catesby's death. When funds for conserving the drawings were generously given by Mrs. Hiroko Usami, the disbinding of the albums provided the perfect opportunity to pursue plans for an exhibition that would illustrate to the scholarly world as well as to the general public the importance of Catesby's original compositions for his *Natural History*.

Curated by Henrietta McBurney, deputy curator of the Print Room at the Royal Library, this exhibition, *Mark Catesby's "Natural History" of America: The Watercolors from the Royal Library, Windsor Castle,* showcased fifty-two drawings from Windsor. Organized in conjunction with the Museum of Fine Arts, Houston, the exhibition traveled across the United States to four venues: the Huntington Library, Art Collections, and Botanical Gardens, San Marino; the Museum of Fine Arts, Houston; the DeWitt Wallace Gallery, Colonial Williamsburg; and the Telfair Museum of Art, Savannah. Finally, an English audience viewed it at the Queen's Gallery, London, in the fall of 1998. A fully illustrated catalog, published to accompany the exhibition, detailed the technical process by which Catesby transformed his field sketches of American flora and fauna into the first extensively illustrated natural history of the British colonies in the Americas, and it established through extensive analytical discussions the importance of his images as among the earliest to portray animals and plants in complex environmental relationships.[50]

A second project prompted by the conservation of the Windsor drawings and their exhibition has been the production of a full-scale color facsimile, published by Alecto Historical Editions. The press has utilized the stochastic printing process (whereby computer technolgy replicates tonal relationships with unprecedented accuracy), which has resulted in the finest reproductions of Catesby's drawings yet available. These excellent reproductions will stimulate scholars of the naturalist's work to make more extensive comparisons of the preparatory drawings for *The Natural History* with the published prints and texts. Such comparisons should shed new light on the complex intellectual and aesthetic decisions made by Catesby in producing *The Natural History* and should further illuminate his relationships with other naturalist-artists upon whose work he depended to complete his publication.[51]

The final project associated with the conservation and exhibition of the Royal Library's drawings has been the publication of this volume. This collection of essays is intended to complement the exhibition catalog by examining, from a variety of perspectives, the cultural forces that moved Catesby to pursue his work as a naturalist-artist and experimental horti-culturist with a special interest in American flora and fauna. It assesses the impact made upon Catesby's own objectives by the desires of the individuals and institutions that backed his expeditions and his collecting activities, the interests of the colonial communities that encouraged his forays into the field, the expectations of the subscribers to his *Natural History,* and the concerns of fellow nurserymen, gardeners, and estate owners who received plant materials from him both in England and in the colonies.

Considering Catesby's Own Objectives

An analysis of the influence of broader cultural forces on Catesby's activities must, ultimately, be based on an understanding of the naturalist's

50. During the same period, another set of drawings for Catesby's *Natural History,* from the Royal Library's collection, traveled to four venues in Japan, accompanied by a reduced version of the English catalog translated into Japanese.

51. These relationships with other naturalist-artists have been described in detail for the first time by Henrietta Ryan in her catalog entries in McBurney, *Mark Catesby's "Natural History" of America.*

own conception of his objectives. Since the production of his *Natural History* absorbed a major portion of his financial assets and the project received the greatest share of his intellectual attention, it is not surprising that Catesby chose to articulate the most coherent explanation of the development of his own interests in the "Preface" to the work. Indeed, Catesby begins the "Preface" by defining his book as the logical outcome of an extended search for the proper place—both geographically and socially—in which to satisfy his personal propensity to study nature. In his opening sentence he tells us that in his youth he had been "naturally bent" to "search after Plants, and other Productions in Nature" but that this "early Inclination" had been "much suppressed" by the distance of his home from London—"the Center of all Science." He goes on to suggest that the lack of opportunities and examples that characterized his youth continued to have a deleterious effect on his first expedition, to Virginia in 1712, to view flora and fauna "in their Native Countries; which were Strangers to *England*." He reports with shame that on this trip he "thought . . . so little of prosecuting a Design of the Nature of this Work, that in the Seven Years I resided in that Country . . . I chiefly gratified my Inclination in observing and admiring the various Productions of those Countries."[52] According to Catesby, only when he moved away from self-absorbed observation to engage in the more communal pursuit of supplying Samuel Dale with plant specimens and seeds did he make the important contacts in London society that would then advance him in his proper undertaking.

Catesby goes on to inform us that Dale "communicated" his plant specimens and observations to the "celebrated" botanist, William Sherard, who, Catesby reports, then

> favoured me with his Friendship on my Return to *England* in the Year 1719; and by his Advice, (tho conscious of my own Inability) I first resolved on this Undertaking, so agreeable to my Inclination.

Catesby believed that only by entering the proper sphere of influence could he ever be directed toward a project so perfectly suited to his native interests and desires: the production of his *Natural History*. And, as he quickly notes, this sphere of influence also determined the financial support necessary to "carrying the Design" of the project.[53]

Catesby's discussion of the importance of appropriate environment to

52. Catesby, *Natural History,* I, v.
53. Ibid., I, v–vi.

the full development of his interests parallels on a deeply personal level the picture of the natural world that he created through his pictures and his texts. The bearing of community on the welfare of animals and plants and the importance of organic relationships to the definition of flora and fauna as they are found in specific environments absorbed Catesby's attention both in the field and back in London as he crafted his *Natural History*. Indeed, Catesby's particular interest in how individual plants and animals survive transplantation from one location to another—either thriving in new physical settings and in relation to new life forms or diminishing in vigor—can be charted not only in *The Natural History* but in the paper on bird migration that he read before the Royal Society in March 1746/7.[54] As is evidenced by his correspondence and by the text of *Hortus Britanno-Americanus,* this interest was also the presiding force that drove his work as a horticulturist, leading him to experiment extensively with the introduction of American plants into English gardens and with the cultivation of flora from the farthest reaches of the frontier in the gardens of colonial planters.

Whether tracing the impact of various environmental relationships on his own career or on the health of an animal or plant, Catesby was fundamentally concerned with the effect of communal interaction on the well-being of the subject at hand. Although in the "Preface" to *The Natural History* he might track a consistent improvement in his own condition, based on his movement from one community to another, he does not always arrive at such encouraging conclusions for the plants and animals—or even peoples (from English colonists to native Americans and African Americans)—who figure as the subjects of his pictures and his texts. It is Catesby's complex conception of the nature and value of communal interaction for the whole of organic creation that serves as a common thread, uniting the essays in *Empire's Nature*.

The Essays

In the first essay, "Mark Catesby, a Skeptical Newtonian in America," Joyce E. Chaplin asserts that an understanding of Catesby's contribution to the study of natural history has been lost over time largely because the intellectual concerns of his own community of naturalists have not been well understood. Catesby self-consciously placed himself among the first

54. Mark Catesby, "Of Birds of Passage," Royal Society, *Philosophical Transactions,* XLIV (1747), 435–444.

generation of post-Newtonian natural philosophers who sought to hypothesize uniform laws of nature for nonmechanical phenomena.

At the same time, however, he was skeptical—though not dismissive—of this enterprise, since he found in America a world of violent, disorderly phenomena that he could not describe as functioning according to predictable tendencies. In that he looked for laws, he was a Newtonian, but his views of natural systems were too diffident and indeterminate to place him at the heart of a community of thinkers who were forming the boldest vision of the material world in the early eighteenth century.

Chaplin contends that, in part, Catesby's predisposition was related to a cultural politics that figured the New World as locus of exotica and tumult. Although as a naturalist he would often describe organisms and natural phenomena, as he observed them in the Americas, in terms of violent interchange, he would leave this interest in chaotic environmental relationships behind when, as a horticulturist, he sought to replant American flora in English gardens. Chaplin concludes that Catesby ultimately "wanted to create within England an American garden that was the opposite of an anarchic mangrove swamp"—a desire that drew upon "a long tradition of recreating humanity's original paradise, a garden that represented the harmony among creatures that antedated the Fall." Although Catesby might have thought that the Americas could never be fully tamed, he believed that "American products could be extracted . . . and naturalized in England" to create a pacific landscape. Indeed, it was in England that Catesby believed he could approximate, through the human arts of gardening, image making, and writing, a prelapsarian order that could never be discerned in the raw wilderness that was America.

Chaplin's essay thus clarifies Catesby's intellectual position within communities of natural philosophers. David Brigham expands on this undertaking, using Catesby's subscription list to *The Natural History* as the starting point from which to place the naturalist within a complex web of overlapping social networks, all with vested interests in his publication. "Mark Catesby and the Patronage of Natural History in the First Half of the Eighteenth Century" examines "the fluid network of labor, capital, and personalities that sustained the study of natural history." Through the close analysis of a broad spectrum of interrelated activities in which Catesby's 155 subscribers engaged, including gardening, the collecting of scientific specimens, membership in various societies, and scientific publication, Brigham portrays the interdependent roles played by people occupying markedly different positions in the social and economic hierarchies of England and the colonies. Indeed, his study illuminates Catesby's own sophisticated understanding of the structure of these relationships, and the ways in which the naturalist was able to parlay many of those connections to his own advantage in producing and marketing his *Natural History*.

One particularly complex community essential to Catesby's publication included members of the political and cultural elite on both sides of the Atlantic who were involved in the creation of gardens for scientific as well as ornamental purposes. A discussion of this transatlantic network of gardeners, which also encompassed nurserymen, horticulturists, and plant collectors, is developed in detail by Therese O'Malley. "Mark Catesby and the Culture of Gardens" shows how Catesby served as a catalyst in the active international exchange of seeds and plants that characterized the period, and, like Chaplin, she draws on passages in *The Natural History* and *Hortus Britanno-Americanus* to highlight his presiding interest in the domestication of American flora in English gardens.

O'Malley describes Catesby's contribution to the planting of these foreign exotics in so-called American gardens that often took the form of a "shrubbery" or "wilderness." These gardens symbolized visually the native habitats in which foreign imports had originally been discovered, if not replicating those habitats precisely. O'Malley contends, however, that the impulse to naturalize American plants in English soil cannot be fully understood unless examined in terms of the culture of gardening in the colonies. And here she finds Catesby's role as an experimental horticulturist most illuminating.

O'Malley suggests that Catesby was part of a transatlantic community that desired England to rid itself of dependence upon foreign monopolies that controlled the supply of agricultural products from other parts of the globe. American colonies were viewed as useful in this endeavor, serving as planting grounds for species that might not thrive in English soil. Noting that Catesby interpreted every landscape through which he moved as an experimental garden, she documents Catesby's close involvement with colonial planters who attempted the cultivation of flora from Asia, the Mediterranean, and other regions of the Americas as well as Britain's own colonial frontier. Whether working in the field, a colonial garden, or an English nursery, Catesby could "observe, describe, and depict those plants in various states of culture" and so gain from this experience an understanding of plant geography and the impact of environmental conditions on the ability of plants to survive.

The actual successes and failures faced by Catesby and the community of gardeners whose interests he served in naturalizing foreign flora to the soil of the British Isles are discussed by Mark Laird in "From Callicarpa to Catalpa: The Impact of Mark Catesby's Plant Introductions on English Gardens of the Eighteenth Century." Through his importations, and perhaps even more through his beautiful published prints, Catesby played a seminal role in stimulating a century-long mania for American plants on the part of English estate owners, horticulturists, and nurserymen. Yet, when the seeds of plants illustrated so dramatically in Catesby's *Natural History* and *Hortus Britanno-Americanus* were germinated in English gardens, more often than not the resulting specimens bore little resemblance to Catesby's magnificent images. Indeed, Laird documents several plants that were nonstarters in English soil. Through a number of examples, he also charts the ways in which plants that began as expensive, high-risk curiosities were transformed by the nursery trade into more easily procurable and affordable commodities by the middle of the eighteenth century.

Laird discusses the different environments in which a variety of Catesby's introductions met with greater or lesser success, from within the protective walls of the Chelsea Physic Garden to frosty planting grounds in the North of England—and he relates the degree to which English planters, cued by Catesby's descriptions as well as those of colonial American suppliers of seeds, experimented with the creation of habitats suited to the needs of particular species. Like O'Malley, Laird is interested in the development of the specialized section of the English garden that came to be known as the "American garden," and he describes the changing form of this section alongside a discussion of Catesby's plant introductions that were characteristically cultivated within it. By the end of the eighteenth century the passion for exotic flora that Catesby had helped to promote was beginning to be considered by some gardeners a liability. Laird also notes, however, that Catesby's significant contribution to "the trial and error of eighteenth-century planting" would continue to determine many aspects of horticultural practice, planting design, and landscape theory for generations to come.

Catesby's own reflections on the practical and moral consequences of transplanting species from one region of the globe to another are assessed by Amy R. W. Meyers in "Picturing a World in Flux: Mark Catesby's Response to Environmental Interchange and Colonial Expansion." Examining Catesby's drawings and published prints in relation to his writings, Meyers shows how Catesby expressed interest not only in environmental interconnections among animals and plants he considered indigenous to the Americas; he also expressed interest in organic relationships that had recently been introduced to the colonies through European settlement and global trade—in which he knew he played a significant role. Although Catesby understood the transplantation of flora and fauna from Europe, Africa, and other parts of the Americas to the British colonies as highly beneficial to agriculture and animal husbandry, he also recognized that such importations would inevitably establish new patterns of organic interchange that might prove detrimental to British interests.

Meyers suggests that Catesby's concern over the results of these shifting patterns of organic interaction reached beyond the realm of flora and fauna to human society. In his texts as well as in his images Catesby produced a provocative commentary on the ways in which British colonial expansion brought together peoples from different regions of the globe who, because of their divergent racial and cultural backgrounds, were benefiting to unequal degrees from the new social order that was emerging in the Americas. In essence, Meyers maintains that the paradigm for interpreting organic interaction that Catesby established in his analysis of animals and plants served also to assess human social relationships.

Catesby's self-consciousness about both his own role in moving organic productions from one region of the globe to another and his own place in the human communities where he himself functioned is, finally, the subject of Meyers's essay. Indeed, the naturalist's reflections upon his own involvement in the many avenues of human endeavor characterizing the historical moment in which he lived are examined from a slightly different vantage point by each essay in *Empire's Nature*. As the very title of the volume suggests, the examination of Catesby's own conception of his life and work yields up signal insights into the development of England's colonial possessions in the Americas during the first half of the eighteenth century, and it is hoped that the book will stimulate further investigations along those lines.

One important avenue of inquiry would involve an exploration of the intellectual, spiritual, and political world of Catesby's childhood as it had bearing upon his interest in the exercise of tolerance toward peoples of different cultural origins who were being forced into contact through Britain's colonial expansion in the Americas. One might hypothesize, for example, that Catesby's father, who twice lost his position as mayor of Sudbury because of his open toleration for Nonconformists, Independents, and Anabaptists, had an influence on the formation of his son's own attitudes toward people who viewed the creation from vastly different points of view and who lived life differently as a consequence. As Frick and Stearns point out, in Puritan East Anglia John Catesby's acts of tolerance might have been a political necessity, but the elder Catesby was apparently so open as to be indiscreet—and he paid for his indiscretions with his post. Mark Catesby was just a small child when his father's mayoral career was compromised in this way, but the young Mark continued to be surrounded by those dissenters whose faith his father had protected. It has been suggested that Samuel Petto, the minister to the Independents of Sudbury, whose controversial residence in the vicarage house of All Saints Church was supported by John Catesby, might have served as Mark's tutor.[55] In fact, Mark's own interest in natural history might have been stimulated by Petto, who published an account of parhelia in the Royal Society's *Philosophical Transactions* and corresponded with Increase Mather on his observations of mock suns.

Mark's exposure, through his father, to toleration for members of dissenting sects might also have been reinforced through his contact with John Ray, who had himself been compelled to leave Cambridge and the ministry over his refusal to subscribe to the Act of Uniformity in 1661. Certainly, as this brief account suggests, a closer look at the attitudes toward toleration voiced by the people who first shaped Catesby's life is warranted if we are to understand the naturalist's own views toward members of societies that differed markedly from his own, as he encountered them in the Americas.

Another valuable question to pursue concerns the impetus that drove Catesby to devote such time and effort to the production of his *Natural History*. While, as the essays in this volume demonstrate, the intellectual and even philosophical incentives that moved Catesby to produce this scientific work are relatively clear, much remains to be learned about the social imperatives that drove him to undertake his project. A discussion of the social standing, if not monetary gain, to be achieved by a young, rural gentleman like Catesby through the completion of such a monumental publication would undoubtedly help to shed light on our understanding of the motivations that drove forward the professionalization of science in England and colonial America during the first decades of the eighteenth century.

There are, of course, many other lines of investigation that might be

55. Frick and Stearns, *Mark Catesby,* 6, 7.

followed in relation to Mark Catesby's life and work—from queries concerning the role of natural science as a transatlantic bond among members of the aristocracy, the gentry, and an emerging professional class to questions about the mechanisms that drove the increasing passion for the collecting of natural productions, including seeds, plants, dried specimens, and animals (both live and preserved) as well as the drawings and descriptions made from them. The essays comprising *Empire's Nature* do not attempt to answer these definitively, nor even to address them all; but they should help to point the way toward a more thorough understanding of Mark Catesby as a man whose interests and pursuits are particularly useful in clarifying the multiple functions of the natural sciences as they were practiced in English and colonial American society during his lifetime.

Joyce E. Chaplin

MARK CATESBY, A SKEPTICAL NEWTONIAN IN AMERICA

Mark Catesby has remained but a footnote in the history of science, even in the realm of eighteenth-century natural history. This is the case, not because Catesby's studies of nature were insignificant, but because his work has been misrepresented within teleological constructions of the history of science that trace the emergence of a single dominant view of nature. Such studies represent modern science as a form of knowledge that progresses diachronically toward an increasingly accurate understanding of the natural world, one that replaces the views that had come earlier or continued to critique this vision. But the eighteenth century had no dominant view of nature, and Catesby's conceptual indecision was in fact symptomatic of his age. Catesby tackled problems of interest to his contemporaries, even as he refused to see easy answers to those problems. He belonged to the first generation of post-Newtonian naturalists who tried to hypothesize uniform laws of nature for nonmechanical phenomena. Because Catesby was skeptical—though not dismissive—of this enterprise, his views of natural systems seemed too diffident and indeterminate to belong to the early eighteenth century's boldest vision of the material world: hence the facile assumption that he must have been a lesser light. Further, by the time many other naturalists like Buffon would question a simplistic, Newtonian vision of biological nature, Catesby's reputation

I would like to thank David Armitage and Arleen Tuchman for their comments on this essay, and Nicolaas Rupke for advice on Alexander von Humboldt. I am also grateful to Dan Slive of the John Carter Brown Library, and the staffs of the Royal Society, British Library, New York Public Library, Columbia University Library Special Collections, Vanderbilt University Library and Vanderbilt Medical Library Special Collections, and the Newberry Library for their assistance with research.

had fallen. He was therefore not seen as one of the precursors of the less mechanical conception of nature that gained purchase in the late 1700s and early 1800s, though he in some ways anticipated that view.

Catesby emphasized phenomena in nature that appeared violent and disorderly, and questioned whether those capacities could be represented as possessing predictable tendencies, let alone laws. For this reason, he was a Newtonian (he did look for recurrent pattern), but a skeptical one: he saw more puzzles than patterns. Philosophical skepticism, particularly as defined by David Hume, was slowly taking shape in the eighteenth century and was a profound attack on the human capacity to predict natural events. It is not clear that many naturalists (including Catesby) accepted philosophical skepticism; most simply conceded some limits on science's ability to generate laws. Historians of science who have considered Catesby have thus found him a difficult subject, eccentric at best. If he could be fitted into any tendency within modern science, he might be considered a remote prophet of nonlinear science or complexity theory, popularly known as chaos theory, which posits that most of nature's laws are far more subtle and complicated than Newton's (or even Einstein's) axioms. Although Catesby's writings definitely support a view of nature's laws as complex—too entangled in multiple variables to permit human understanding—he seemed also to believe in real chaos, a primordial disorder that could not be seen, from any perspective, to have integrative properties. In part, Catesby's predisposition was related to a cultural politics that figured the New World as locus of exotica and tumult and the Old World as site of regularity and regulators. Further, he believed that human art might create order where nature had failed. Catesby's faith in human artifice was reflected in his entrepreneurial efforts at scientific illustration and in gardening, which gave fixed and understandable form to American flora and fauna within elaborate engravings and English gardens.[1]

Catesby's intellectual diffidence made sense within his intellectual context, which encouraged multiple and nondogmatic opinions. His theoretical caution has made it easy, however, for historians to focus on his discrete observations rather than to understand his larger vision. Catesby's ornithology and taxonomy thus appear as evidence of his limited

1. On complexity theory, see James Gleick, *Chaos: Making a New Science* (New York, 1987); Stephen H. Kellert, *In the Wake of Chaos: Unpredictable Order in Dynamical Systems* (Chicago, 1993). On skepticism, see Richard H. Popkin, "New Views on the Role of Scepticism in the Enlightenment," in Popkin, Ezequiel de Olaso, and Giorgio Tonelli, eds., *Scepticism in the Enlightenment* (Dordrecht, 1997).

scope. Catesby is best known for his ornithology, hence the description of him as the "colonial Audubon." In part he has gained this reputation because of his *Natural History*'s many and eye-catching plates that contain birds; because most of these plates appeared in the first volume of the work, Catesby's initial appearance before the public appeared to be as an expert on these creatures. Further, the later fame of illustrator-ornithologist John James Audubon would make Catesby seem a mere harbinger of ornamental bird illustration rather than a producer of a more comprehensive natural history in his own right. Reduction of Catesby's *Natural History* to a mainly ornithological study has made it seem a narrow and easily eclipsed work. Scholars have pointed out that, because Catesby depended on old methods of classifying birds (he employed the late-seventeenth-century system of Francis Willughby), he was outdated by the time Carolus Linnaeus promulgated his more successful taxonomy for animals in 1758. Catesby's nomenclature was superseded, with the consolation that the Swedish scholar at least utilized other material in Catesby's *Natural History* to describe American species. Catesby's reputation therefore declined in the nineteenth century after, first, Alexander Wilson and, then, Audubon assigned Linnaean names to American birds.[2]

This emphasis on ornithology and taxonomy obscures Catesby's contribution to other areas of natural history and ignores his desire to make larger, systematic statements about nature. More could be done, for example, to emphasize Catesby's importance to botany. The *Natural History* in fact contained only 109 varieties of birds, but 171 species of plants, by far his largest category of biota.[3] And the even more dismissive idea that an antiquated Catesby was swept aside by Linnaean naturalists drastically simplifies eighteenth-century natural history. To place Catesby's work outside a single trajectory leading to the triumph of Linnaean nomenclature is to guarantee his irrelevance at the expense of understanding the multiple strands that make up the history of science. Classification was only one

2. George Frederick Frick and Raymond Phineas Stearns, *Mark Catesby: The Colonial Audubon* (Urbana, Ill., 1961), 55–60; Russell W. Peterson, foreword, in Alan Feduccia, ed., *Catesby's Birds of Colonial America* (Chapel Hill, N.C., 1985), xi (see also 9, 10); Kevin R. McNamara, "The Feathered Scribe: The Discourses of American Ornithology before 1800," *William and Mary Quarterly*, 3d Ser., XLVII (1990), 226–227—see 211 on Willughby, who authored the first modern ornithological work in English. Raymond Phineas Stearns gives a good description of Catesby's activities without untoward judgment of his limitations; see *Science in the British Colonies of America* (Urbana, Ill., 1970), 286–288, 317–322.

3. Feduccia, ed., *Catesby's Birds of Colonial America*, 5.

development in the emergence of a recognizably modern form of science. In fact, it resembled an older preoccupation of natural history, which had used herbals and bestiaries to identify, describe, and categorize as many things within nature as possible. Other modern naturalists instead wanted to theorize nature as a set of *functions* (rather than as discrete objects) and thereby identify systemic qualities of the material world. Catesby's science was marked by this latter interest.

His theoretical work included inquiry into three questions. First, Catesby hypothesized that nature might be a system or set of systems for which universal laws could be derived; he looked particularly at laws related to climate. Second, he addressed the question of whether nature's systems were teleological, that is, running in a more or less linear fashion toward some final state. Third, he considered whether the cosmos was anthropocentric; this last question could include the possibility that nature was actually centered on humans, or that it was recognizable as a set of laws when focused through the human perspective, or that it was reducible to an order determined by humans, though not originally present in nature itself. Catesby did not provide a direct answer to the anthropocentric question, though his interest in gardening revealed his belief that human actions—within specific political networks—did provide order over nature, an order perhaps needed because of nature's lack of predictable system.

Catesby's vision thus contained both belief in natural laws and skepticism that such laws expressed universal principles, a skepticism that structured his confidence that human artifice could provide an order and predictability that the creation itself lacked. Though he perceived and described some orderly patterns in nature, Catesby suspected that many natural phenomena tended toward a seemingly purposeless destruction. Catesby did not always see stability and pattern: he employed catastrophist views of the earth, and he blurred differences between categories of creatures (meaning all things created), even between animate and inanimate phenomena. Catesby's descriptions of nature's disintegrative forces and of the instability of its categories nonetheless existed alongside his serious desire to make some coherent sense of the world. He sought to describe accurately his individual specimens, to define ecological connections between these specimens, to trace nature's recurring patterns (like animal migration), and to postulate mathematically definable relationships—like degrees of latitude and biodiversity. In short, he entertained the possibility of destruction surprisingly cheerfully, and it did not impede his interest in describing order elsewhere. He lacked faith that humans could eventually decode this disintegration as part of a cognizable pattern. He therefore rejected the position, associated with but not unique to Linnaeus, that the naturalist should impose an intellectual order over a nature that itself lacked clear pattern. In the end, he seemed to believe that human effort, specifically his own entrepreneurship, could create a real order lacking in unattended wilderness. He accordingly *made* order appear within his illustrations and also within English gardens of American plants. What nature lacked in laws of predictability could be mitigated by human activities. In this way, science and empire interacted, though in an unexpected way. Catesby's science did not predict chaos in America because of that science's totalizing or imperialistic view of the natural world. Instead, because of natural history's disinclination to posit universal laws, it was possible for naturalists to conceive certain parts of the world as more disorderly by nature. Intellectual openness, paradoxically, encouraged rigid stereotyping of the New World.

Catesby's contribution to natural history stood between the work of John Ray (1627–1705) and the work of the contemporaries and rivals Linnaeus (Carl von Linné, 1707–1778) and Buffon (Georges Leclerc, comte de Buffon, 1707–1788). Despite the lasting prestige of Ray and the accretion of naturalists' studies that enabled Linnaeus and Buffon to advance more theoretical statements, these years formed a period in which natural history had an uncertain relation to more positivistic views of the creation. Ray's empirical studies, his collections and nomenclature, remained a benchmark for British naturalists. But mechanical and mathematical science had since garnered the most praise and attention in the wake of Isaac Newton's accomplishments. After the Newtonian revolution, England's Royal Society (chartered in 1662) became the model of a scientific organization that defined what the correct method of inquiry into nature should be and rewarded practitioners of this method; it was, to use Bruno Latour's useful concept of scientific organization, a powerful "center of calculation." Catesby therefore belonged to the first generation of post-Newtonian naturalists.[4]

4. Charles E. Raven, *John Ray, Naturalist: His Life and Works* (Cambridge, 1950); Margarita Bowen, *Empiricism and Geographical Thought: From Francis Bacon to Alexander von Humboldt* (Cambridge, 1981), 91–122; John Gascoigne, *Joseph Banks and the English Enlightenment: Useful Knowledge and Polite Culture* (Cambridge, 1994), 73–74; Stearns, *Science in the British Colonies of*

Even though the Royal Society included naturalists in its ranks, studies like botany and natural history appeared inferior to physics because they had not yet generated universal and mathematically expressed laws. Naturalists contemporary to Catesby had to decide whether mechanical science provided a model for the rest of nature. One way to solve the problem was to rely on probability theory. This strategy rendered laws, not as absolutes, but as matters of statistical likelihood. Probability theory had gained sophistication over the course of the seventeenth century; and, by the time the Royal Society took a defining role over modern science, probability was an accepted way to posit natural laws. Newton, for instance, used statistical laws to define phenomena like gravity. In this way, he and others modified the program they felt they had inherited from Francis Bacon, to describe nature's predictable patterns without artificial rigidity. Probability theory shifted science away from positivism, but scientists remained more sanguine about understanding nature than would be the case with David Hume, the eighteenth century's most famous skeptic. Hume's *Treatise of Human Nature* (1739–1740) denounced probabilistic statements as mere opinion. Inductive logic, which used repeated phenomena to predict future events, merely recounted human experience without revealing any true, natural process. Few agreed with Hume, who admitted his *Treatise* fell "stillborn" from the press. Yet Newtonian science continued to struggle with the extent to which it might trace the laws of nature.[5]

The most successful practitioner of a Newtonian inquiry into living nature was the Cambridge physiologist Stephen Hales (1677–1761). Hales defined mathematically the functional equilibria that operated within plants and within the human body; his two key works, *Vegetable Staticks* (1727) and *Haemastaticks* (1733) calculated the laws of such equilibria. Most

America, 171–176; John Gascoigne, *Cambridge in the Age of the Enlightenment: Science, Religion, and Politics from the Restoration to the French Revolution* (Cambridge, 1989), 142–184 (on Newtonian science); Bruno Latour, *Science in Action: How to Follow Scientists and Engineers through Society* (Cambridge, Mass., 1987), 215–257.

5. On probability theory, see Ian Hacking, *The Emergence of Probability: A Philosophical Study of Early Ideas about Probability, Induction, and Statistical Inference* (Cambridge, 1995), 122–142, 166–175, 176–185 (Hume); Barbara J. Shapiro, *Probability and Certainty in Seventeenth-Century England: A Study of the Relationships between Natural Science, Religion, History, Law, and Literature* (Princeton, N.J., 1983), 15–73; Alexander Rosenberg, "Hume and the Philosophy of Science," and Robert Fogelin, "Hume's Scepticism," in David Fate Norton, ed., *The Cambridge Companion to Hume* (Cambridge, 1993), 64–89, 90–116.

naturalists hailed Hales's accomplishments. Buffon translated Hales's work on plants in 1735, after which discussion of Newtonian natural history influenced French circles. Some naturalists went to an extreme and defined all of nature as mechanical. Buffon's translation had in fact blurred Hales's distinction between the living atoms that made up plants and animals and the merely "brute" particles that constituted other matter. The Newtonian (and Cartesian) Julien Offroy de La Mettrie went further and posited that animals, plants, and even humans were machines that operated in a mechanical universe. Other naturalists rejected this vision and began to identify an *organic* nature, one that had universal laws but was not equivalent to physics; Buffon was the first to define nature in this way. After Hales and La Mettrie, naturalists who thought of themselves as scientists in the Newtonian sense diverged from naturalists who looked at the creation as a vital, organic, even mystical system. The latter tradition was most apparent in Jean-Baptiste Pierre Antoine de Monet de Lamarck (1744–1829), whereas Alexander von Humboldt (1769–1859) would revive a Newtonian program to reduce nature to numerically calculable formulae. What Hales began, therefore, was argument over the degree to which naturalists should model themselves on mechanical scientists.[6]

In the meantime, many naturalists contemporary with Catesby insisted on the significance of organic nature (as opposed to mechanics) and

6. On Hales, see D. G. C. Allan and R. E. Schofield, *Stephen Hales: Scientist and Philanthropist* (London, 1980), 10–19 (education and influence of Newton), 30–64 (work on statics), 119–140 (influence). On blurring of boundaries between animate and inanimate, see Arthur O. Lovejoy, *The Great Chain of Being: A Study of the History of an Idea* (New York, 1963), 232–233; Barbara M. Stafford, "Images of Ambiguity: Eighteenth-Century Microscopy and the Nei-ther/Nor," in David Philip Miller and Peter Hanns Reill, eds., *Visions of Empire: Voyages, Botany, and Representations of Nature* (Cambridge, 1996), 230–257.

On British debate over mechanical representations of nature (especially human nature), see Otto Mayr, *Authority, Liberty, and Automatic Machinery in Early Modern Europe* (Baltimore, 1986), 81–92, 187–189. On La Mettrie and Buffon, see Paul L. Farber, "Buffon and the Concept of Species," *Journal of the History of Biology*, V (1972), 259–284; Emma Spary, "Political, Natural, and Bodily Economies," in N. Jardine, J. A. Secord, and E. C. Spary, eds., *Cultures of Natural History* (Cambridge, 1996), 181–186; D. G. Charlton, *New Images of the Natural in France: A Study in European Cultural History, 1750–1800* (Cambridge, 1984), 71–86; Jacques Roger, *Buffon: A Life in Natural History,* trans. Sarah Lucille Bonnefoi, ed. L. Pearce Williams (Ithaca, N.Y., 1997), 25–27 (trans. of Hales), 65–75 (mechanical vs. natural). On Lamarck, see Richard W. Burkhardt, Jr., "The Inspiration of Lamarck's Belief in Evolution," *Jour. Hist. Bio.*, V (1972), 413–438; L. J. Jordanova, *Lamarck* (Oxford, 1984), esp. 44–57; Pietro Corsi, *The Age of Lamarck: Evolutionary Theories in France, 1790–1830,* rev. ed., trans. Jonathan Mandelbaum (Berkeley, Calif., 1989), esp. 1–39, 68–76.

collected and described specimens without hypothesizing universal laws. The most important British figure in this regard was John James Dillenius, Oxford's foundation professor of botany between 1728 and 1747, one of Catesby's professional contacts. Nevertheless, the specter of Newton hovered over natural history; certainly, Catesby must have known of Hales and his work, if not directly, at least through others. The naturalist Peter Collinson, who presented Catesby for membership in the Royal Society in 1733, also wrote Hales's obituary in the *Gentleman's Magazine* in 1764.[7]

Catesby's work took shape in this context of intellectual indecision or openness, which would have particular consequences for his subject matter, nature in the New World. Britain's colonies were an important arena for the collection of new flora and fauna, which had long seemed too myriad and foreign to describe with accuracy. Ray had been one of the first authors to take seriously the task of integrating American specimens into European writing on nature. His scholarship inspired others to accelerate the process of detecting and describing America's products. Colonial merchants (including Peter Collinson and John Ellis) were instrumental thereto, and some Britons traveled to the colonies as semiprofessional naturalists. This was the case with Hans Sloane and John Lawson, who produced, respectively, *A Voyage to the Islands Madera, Barbados, Nieves, S. Christophers, and Jamaica* (vol. I, 1707) and *A New Voyage to Carolina* (1709). An increasing number of colonists themselves entered the learned circle of British natural history—some (including John Winthrop and Benjamin Franklin) even became fellows of the Royal Society. By the 1730s, when Catesby was issuing the first parts of his *Natural History,* John Bartram would be considered the colonies' most adept botanist. (His son, William, would be America's most influential naturalist of the post-Revolutionary period.) Like Catesby, these men regarded their primary task as the accumulation of specimens and information; they made occasional gestures toward theorizing about what they gathered and described, but no totalizing visions resulted.[8]

---

7. On Collinson's patronage of Catesby, see Feduccia, ed., *Catesby's Birds of Colonial America,* 5; see also Collinson, "Some Account of the Life of the Late Excellent and Eminent Stephen Hales, *D.D.,* F.R.S.," *Gentleman's Magazine, and Historical Chronicle,* XXXIV (1764), 273–278.

8. Antonello Gerbi, *Nature in the New World: From Christopher Columbus to Gonzalo Fernandez de Oviedo,* trans. Jeremy Moyle (Pittsburgh, 1985), 3–11, 15–18, 68–73; Stearns, *Science in the British Colonies of America;* Frans A. Stafleu, *Linnaeus and the Linnaeans: The Spreading of Their Ideas in Systematic Botany, 1735–1789* (Utrecht, 1971), 201–202; Gascoigne, *Joseph Banks*

More ambitious naturalists emerged toward the end of Catesby's life, most evidently Linnaeus and Buffon. Each man articulated a systematic theory of nature—and each claimed his theory was opposed to the other. Linnaeus's contribution came with a convincing compartmentalization of all natural entities within a single taxonomy that had a universally applicable binominal nomenclature. The Linnaean system thus sidestepped Newtonianism by imposing a universal order over nature rather than theorizing functions within it. Buffon distrusted the artificiality of taxonomic systems and decried the Linnaean craze to reduce nature to articles that seemed to exist in isolation from each other. Taxonomy not only represented organisms as discrete but did so by focusing on discrete parts of them; Buffon and others emphasized instead the "natural" connections between organisms and examined phenomena like climate that seemed to encompass a field or network of creatures. Even more than Linnaeus, Buffon specified that science was the determination of a set of laws (defined probabilistically) that regulated nature. Linnaeus and Buffon were significant not only as promoters of theories but also as impresarios of institutions: gardens, libraries, schools of protégés, factions—"centers of calculation" modeled on and in contact with the Royal Society.[9]

Factionalization among naturalists promoted multiplicity of theories. The continuing indeterminacy was especially apparent in Britain. The Royal Society did not have a figurehead comparable to Linnaeus or Buffon who provided a united program. (No Newton of the organic world would emerge until Charles Darwin.) Further, Britons remained unconvinced of Linnaeus's and Buffon's theories until a period of takeoff from the 1750s to the 1770s. A search for an integrated view of nature

---

and the English Enlightenment, 76–79; Henry Lowood, "The New World and the European Catalog of Nature," in Karen Ordahl Kupperman, ed., America in European Consciousness, 1493–1750 (Chapel Hill, N.C., 1995), 306–317.

9. On the classificatory impulse, see Lovejoy, Great Chain of Being, 227–241; Michel Foucault, The Order of Things: An Archaeology of the Human Sciences (New York, 1970), esp. 125–165. On Buffon and natural laws, see John Lyon and Phillip R. Sloan, eds., From Natural History to the History of Nature: Readings from Buffon and His Critics (Notre Dame, Ind., 1981), 1–32; Roger, Buffon, trans. Bonnefoi, ed. Williams, 84–92, 309–335. On both naturalists, see Stafleu, Linnaeus and the Linnaeans, 302–310; Phillip Sloan, "The Gaze of Natural History," in Christopher Fox, Roy Porter, and Robert Wokler, eds., Inventing Human Science: Eighteenth-Century Domains (Berkeley, Calif., 1995), 113–139; Dirk Stermerding, Plants, Animals, and Formulae: Natural History in the Light of Latour's "Science in Action" and Foucault's "The Order of Things" (Amsterdam, 1991), pt. 1.

was nevertheless a preeminent goal. Much of this desire for integration achieved expression in the *form* of British naturalists' accounts: they were narratives. In this regard, natural history was related to the genre of the travel narrative. Indeed, contemporaries of Catesby titled their works as if they were predominantly travel accounts. In such narratives, authors merged assessments of people (especially aboriginal inhabitants of places outside Europe) with their treatment of material nature. Cataloging the manners and customs of people was still part of the description that naturalists did; in this way, the narrative style connected nature to humanity. This was true of Sloane's *Voyage to the Islands* and Lawson's *New Voyage to Carolina* as well as of the most famous eighteenth-century example of the naturalist narrative, William Bartram's *Travels through North and South Carolina* (1791).[10]

Though Catesby belonged to the British world of empirical naturalists who were skeptical of theories, he did *not* take up the narrative solution to providing a reader with an orderly representation of nature's phenomena. His *Natural History* focused tightly on natural entities and properties and eschewed narration of discovery of them. To be sure, the introduction and appendix of *The Natural History* gave a somewhat narrative frame to the main body of illustrations, each of which was itself annotated. But Catesby was clearly not as interested as someone like Lawson in constructing an account that showed him, the reader's witness, moving through space and time. Indeed, as a piece of haphazard intentionality, his stated reasons for initially traveling to America—"*Virginia* was the Place (I having Relations there) suited most with my Convenience to go to"—rivals Laurence Sterne's offhanded desire to commence his *Sentimental Journey* (1768) because "they order this matter . . . better in France." Even more telling was Catesby's lack of interest in establishing America's native residents as natural features of the landscape—again, in contrast to writers like Lawson and Bartram. Catesby instead pillaged Lawson for material on Indians and declared his own view that he thought it "impertinent to relate tedious

10. On travel writing's connection to writing on nature, see P. J. Marshall and Glyndwr Williams, *The Great Map of Mankind: Perceptions of New Worlds in the Age of Enlightenment* (Cambridge, Mass., 1982); David Philip Miller, "Joseph Banks, Empire, and 'Centers of Calculation' in Late Hanoverian London," in Miller and Reill, eds., *Visions of Empire*, 21–37; Pamela Regis, *Describing Early America: Bartram, Jefferson, Crèvecoeur, and the Rhetoric of Natural History* (DeKalb, Ill., 1992), 25–39; Joyce E. Chaplin, *An Anxious Pursuit: Agricultural Innovation and Modernity in the Lower South, 1730–1815* (Chapel Hill, N.C., 1993), 71–91.

Narratives of Religious Ceremonies, Burials, Marriages, etc. which are too often the Product of Invention, or Credulity in the Relater."[11]

The words "tedious Narratives" foreground Catesby's interest in description and in the physically concrete. He spent his energies on illustration and on text that glossed the illustrations. In a sense, therefore, Catesby's spare and scattered prose did not supplement his illustrations, but functioned like them: as instances of portraiture that the reader could turn to and enter at will, without being led along a narrative pathway to the spot. Catesby was a retiring docent rather than a vigorous frontier guide— hence his verbal instructions allowed the reader considerable freedom to roam and reinterpret.

Catesby's distaste for narration did not, however, make him avoid other ways of making discrete phenomena cohere with each other in recognizable patterns. He was too ambitious to avoid making any bold statement. He was not interested in being a little-known collector of material things who lacked larger and more abstract ideas about nature. Catesby's ambitions were high, partly because of his high social position. It is worth remembering that, of all Britons who visited colonial America as trained naturalists, Catesby was the highest born. (Hans Sloane might have received a title because of the prestige he won, but had been born in rather humble circumstances.) Catesby, in contrast, was a gentleman who inherited property and was descended from an old English family. His social and intellectual confidence are apparent in his letters to his patrons. He disdained the role expected of him by these men, who wanted him to be a dutiful supplier of specimens to them and who would do the intellectual work of attaching scientific names to them. Catesby's intellectual confidence showed the powerful role social status played in early science; as Steven Shapin has argued, the Royal Society expected that, because a gentleman's word was his honor, genteel practitioners of experimental science (and observers of nature, generally) were the most trusted of informants.[12]

Catesby was impatient of the request of his patrons to send boxes and bottles of specimens to each of them. He complained to Sloane in 1724

11. Mark Catesby, *The Natural History of Carolina, Florida, and the Bahama Islands . . .*, 2 vols. (London, 1731–1747), I, v, II, "An Account of Carolina, and the Bahama Islands," xvi.

12. On Catesby's social level, see Frick and Stearns, *Mark Catesby*, 3, 5; Feduccia, ed., *Catesby's Birds of Colonial America*, 3. Steven Shapin, *A Social History of Truth: Civility and Science in Seventeeth-Century England* (Chicago, 1994).

that his "sending Collections of plants and especially Drawings to every of My Subscribers is what I did not think would be expected from me." His desire to retain his drawings, his personal representations of the specimens, is especially telling. Catesby seemed to envisage his role as that of interpreter and entrepreneur on his own terms. He specified to Sloane that he wanted to keep his drawings and get them engraved, "in order to give a gen'll History of the Birds and other Animals, which to distribute Seperately would wholly Frustrate that designe, and be of little value to those who would have so small fragments of the whole." Unlike the humbly born John Lawson and John Bartram, who addressed patrons with deference, Catesby knew he was a gentleman's son. He expressed himself boldly to his patrons and had confidence in his ability to "give a gen'll History," not grub up mere pieces to be owned and named by others. Catesby was not highborn enough to establish his own sphere of influence, as aristocrat Buffon did. But he could confidently seek the patronage of his betters (as he did when he dedicated the volumes of his *Natural History* to Queen Caroline and the Princess Augusta) and could pitch his products—his books and, later, his horticultural items—to a luxury market for the genteel and noble.[13]

At the same time, Catesby had little respect for nonsystematizers or (worse) men interested in American specimens for their mercantile promise. Catesby opened his *Natural History* with the lament that few of South Carolina's natural products were yet known, "except what [are] barely [merely] related to Commerce." Catesby's disdain for the crassly commercial and his exasperation over the unsystematic mind united in his assessment of a Dr. Sinclair who emigrated to Charleston with a patent and the supposed patronage of Archibald Campbell, earl of Islay (later third duke of Argyll), and Robert Walpole, to raise cochineal, nutmeg, cloves, pepper, rhubarb, and opium—the usual list of improbable exotics. Catesby complained to William Sherard (his main patron and the overseer of the duchess of Beaufort's garden), "You will gues at the Man by the undertaking," and concluded, that "Such an Emperick and so ignorant a person can impose on Such Men [as Islay and Walpole] is unaccountable to me." He

13. Catesby to Sloane, Aug. 15, 1724, Sloane MSS 4047, 213ʳ, British Library, London. On the strategy of publishing a work independent of one's patrons, see Regis, *Describing Early America,* 8–9. On patronizing treatment of nongenteel naturalists, see Thomas P. Slaughter, *The Natures of John and William Bartram* (New York, 1996), 95–98.

was clearly stating a claim to be considered a different sort of person, one who was learned and rational rather than vulgarly empirical.[14]

Catesby's self-assertion was a reminder of the competitive nature of eighteenth-century science, in which social rank and school of opinion provided strategic advantage. Naturalists were supposed to decide which theories they found useful and reject those they found wanting. Indeed, the received view of Catesby as a clumsy empiric, especially as a pre-Linnaean, has not taken full account of his knowledge of the Swedish naturalist's work. Linnaeus's first important statement on taxonomy, *Systema Naturae*, appeared in its initial form in 1735—during the very time Catesby was preparing his *Natural History*. Indeed, Catesby received a copy of the work in 1735, via Johann Friedrich Gronovius (Dutch coauthor of John Clayton's *Flora Virginica* [1739]), to whom he had been sending specimens. This must in fact have been one of the first copies of Linnaeus in England. Catesby reported his acquisition to the Royal Society in December 1735 and promised to "give an account of its contents." (Like many a book reviewer, Catesby defaulted.) It is also possible that Catesby encountered Linnaeus when the Swedish scholar visited Britain in 1736 and met other naturalists known to Catesby, like Dillenius.[15]

It is therefore worth reconsidering why Linnaeus had no impact on Catesby. He was not ignorant of Linnaean taxonomy, in its early form, but had instead made a decision not to mention or use it. Certainly, it would have been awkward had Catesby tried to model any part of his *Natural History* according to Linnaean principles. The 1735 *Systema Naturae* appeared after publication of all the installments of Catesby's first volume (1729–1732) and during those of the second (1734–1743; the appendix appeared in 1747). The close timing of Linnaeus's and Catesby's publications could partly explain the latter's reluctance to alter his mostly formed project to refer to the scholarship of the former. But it is also likely that Catesby, with many of his English contemporaries, was not entirely con-

14. Catesby, *Natural History*, I, vi; Catesby to Sherard, Nov. 20, 1724, Sherard Letters, CCLIII, 182, Royal Society, London. On Sherard, see Frick and Stearns, *Mark Catesby*, 16–17, 19.

15. Journal Book, XVI, meeting of Dec. 18, 1735, 219, Royal Society, London; Gascoigne, *Joseph Banks and the English Enlightenment*, 99–100. Frick and Stearns (*Mark Catesby*, 40) claim that Catesby declined to review Linnaeus, but the records they cite give no such evidence and, in contrast, record Catesby's promise to do so. Linnaeus had already sent a copy of his *Musa Cliffortiana Florens Hortecampi* in the spring of 1735—see Journal Book, XV, entry for Mar. 11, 1735, Royal Society.

vinced by Linnaeus's taxonomy. The Linnaean system did not have wide support in Britain until the 1750s, after Catesby's death. Philip Miller, superintendent of the Chelsea Physic Garden and author of the influential *Gardeners Dictionary,* used the Linnaean system only upon the seventh edition (1759) of his work. Nor did advocates of pre-Linnaean taxonomies give up the fight: Ray's system continued to have its defenders.[16]

In any case, as Ray and Buffon made clear, lack of Linnaeus was not equivalent to lack of interest in systematizing. First, Catesby did utilize classification, thereby participating in one of the dominant scientific impulses of his era; the extinction of his system is not sufficient evidence of intellectual backwardness. Second, a science of natural history emerged from theories other than classification; Newtonians like Hales demonstrated other possibilities.[17] Many other attributes of the earth drew critical attention from observers interested in generating laws of nature. Without a doubt, Catesby's boldest attempts at theory had to do with climate. He attacked old notions of climate and proposed at least one replacement, a new and systematic view of the earth's latitudinal variation. He was most critical of the long-established view that climates were roughly equivalent to latitudes and that the globe could therefore be divided into vertical bands in which the climate on one side of the globe was similar to that of its geographic opposite. Such thinking had guided many European expectations on colonization and production of colonial commodities, sometimes with disastrous consequences.[18]

The idea of latitude as climate, though it enjoyed a prestigious classical pedigree, was already questioned by the time Catesby challenged it. By the early 1700s, sophisticated theories of climatic variation had emerged, and discussion of differences between hemispheres was raised though often refuted. Some speculations were simple glosses on ancient medical thought, which had its most notable modern revival in neo-Hippocratic theory. Hippocratic ideas suggested that climates existed more as patches

---

16. Stafleu, *Linnaeus and the Linnaeans,* 199–210 (205–207 discuss Miller); Gascoigne, *Joseph Banks and the English Enlightenment,* 99–101, 104. On the publication dates for the *Natural History,* see Feduccia, ed., *Catesby's Birds of Colonial America,* 5.

17. See Stermerding, *Plants, Animals, and Formulae,* pt. 2.

18. On climate, see *Oxford English Dictionary,* 2d ed., s.v. "climate"; Clarence J. Glacken, *Traces on the Rhodian Shore: Nature and Culture in Western Thought from Ancient Times to the End of the Eighteenth Century* (Berkeley, Calif., 1967), 80–95, 551–622; Karen Ordahl Kupperman, "The Puzzle of the American Climate in the Early Colonial Period," *American Historical Review,* LXXXVII (1982), 1262–1289.

than as global bands; latitude combined with a place's altitude, soil, water, vegetation, and human population to create medically unique localities. Hippocratic assumptions guided Hans Sloane's attention to the impact that physical place (temperature, moisture, quality of air, barometric pressure, water, and soil) had on human health. Despite Sloane's pains to establish the unique details of Caribbean climates, he nevertheless maintained that the diseases people had there were the same as in Europe.[19]

Modern theorization about climate updated Hippocratic theory by defining and measuring atmospheric variables that contributed to climatic variation. By the late seventeenth and early eighteenth centuries, colonized islands were foci for European studies of climate, because such islands provided small units of analysis as well as territory where variables (such as forests and deforestation) could be manipulated by imperial policy. One key work for this field was Hales's *Vegetable Staticks,* which connected vegetation to the heat and moisture of a climate. Discussion of climate became more specialized, distinguished from medical theories, and mathematicized and was often connected to discussions of the character of human populations and political regimes. Montesquieu's *Spirit of the Laws* (1748) would contribute to the politicized debate. And from this ferment Buffon crafted the eighteenth century's most famous contention about climate's consequences: that America, prone to extremes of temperature and tending toward excessive damp, gave rise to species of plants and animals not only distinct from those in Europe but clearly inferior in variety, size, and vigor. The old view of hemispherically similar climates had united Old and New Worlds; attacks on this view allowed Europeans to distance themselves from colonial peoples and cultures, and to employ up-to-date science to do so.[20]

19. Hans Sloane, *A Voyage to the Islands Madera, Barbados, Nieves, S. Christophers, and Jamaica* . . . , 2 vols. (London, 1707, 1725), I, B^r, viii–x (climate), xc–cliv (medical case studies), xc (diseases same as in Europe), II, xv (ditto). On Hippocratic theory, see L. J. Jordanova, "Earth Science and Environmental Medicine: The Synthesis of the Late Enlightenment," in Jordanova and Roy S. Porter, eds., *Images of the Earth: Essays in the History of the Environmental Sciences* (Chalfont St. Giles, 1979), 119–146; James C. Riley, *The Eighteenth-Century Campaign to Avoid Disease* (New York, 1987); Roy Porter, "Medical Science and Human Science in the Enlightenment," in Fox, Porter, and Wokler, eds., *Inventing Human Science,* 65–68.

20. On atmospheric theories and Hales's work, see Lyon and Sloan, eds., *From Natural History to the History of Nature,* 35–49; Richard H. Grove, *Green Imperialism: Colonial Expansion,*

Catesby evidently knew enough about new views of climate to enter his own suppositions, though they were not as sophisticated as those of Hales and Buffon. He did not entirely discount the old latitudinal theory, but instead complicated its applicability. Indeed, his indeterminacy makes it difficult to assess his beliefs. He stated that, because South Carolina was "happily scituated in a Climate parallel to the best Parts of the Old World, [it] enjoys in some Measure the like Blessings." But he next asserted that the entire continent of North America was, however counterintuitively, "much colder than those Parts of *Europe* which are parallel to it in Latitude." The frosts in Virginia were, for example, much worse than those in England. Newfoundland was, in Catesby's opinion, "not habitable for Cold, tho' in the Latitude of the South parts of *England.*" His speculation contributed to puzzlement over lack of latitudinal consistency that would end with Benjamin Franklin's identification of the Gulf Stream and in the scientifically more dubious isothermic lines of Alexander von Humboldt.[21]

After Catesby had questioned the old latitudinal understanding of American climates, he began to reconceptualize climatological differences. He described a north-south continuum through the Americas that, rather than latitudinal bands that looped around the globe, explained nearly all differences among American climates. Catesby was particularly interested in using this continuum to explain biological diversity. "Animals in general," he declared, "and particularly Birds, diminish in number of species so much the nearer they approach the Pole." Birds therefore had the greatest diversity of species above the forty-fifth latitude. Catesby gave a strikingly mathematical method of determining species variety. "As the Productions of Nature in general are very Scanty near the *Arctic Circle*," he concluded, "there is a Gradation of Increase at every Degree of Latitude approaching the Tropick." One degree's variation was not perceptible even to the adept naturalist, but four or five degrees "makes it evidently

Tropical Island Edens, and the Origins of Environmentalism, 1600–1860 (Cambridge, 1995), chap. 4. On Buffon's critique, see Antonello Gerbi, *The Dispute of the New World: The History of a Polemic, 1750–1900,* trans. Jeremy Moyle (Pittsburgh, 1973), esp. chap. 1; Roger, *Buffon,* trans. Bonnefoi, ed. Williams, 178–180.

21. Catesby, *Natural History,* II, "Account," i, ii. Franklin worked on the problem of the Gulf Stream between 1769 (when he first used the term) and 1786, when he published his conclusions. See Benjamin Franklin, *Maritime Observations . . .* (Philadelphia, 1786); T. F. Gaskell, *The Gulf Stream* (New York, 1973), 5–7, 47–50.

appear." Size as well as numbers of flora and fauna varied with latitude, even if the specimens were of the same species. "Many other Instances may be produced of Vegetables, and Animals of the same Species abiding in different Climates, that are diminutive in their Northern Situation."[22]

Variation from north to south was not, for Catesby, an absolute law. It is not even clear whether he meant his rules to apply to other divisions of the globe, or whether this continuum was particular to America. His declarations that latitudinal bands did not uniformly describe climate would argue for an attribute unique to America. (It would have been helpful had Catesby explained this, given that he was later seen as *both* pro- and anti-Buffonian.) Nor did the same principle hold for humans, an intriguing codicil that revealed Catesby's determination to see people as creatures above nature. He specified that northern Indians differed little from those "near the *Equinoctial*." If anything, cold had the opposite effect on humans to what it had on other creatures. Thus northern Indians were "not altogether so swarthy, and generally somewhat of a larger stature." The first part of the statement was of a piece with much reasoning about climate and human complexion, but the latter phrase directly contradicted Catesby's idea that plants and animals were larger in warmer climates. To some extent, Catesby might have thought he lacked the expertise to speculate about climate and humans; he trusted such matters to observers trained in medicine. Indeed, he had wished to make a survey of Central and South America with a Dr. Thomas Cooper of Charleston. Catesby said Cooper's "Genius bends most to the Mathematicks, [and] he proposes to communicate to the R. Society what observations he makes in Astronomy. And perticularly in his way of practice," that is, to correlate precise measurements of location with their effects on the human body. Without such precision, latitudinal variation had only the rough medical effects that even ancient philosophers had managed to see.[23]

Catesby did not believe that latitude determined all global variation. Hemispheric differences also existed. Though his view prefigured the critical position Buffon would hold of American flora and fauna (as inferior in size and variety), Catesby did not see all hemispheric variation as revealing the New World's lack of distinction. Like earlier commentators,

22. On Catesby's ideas of climates, see Feduccia, ed., *Catesby's Birds of Colonial America*, 5; quotations from Catesby, *Natural History*, II, Appendix, 16 (birds), "Account," xli (size of specimens), xlii (number of species).

23. Catesby, *Natural History*, II, "Account," vii; Catesby to Sloane, Aug. 15, 1724, 212ᵛ, Sloane MSS, 4047.

he believed that American birds "excell those of *Europe* in the Beauty of their Plumage, but are much inferior to them in melodious Notes."[24]

Even if Catesby's views did not resemble Buffon's later attacks on the Western Hemisphere, they disturbed the perceived relation of New World to Old and reconfigured Europe's presumed cultural superiority to America in naturalistic terms. Virginia colonist William Byrd II, for one, feared that the loss of a latitudinal analogy would lower the economic value of American territory and products. He therefore questioned Catesby's skepticism. Byrd, in a letter that Catesby obligingly read to the Royal Society in January 1737, wrote, "I cannot be of your opinion, that wine may not be made" in Virginia. Byrd maintained his belief in the circumglobal properties of a given "latitude"; even if production of a given commodity "may be more difficult in one place than another, yet those difficulties may be overcome by good management." Careful Chesapeake husbandmen could compensate for their region's frosty winters.[25]

But the temperature of the climate was not the only variable of interest. Catesby was aware that myriad natural forces shaped phenomena. In this way, he prefigured the position taken by complexity theorists, that nature might have predictable patterns but that some of these might be difficult for humans to grasp because variables were so multiply intertwined. Catesby therefore noted that atmospheric factors other than temperature affected life. He pointed out that mahogany trees were not as large in the Bahamas as they were on the cooler American continent, because the island trees had to grow on rock. He also maintained that waterfowl were not more abundant in the South, because these warmer climates bred more predators; the fowls' "Sagacity for their Preservation" therefore made them avoid climates with "voracious Animals." These observations about birds and trees reveal two other areas about which Catesby wished to hypothesize: habitat (natural interconnections among creatures) and animal behavior (including search for an optimal habitat).[26]

Though the terms "ecology" and "habitat" would not have been part of the naturalist's vocabulary during the eighteenth century, a concept of the interconnectedness of nature was acquiring both richness and precision.

24. Catesby, *Natural History,* II, "Account," xxxv.

25. Marion Tinling, ed., *The Correspondence of the Three William Byrds of Westover, Virginia, 1684–1776* (Charlottesville, Va., 1977), II, 518.

26. Catesby, *Natural History,* II, "Account," xl, xxvi. On Catesby's representation of ecological relationships, see Amy R. W. Meyers, "Environmental Interchange and Colonial Expansion in the Americas," below.

Catesby expressed his goal in rather open-ended terms: "I have adapted the [illustrated] Birds to those Plants on which they fed, or have any Relation to." This is not yet a tightly knit natural world; subjects must be "adapted" by humans to seem natural in their relations, and their connections to each other might take on "any" number of qualities. This vague view of harmonious connections between things was partially derived from the concept of the chain of being, in which the plenitude of the material world rested on the benevolence of its creator. This older idea received new form from naturalists like Ray (especially in his 1691 *Wisdom of God*) and from Linnaeus, whose chain of being was an integrated set of species. Theorists like Buffon continued to assert that a primarily taxonomic emphasis obscured nature's integral character and systemic qualities.[27]

Catesby's representation of ecological relationships has already received some comment, especially in relation to his art. Scholars have noted that his was an unusual method of illustration, as there had been only a few naturalists who had this vision, such as its pioneer, painter Maria Sibylla Merian (1647–1717), Catesby's near contemporary. Merian's tactics derived from traditions as much in art as in science; her interconnected plants and animals had ancestors in Dutch still lifes that combined insects with flowers, and she questioned her naturalism by experimenting with trompe l'oeil representations of sheets of paper pinned up and containing her paintings. By Catesby's time, representation of relations among natural phenomena was a recognized strategy for scientific illustrators, though not one they always employed. Despite Buffon's emphasis on nature as systemic connections rather than typologized entities, the illustrations in his monumental *Histoire naturelle* (1749–1789) emphasized isolated and inactive animals; even his predators simply stand against a background—sometimes even elevated a little, as on a platform—as if waiting for a dish of food to be set down (Figure 1). It is unclear whether representations that placed specimens in situ were seen as giving a better understanding of nature, for the ecological perspective was far from dominant. The distinguished German naturalist Johann Philip Breynius confessed to William Sherard that, while he admired Eleazar Albin's *Natural History of English Insects* (1720), he disliked Albin's use of plants in his illustrations. "I wonder he has not made use of some rare Vegatables in compagnie of the Insects," Breynius wrote, "in place of the common

---

27. Donald Worster, *Nature's Economy: A History of Ecological Ideas,* 2d ed. (Cambridge, 1994), 34–39 (Linnaeus and Ray), 44–47; quotation from Catesby, *Natural History,* I, xi.

1. Cougar. *Buffon, Natural History, General and Particular, by the Count de Buffon, trans. William Smellie (London, 1812), VI, pl. 171 (after p. 322). From the Jean and Alexander Heard Library, Vanderbilt University*

[plants], very often repeated and not exactly figured." Breynius's concern seemed to be over the use of commonplace and sketchy figures rather than over the accuracy of the relation between animal and vegetable.[28]

If Catesby knew that some among his audience might be indifferent to the correct relations between creatures, he was also aware that such accuracy was a shibboleth to other naturalists, and one he himself did not share to the same degree. Although nearly all the illustrations for his *Natural History* contain more than one specimen, not all of these pictures assert a natural connection between the creatures. Other naturalists would not, unlike Catesby, group phenomena together *unless* they had some functional relationship. One such naturalist, whom Catesby is known to have studied, was René Antoine Réaumur (1683–1756). Catesby's knowledge of Réaumur is intriguing (though heretofore unexamined) because he shared certain interests with the distinguished French scientist, including attention to temperature and its effects on animals. Catesby reviewed the first four volumes of Réaumur's six-volume *Mémoires pour servir à l'histoire des insectes* (1734–1742) for the Royal Society. He read the reviews to the society's members, though they were not published in the *Transactions*. Catesby gave an astonished and revealing assessment of the amount of material Réaumur covered when he stated that "twelve or thirteen thousand Species of vegetables have perhaps each its peculiar Insects"; the

28. "Habitat" as a term for naturalists made its appearance in Latin by 1762, and in English by 1796 (*OED*, s.v. "habitat"). On Catesby's view of habitat, see also Amy R. W. Meyers, "The Perfecting of Natural History: Mark Catesby's Drawings of American Flora and Fauna in the Collection of the Royal Library, Windsor Castle," in Henrietta McBurney, ed., *Mark Catesby's "Natural History" of America: The Watercolors from the Royal Library, Windsor Castle* (London, 1997). Quotation from Breynius to Sherard, Aug. 15, 1722, Sherard Letters, CCLII, 93. On Catesby's habitats, see Frick and Stearns, *Mark Catesby,* 60–61, 63–64; but cf. Slaughter, *Natures of John and William Bartram,* 112.

On Merian, see William T. Stearn, "Maria Sibylla Merian (1647–1717) as a Botanical Artist," *Taxon,* XXXI (1982), 529–534; Sharon Valiant, "Maria Sibylla Merian: Recovering an Eighteenth-Century Legend," *Eighteenth-Century Studies,* XXVI (1993), 467–479 (both articles make clear that Merian's illustrations had great scientific accuracy); Natalie Zemon Davis, *Women on the Margins: Three Seventeenth-Century Lives* (Cambridge, Mass., 1995), 140–202. See the illustrations in the posthumous 1726 edition of *Metamorphosis* (1706), Maria Sibylla Merian, *Dissertation sur la generation et les transformations des insectes de Surinam / Dissertatio de generatione et metamorphosibus insectorum surinamensium* (The Hague, 1726), pls. LXVIII, LXXI (trompe l'oeil). That Merian did not include the trompe l'oeil images in her work during her lifetime indicates that she did not consider them of the same significance as her naturalistic images of habitats.

relation between plant and animal was not accidental, nor was its representation to be done merely as ornamental flourish or general indication of the way insects lived on plants. This precision was clear in Réaumur's illustrations, one example of which showed different caterpillars and butterflies, each on a different plant (Figure 2).[29]

Catesby did not, however, use habitat merely as an accepted trope or a device to present multiple entities in efficient, visual packages; his difference from Réaumur was a matter of degree. He paid attention to relations between animals and plants in his writings, not just in his illustrations. Further, he postulated habitats that were not visible to him—or to any human observer. Even in his unpublished writing he noted that some creatures seemed designed to accompany and assist each other, either in mere survival or even in propagation. Catesby explained to Sherard that laurel and umbrel seeds seemed to grow only if eaten "and voided by fowls." When he sent some of these seeds to England, he recommended that Sherard wash the mucilage from the seeds to approximate the same process. In the case of voracious creatures that seemed to protect their own parasites, Catesby was puzzled. He saw remora detach themselves from sharks and swim near them. Remora could be quite close to a shark's mouth "without his attempting to swallow them, the Reason of which I am not able to give." Here, it is clear that Catesby was reluctant to generalize from his observations; hence, some of his diffidence in presenting systemic connections within nature as the norm.[30]

His willingness to posit the existence of such relations is nonetheless striking. He was truly innovative when he hypothesized that habitats existed under the sea. "Every Species of Shell-fish inhabit particular Parts of the Sea agreeable to their Natures," he declared. "This seems to have some Analogy to Plants, whose different Kinds affect a different Soil and Aspect." Unseen relations between marine creatures could even explain certain dangers to humans. Catesby held that some Bahamian fish were poisonous only if they were caught in specific locations. He postulated

29. Catesby's account of vol. I of Réaumur, Register Book (Copy), RBC 20, p. 30, Royal Society; René Antoine Ferchault de Réaumur, *Mémoires pour servir à l'histoire des insectes* (Paris, 1734–1742), II, pl. 2, 120. On Réaumur's entomological work, see S. L. Tuxen, "Entomology Systematizes and Describes: 1700–1815," in Ray F. Smith et al., eds., *History of Entomology* (Palo Alto, Calif., 1973), 96–104.

30. Catesby to Sherard, Oct. 30, 1724, Sherard Letters, CCLIII, 179; Catesby, *Natural History*, II, 26. On marine habitats, see Frick and Stearns, *Mark Catesby*, 78.

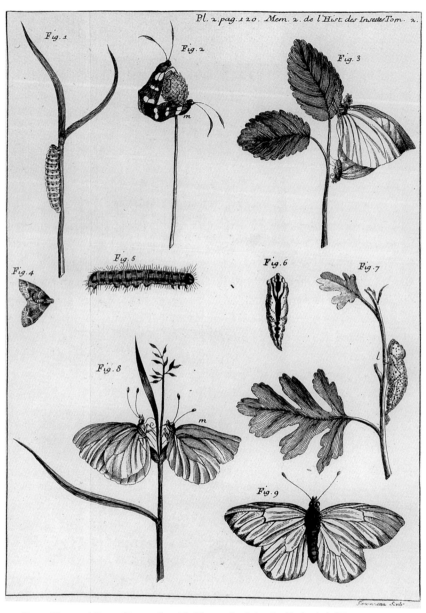

Pl. 2. pag. 120. Mem. 2. de l'Hist. des Insectes Tom. 2.

2. Caterpillars and Butterflies on Specific Plants. *René Antoine Ferchault de Réaumur,* Mémoires pour servir à l'histoire des insectes, *6 vols. (Paris, 1734–1742), II, pl. 2, p. 120. This item is reproduced by permission of* The Huntington Library, San Marino, California

that it was only when the fish came into contact with poisonous coral that they acquired poisonous properties themselves.[31]

Habitat and interconnection among subjects were not the only guides to Catesby's vision—the variety of methodological and theoretical frames he used in his illustrations reveals, if anything, the absence of any orthodox opinion. Unlike Merian, for instance, Catesby did not represent nature only as if he were constructing a frame around part of it in order to point out its interrelated residents to an observer who happened by the scene. Some of his images were, instead, beholden to styles of scientific illustration that depended on dissection and microscopy; they laid out or cut apart dead specimens or presented disembodied parts of subjects as if magnified. The dead specimen was the mode Catesby used in his illustration of the Carolina fieldfare, which had expired and was lying on its back. Catesby's closeup view of a flamingo's bill both isolated a part of this animal and enlarged the pertinent detail, a sievelike construction that filtered food from water and mud; the bird's internal constitution, rather than its relations to external phenomena, was most important, and a part of it appeared as if dissociated from the animal's very body (Figure 3). Finally, his rattlesnake showed not only the animal itself but a detached fang, a detached rattle, and a rattle cut through to show the interior structure (Figure 4).[32]

Some of Catesby's illustrations were unsettling combinations of relation and disembodiment. Such was his image of the yellow-breasted chat, which he pictured as if flying over an uprooted plant: part of nature appeared in its actual motion, yet another part was laid out like a disassociated specimen (Figure 5). This was true as well of Catesby's portrayal of the Jamaican blackbird, which he showed gripping a ladyslipper in its claws. Its perch is, however, not steadily fixed in the material world, as its roots are represented as exposed through transparent earth (Figure 6). Some phenomena are rather oddly disconnected or unnaturally connected. For instance, Catesby's seven-year apple and its avian inhabitant appear to be naturally in contact, even though parts of the tree are working against nature: the bird sits in the tree, which improbably (but conveniently for an illustrator) bears both fruit and seedpod. Another seed is suspended as if in midair, less connected than the bird to the tree itself. The same is true of the red-flowering maple, which has both seedpods and

---

31. Catesby, *Natural History*, II, "Account," xlii, xliii.
32. Ibid., I, 29, 74, II, 42.

Caput Phœnicepteri.   *Keratophyton &c.*

3. Flamingo's Bill. *Mark Catesby,* The Natural History of Carolina, Florida, and the Bahama Islands . . . *(London, 1731–1747), I, pl. 74. Courtesy, Colonial Williamsburg Foundation*

4. Rattlesnake. *Catesby,* Natural History, *II, pl. 41. Courtesy, Colonial Williamsburg Foundation*

blossoms, though these should be present in different seasons. Further, a branch has just snapped off from the bird's perch, again making the plant into a disconnected series of specimens even while the animal is firmly attached to part of the series (Figure 7).[33]

These images reveal Catesby's underlying eclecticism, his unwillingness to make nature appear to fit one model of representation; nature did function according to relations among specimens, but these relations were not always essential for humans to visualize how nature worked. Certainly, some of Catesby's more bizarre images do not fit well with the premise of habitat. This was true of his plate of a flamingo against a background of coral (which would not have grown on the dry land on which the flamingo stands) and of a globefish he made float in the air surrounding the branches of a tree. In these images, Catesby was not interested in the relations of the specimens, but in the visual play they established against each other: the elongated coral and flamingo mirror each other; the globe-fish's inflatable quality is emphasized as it sails in the treetops.[34]

33. Ibid., I, 50, 59, 62, II, Appendix, 3 (blackbird and ladyslipper).
34. Ibid., I, 73, 74 (flamingo), II, 28 (globefish).

5. Yellow-Breasted Chat. *Catesby,* Natural History, *I, pl. 50. Courtesy, Colonial Williamsburg Foundation*

Even when Catesby focused on natural relations among his subjects, he was also at least as interested in how these relations might change. Change in habitat due to animal behaviors like migration was significant for him. His interest in animal behavior took its boldest form in his theory of avian migration. Seasonal variation of bird populations had received comment since ancient times, but the reasons for it, and the predictability of its

6. Jamaica Blackbird. *Catesby,* Natural History, *II, Appendix, pl. 3. Courtesy, Colonial Williamsburg Foundation*

pattern, awaited modern commentators, of whom Catesby was one of the earliest and most interesting. Many modern naturalists believed birds vanished in winter because they hibernated in caves or were in another state of suspended animation in bodies of water. Discovery of heavy deposits of guano in caves or ponds seemed evidence for this premise. Catesby argued instead that birds did not hibernate, but, as suited their nature, took to the air when the weather turned too cold for them. (He considered the possibility quite early; the first sign of it appeared in a May 1723

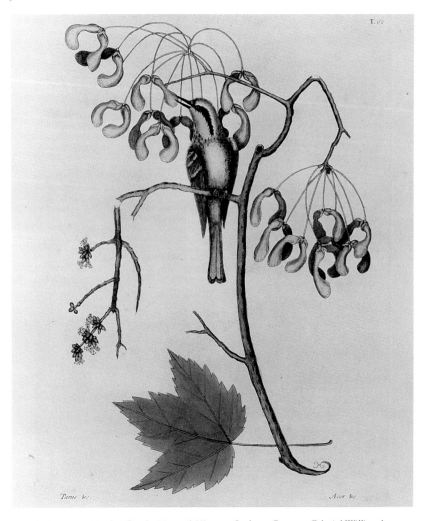

7. Red-Flowering Maple. *Catesby,* Natural History, *I, pl. 62. Courtesy, Colonial Williamsburg Foundation*

letter to Sloane.)[35] Climate explained the reason for and the pattern of migration; seasonal process took place so that the animals might out-maneuver changes in season. Birds migrated to "the same Latitude of the southern Hemisphere" as they dwelt in in the northern, so "they live in perpetual Summer." This was indeed the correct hypothesis, and it is surely significant that Catesby's other major premise about nature—biodi-

35. Catesby to Sloane, May 10, 1723, Sloane MSS 4046, fol. 353ʳ. On avian migration, see Feduccia, ed., *Catesby's Birds of Colonial America,* 5.

versity in relation to latitude—was related to avian migration. Catesby had said that, of all cases of species variation, the connection between birds and their environment was most striking. Birds had the closest relation to place and therefore needed the ability to uproot themselves in search of the optimal place. One law (of fixed physical conditions that varied by mathematical degree) was modified by another tendency—animal sagacity and ability to control physical surroundings through movement.[36]

In his attention to the migration of animals, Catesby extended old understandings about climate and the human body to a wider inquiry into climate and all animal bodies. Unlike Sloane, he did not give medicalized details about climate, movement, and physical adaptation; he instead used broad strokes to define areas broader than the smaller units of Hippocratic theory. It is frustrating that Catesby did not give sustained attention to the question of human travel, as other narrative writers on nature did. He seemed elliptically to register the significance of increased colonization and its consequences for the integrity of bodies that had moved to new climates. But not until Catesby discussed the project of moving plants did he have a manifest interest in proving what he only indicated in his discussion of migration: natural bodies could be moved to seemingly alien climates without damage.[37]

Catesby, with characteristic caution, was nonetheless reluctant to make animal migration into a law rather than a tendency, and he gave generous examples of phenomena that did not suit his hypothesis. He did show that other animals like fish fitted in his theory of migration; sturgeon did so. But the universal properties of animal migration remained elusive. Some examples of bird migration baffled him. Catesby related that an owl had appeared on his ship midway between Africa and America, and he could not determine how or why it had flown so far from land. Passenger pigeons migrated south in winter, but they evidently took a different route back, because they were not "ever seen to return, at least this [same] way." Catesby was most mystified by the question of the origin of American birds. He agreed with most naturalists that America had been populated by people and animals from Asia. But Asian birds would had to have flown a prodigious distance (like the transatlantic owl) through a climate

---

36. Catesby, *Natural History*, II, "Account," xxvi, Appendix, 16 (see also II, 57, which discusses plants' habitats occurring in comparable latitudes, north and south).

37. Cf. Anthony Pagden, *European Encounters with the New World: From Renaissance to Romanticism* (New Haven, Conn., 1993), 141–181.

too cold for most of the species that ended up in America: "The Climate and their Inability of performing a long Flight may reasonably be objected." Catesby hypothesized that the migration from Asia and America might only have been possible if the continents had once been closer together. This is an intriguing bit of speculation, which held that animals had retained the same qualities since they originated (birds had not grown less tolerant of cold) yet postulated that the structure of the earth might once have been quite different.[38]

In his examination of avian migration, Catesby revealed his interest in the sort of questions Buffon would again raise about physical environment and its effects on everything from plants to people. Catesby's premise that birds migrated, moreover, showed early speculation about animals' intelligent reaction to physical conditions. Although not as striking as the kind of hypotheses Lamarck would define about physical adaptation, attention to animal behaviors like migration nevertheless showed that the question of animal adaptation (behavioral or physical) was gaining intellectual purchase over the course of the eighteenth century, eroding the premise of the chain of being that each part of creation had a fixed place suited to it by the creator. Catesby defined shifting patterns—climate, availability of food, animal migration—that complicated the older view of nature as static.

Though his explanation of bird migration was one of Catesby's most distinctive contributions to natural history, it was part of a wider consideration of the question whether animals had anthropomorphic intelligence or whether their rudimentary instinct remained characteristically bestial. Animal artifice was a standard topic of naturalists. It was, for instance, a question that Catesby knew Réaumur had discussed at length, as one of the keys to animal survival. In one typical illustration, the French naturalist showed a caterpillar winding leaves around itself into a protective cover (Figure 8). Even before he reviewed Réaumur, Catesby had already, in the first volume of his *Natural History*, showed that the red-winged starling built nests using water grasses, "the tops of which they interweave very artfully, and under fix their Nests." Using this analysis within entomology, Catesby related that the largest Carolina moth had "Bags" that are "found artfully fixed to the Twigs of Trees."[39]

Some of Catesby's most detailed analyses of the relations between

38. Catesby, *Natural History,* I, vii, 23, II, "Account," xxxiii (sturgeon), xxxv.

39. Réaumur, *Histoire des insectes,* II, pl. 16, p. 252; Catesby, *Natural History,* I, 13, II, 86.

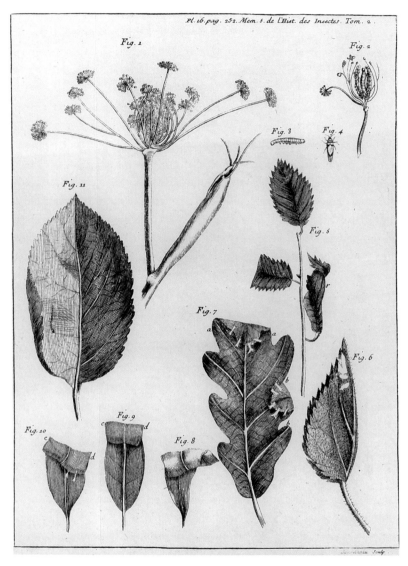

8. Caterpillars Using Leaves to Make Cocoons. *Réaumur,* Histoire des insectes, *III, pl. 16, p. 252. This item is reproduced by permission of* The Huntington Library, San Marino, California

plants and animals described fortuitous connections between the natural properties of one subject and the artifice of another, making *both* partake of art and nature at once. This was the case with the Baltimore oriole and the tulip tree. The bird made its nest "in a particular Manner, supported only by two Twigs fix'd to the Verge of the Nest, and hanging most commonly at the Extremity of a Bough." The tulip tree was well suited to this manner of house building, as it had boughs "very unequal and irregular, not streight, but making several Bends or Elbows" of use to the precarious positioning of the oriole's nest. Here, bird and tree are complementary, as if both animate and inanimate nature bent themselves toward the same purpose.[40]

Indeed, Catesby registered contemporary puzzlement over whether the large kingdoms of natural beings were or were not categorically distinct. The sea polyp was the premier example of an entity that seemed to be both plant and animal, one of the puzzles that led La Mettrie to postulate that all were mechanisms anyway, and Buffon to argue that living matter had laws of form and function that were similar to Newtonian laws about brute matter but that did not make life simply a form of machine. Catesby had read Réaumur's account of insects that demonstrated a polyplike hybrid condition. Catesby's 1740 review of Réaumur's fourth volume (1738) outlined Réaumur's discussion of gall insects: "The more their growth advances, and the nearer they reach to their state of perfection, the more they lose of the animal figure." This was paradoxical: approaching perfection, for animals, could mean resemblance to lower forms of life. Gall insects nevertheless looked "like tubercles of the rind of the plant they are fix'd to" (Figure 9). Some *progall insects* (similar to those that formed galls on plants) were "easier" to recognize as "animals," but the puzzle of their classification was not simple, especially as they lived off (as well as resembled) plants.[41]

Not only did animals resemble plants, but the reverse could appear to be true. Catesby discussed this latter possibility in his description of mahogany trees in the Bahamas. The trees' seeds were winged and so, like birds, dispersed in the wind in order to secure the maximum amount and optimal quality of territory. After falling to earth, the seeds' behavior seemed almost willful: "If the [root] Fibres find Resistance from the Hardness of the Rock, they creep out on the Surface of it, and seek another Chink."[42]

Given these surprisingly animate qualities of plants, it would have been

40. Catesby, *Natural History,* I, 48.

41. "An account of the 4th volume of Mons.r de Reaumur's Memoirs for the history of Insects . . . ," entered into Royal Society Register Book, May 19, 1740, Add. MSS 4436, fol. 188, British Library. See also Réaumur, *Histoire des insectes,* III (1737), pl. 40, p. 532. On the elusive plant/animal distinction, see note 6, above, and Slaughter, *The Natures of John and William Bartram,* 63–64.

42. Catesby, *Natural History,* II, 81.

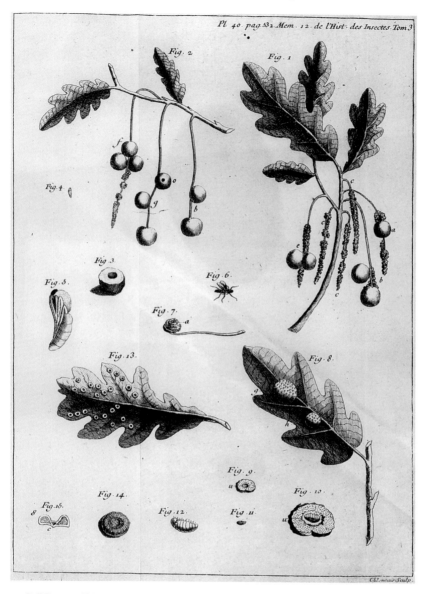

9. Gall Insects. *Réaumur,* Histoire des insectes, *III, pl. 40, p. 532. This item is reproduced by permission of* The Huntington Library, San Marino, California

logical for Catesby to proceed to a systemic or even teleological view of nature, as operated by one animated principle (of survival?) and proceeding toward an ordained end. He did not, however, consistently incline toward such a position, though neither did he openly criticize it. He related, without commentary, Réaumur's strong rejection of teleological views of nature. The French naturalist scoffed at people who had "ascribed all the moral virtues to Insects," and dismissed the Cartesian debate over whether animals were "Machines" or "intelligent Beings." Réaumur stated that the task of the natural historian was, not to think of "ends," but to "describe" with "accuracy."[43]

Catesby went somewhat beyond this position—he described animal behavior in terms of ends, but he had short-term goals rather than cosmic teleology in mind. The sea dotterel, for example, used its bill to overturn stones: "This Property Nature seems to have given it for the finding of its Food." Catesby discussed the flamingo's bill in similar fashion: "Nature has provided the Edges of their Bill with a Sieve, or Teeth, like those of a fine Comb, with which they retain the Food, and reject the Mud."[44] Still, the final emphasis was on the actual intelligence of the subjects, not the hypothetical intelligence of their creator or of surrounding "Nature." Catesby's arguments in this line were sometimes commonplaces, as with his praise for beavers' greater "sagacity," compared to other animals. But he also seemed to want to determine the proportions of intelligence distributed to animals and the conditions under which it varied. He concluded that the wood pelican was "a stupid Bird and void of fear, easily to be shot," and that skunks, when tamed, did not exercise their odoriferous "Faculty, which Fear and Self-Preservation perhaps only prompts them to." Here is a contrast between stupidity and intelligence, yet Catesby admitted that the latter, in animals, was, not intrinsic, but a "faculty" dependent on external stimuli like danger. In Catesby's analysis, however, avoidance of danger was no small sign of intelligence, since violence was so integral to his ideas about the natural world.[45]

Catesby's conviction of the violence of the natural world revealed his fascination with glimpses of primordial chaos and was guided by his experience in tropical and semitropical regions of America. It was a standard trope of natural history that such places were, in comparison to cooler areas, teeming with noxious and dangerous creatures. This was certainly the way Merian had assessed Surinam, and the opinion would take classic form with John Bruckner's *Philosophical Survey of the Animal*

43. Catesby's review of Réaumur's first volume, Register Book (Copy), RBC 20, pp. 32–34, Royal Society. On *telos* in science, see Glacken, *Traces on the Rhodian Shore*, 517–537.

44. Catesby, *Natural History*, I, 72, 74. See also Stephen Jay Gould, *The Flamingo's Smile: Reflections in Natural History* (New York, 1985), 23–39.

45. Catesby, *Natural History*, I, 81 (pelican), II, 62 (skunk), "Account," xxx (beaver).

Creation (1768); Bruckner's tropics were swarming pools of reptiles and other vermin. Though Humboldt would later hold that the creation was harmonious even in Latin America, suspicion that warm climates were by nature more spectacularly violent died hard. A new element of this suspicion held, however, that the truly destructive force within the tropics was human—particularly tropical islands deforested by colonists, which thereafter suffered drought and species extinction.[46]

Catesby's views of climate supported the premise of tropical violence; if more species emerged nearer the equator, so did predatory species as well. Some of Catesby's most violent images came from southern latitudes. He described how small alligators were prey even to their "own Species," and he presented their mangrove swamp habitat as site of a war of all against all. Although the mangrove provided dense thickets where young alligators could find refuge, they were still prey even to "the Jaws of their voracious Parents." In the swamp, "ravenous Fish, Turtles, and other Animals . . . prey continually one upon the other, and the Alligators on them all, so that in no Place have I ever seen such remarkable Scenes of Devastation as amongst these Mangroves, in *Andros,* one of the *Bahama* Islands, where the Fragments of half devoured Carcasses were usually floating on the Water." This is indeed a compelling image of destruction and waste—it is the "usually" in this sentence that conjures up the frequency of tropical predation.[47]

But Catesby saw violence even in northern regions and had characterized it as a principle of nature even before he ventured very far south. He noted in a 1723 letter to Sloane that the "King Bird" was so called either from "it's Golden Crown or from it's tyrannizing Quality for it persues and put[s] to the rout all Birds." He also noted predation while he was at sea. He remarked on the dilemma of the flying fish, which traveled in water and air: "At some Times neither Element aford them safety, for no sooner do they escape their Enemies in the Water, but they are caught in the Air by voracious Birds."[48]

In part, this omnipresent violence functioned as a method of relating one creature to another: they ate each other. The image of nature as one

46. Merian, *Dissertation / Dissertatio,* pls. XVIII (predatory spiders), LXIX (cayman and snake fighting); Davis, *Women on the Margins,* 183; Worster, *Nature's Economy,* 47–48 (Bruckner), 137 (Humboldt); Grove, *Green Imperialism,* 95–152.

47. Catesby, *Natural History,* II, 63.

48. Catesby to Sloane, May 10, 1723, Sloane MSS 4046, 353ʳ; Catesby, *Natural History,* I, vii.

long food chain pervaded the illustrations of the *Natural History* and included even humans. Thus the fish hawk appeared with a captured fish, and the "goat-sucker" had its mouth open and ready to engulf a flying insect. For some creatures, feeding patterns were more complicated and had consequences for humans. The iguana's abdominal fat took on the color of the "Fruit they last eat"; Carolina turtle doves ate poison berries yet "are accounted good Meat"; Carolina's ricebirds arrived in fall "in infinite swarms, to devour the Rice," and Catesby, presumably hungry from watching these birds eat, had "some scores [of them] prepared for the spit." This was a vision, avant Burke, of a sublimity that ended with the cooking pot—an image, anticipating Darwin and Tennyson, of nature "red in tooth and claw."[49]

Catesby's interest in predation was influenced by microscopy. The otherwise invisible cosmos was surprisingly unpacific. Microscopists from Anton van Leeuwenhoek onward had presented even the tiniest parts of nature as teeming with creatures, which fed off each other and off their plant and animal hosts. Microscopes could, therefore, strengthen any inclination to view nature, not as fixed and pacific, but as hostile, predatory, and capable of extinguishing vulnerable species. (Some early accounts of spermatazoa speculated, for instance, that they were parasites within animals' seminal fluid rather than the key element of it.) Catesby's vision was of a piece with naturalists' microscopic images that he saw elsewhere. One engraving in Réaumur, for example, showed the microscopic carnage inflicted by a biting insect. Its proboscis pierced flesh in an image that was repeated again and again, as if to reiterate the myriad lines of attack a bloodthirsty animal could take (Figure 10).[50]

Fascination with the microscopic may seem paradoxical, given Catesby's dominant orientation toward the visible world. But this interest supported his determination to display to a European audience American phenomena that would otherwise be "invisible" to them. Microscopy was a technology that begged as well as answered questions: Were there worlds even smaller than those revealed under a microscope? Was it the nature of

49. Catesby, *Natural History,* I, 2, 8 (hawk and goatsucker), 14 (ricebirds), 24 (turtle), II, 64 (iguana).

50. Svetlana Alpers, *The Art of Describing: Dutch Art in the Seventeenth Century* (Chicago, 1983), 16–25; Catherine Wilson, *The Invisible World: Early Modern Philosophy and the Invention of the Microscope* (Princeton, N.J., 1995), esp. chap. 5; Réaumur, *Histoire des insectes,* IV (1738), pl. 41, p. 636.

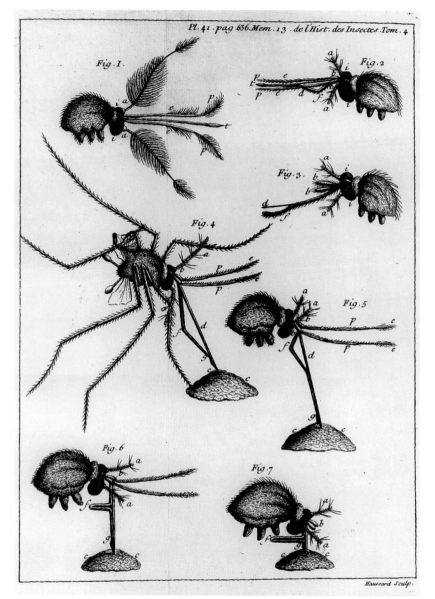

Pl. 41 . pag .636.Mem .13 . de l'Hist. des Insectes.Tom. 4

10. Insect Biting. *Réaumur,* Histoire des insectes, *IV, pl. 41, p. 636. This item is reproduced by permission of* The Huntington Library, San Marino, California

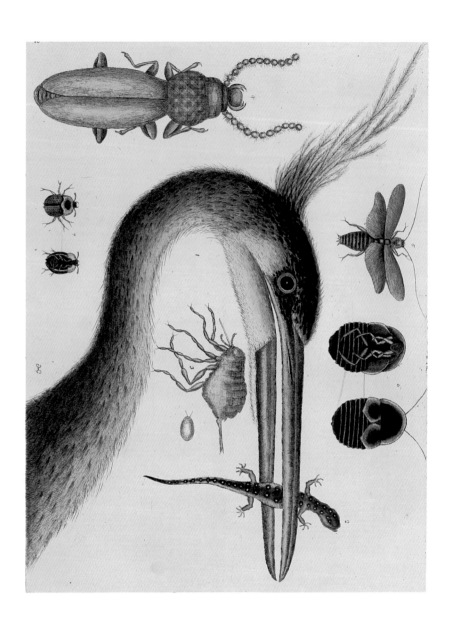

11. Chiggers, Heron, and Eft. *Catesby,* Natural History, *II, Appendix, pl. 10. Courtesy, Colonial Williamsburg Foundation*

nature to be invisible, to have layers and depths humans would never comprehend? New knowledge was always emerging. The hungry, painful world that the microscope revealed gave Catesby the opportunity to show some heretofore unseen aspects of American nature. Catesby thus remarked of the porcupine, "The Point of [its] every Quill is very sharp and jagged, with very small Prickles, nor discernable but by a Microscope."[51]

One of his most complicated plates showed the world of eater and eaten that existed in micro- and macroscopic form. "In the year 1725," Catesby explained, "I being at the house of his Excellency Mr. *Phinney* [George Phenney], then Governor of the *Bahama* Islands, who as he was searching of his feet for Chegoes [chiggers], at the time we were viewing them through a Microscope, produced an odd Insect on the point of his needle as at Fig. 4 which he then picked out of his foot." This intriguing scenario (which revealed, if nothing else, the simplicity of life in the first British Empire) showed a food chain that ran from colonial governor to burrowing insect. Catesby rendered an image of the latter with its egg "magnified by a glass, [which] appeared as here represented" (Figure 11). Despite the connections among the creatures implied by this description, the plate challenges any vision of a (rather bloodthirsty) continuity by representing each specimen discretely, not in the connected manner typical of some of Catesby's other plates. The plate with the chigger also represented the disembodied head of a heron with an eft (newt) in its mouth—a demonstration that to rend living beings into smaller pieces was to sustain life.[52]

As with much else, Catesby was indeterminate in his final assessment of violence, seeing it neither as essentially disintegrative nor as serving part of a larger and more subtle function within nature's systems. A food chain could have implied a kind of order. Insects bit into human flesh and porcupines carried jagged quills in order to propagate and protect themselves. Catesby might have left his images of violence at that, but he instead presented some purely destructive tendencies in nature, and did so without representing them as steps toward an intrinsic order in or final condition for the cosmos. Here he showed that he was aware of contemporary debates over the catastrophist view of the earth: Evidence of extreme change on the planet (of floods, earthquakes, fragments of fossilized animals) was being drawn into controversies about the age of the earth—and the possible extinction of species that would explode tradi-

51. Catesby, *Natural History,* II, "Account," xxx.
52. Ibid., II, Appendix, 10.

tional understandings of nature either as static (existing always as the creator had intended) or as historically linear (existing within a narrative intended by the creator). Catesby was, however, reluctant to take any side, and he especially avoided any teleological intepretation of natural disasters. Even in his repeated attentions to floods, for instance, he was wary of invoking the Deluge. For him, nature simply had violent tendencies whose purposes were as yet not known.[53]

Much of Catesby's vision of nature's disintegrative powers came out of his experiences in South Carolina, where, in 1722, the colony suffered a coastal hurricane and an inland flood of the Savannah River. Of the hurricane, Catesby said, "The Deer were found frequently lodged on high trees, the wind was so violent that it tore up by the roots great numbers of Trees."[54] When the river near Fort Moore (present-day Augusta) flooded, its damage was so remarkable that news of the event quickly spread to the mother country; Catesby's uncle did not hear from his nephew shortly thereafter and feared the worst. (Catesby had serendipitously fallen ill, so was safe in bed in Charleston.) In his *Natural History,* Catesby described the "great Inundation" and the havoc it wreaked among animals and vegetative matter: "The voracious and larger Serpents were continually preying upon the smaller, as well those of their own Kind, as others, which in that Confusion were more easily surprized." His accompanying plate of a viper about to eat a newt underscored how natural disaster encouraged predation and furthered destruction. After the flood: "Panthers, Bears, and Deer, were drowned, and found lodg'd on the Limbs of Trees. The smaller Animals suffered also in this Calamity; even Reptiles and Insects were dislodged from their Holes, and violently hurried away, and mixing with harder Substances were beat in Pieces, and their Fragments (after the Waters fell) were seen in many Places to cover the Ground."[55]

---

53. Roy Porter, *The Making of Geology: Earth Science in Britain, 1660–1815* (Cambridge, 1977), chaps. 2–4; Bowen, *Empiricism and Geographical Thought,* 106–122; Paolo Rossi, *The Dark Abyss of Time: The History of the Earth and the History of Nations from Hooke to Vico,* trans. Lydia G. Cochrane (Chicago, 1984), pt. 1; Stephen Jay Gould, *Time's Arrow, Time's Cycle: Myth and Metaphor in the Discovery of Geological Time* (Cambridge, Mass., 1987), esp. chaps. 2, 3; Charlton, *New Images of the Natural in France,* 82–86; Roger, *Buffon,* trans. Bonnefoi, ed. Williams, 93–105, 402–413.

54. Catesby to Sherard, Sherard Letters, CCLIII, 165.

55. Catesby, *Natural History,* II, 45 (predatory viper), vii. On Catesby's illness, see Frick and Stearns, *Mark Catesby,* 23. Catesby's uncle's fears were reported in Samuel Dale to William Sherard [ca. 1723], Sherard Letters, CCLIII, 231.

As with the Bahamian mangrove swamps—strewn with parts of carcasses—Catesby used Carolina's terrible year of 1722 to delineate an uncompromising view of nature's violence, of a world reduced nearly to atomized fragments of matter. This was the only opportunity he took to relate such small catastrophes to a larger vision of destruction as prelude to regeneration. Following his image of dead animals beaten into pieces, the very next paragraph of the *Natural History* explained that signs of the Deluge were clear in North America; specifically, Catesby mentioned the presence of glossopetrae (fossilized sharks' teeth) in a well recently dug in Virginia—but did not elaborate any analysis of these items or of the Deluge. This noncommittal attitude was typical of Catesby's examination of the hard-to-place data of fossils. He collected few such specimens, though he had remarked at the start of his Carolina sojourn, "I am told up the rivers there are abundance of fossils and petrifactions."[56]

By not relating nature's puzzles and eruptions to a grand vision of deluge, regeneration, and future destruction, Catesby again seemed, at least by default if not by manifest design, to reject the teleological view of nature. He reported disorder without providing soothing codicils about its real or ultimate function. He seemed in sympathy with the emerging vision of the earth as existing in "deep time": it was created long ago and endured a continual process of eruptions that showed the earth itself had a history, a natural history, that, due to its extreme age and constant shifting, was indifferent to the brief and shallow history of humans. Certainly, Catesby's supposition that the continents of Asia and America had once been closer together showed confidence in the proposition of slow, geological change.

What is interesting about Catesby's understanding of this disorderly world is his sense of ease with it—not a position held by all of his contemporaries. To be sure, he sometimes interpreted incidental violence as part of overall stasis; some seemingly destructive natural motion was balanced by opposite and integrative forms of motion. So Catesby reasoned about some hydrological cycles: Carolina's rivers had their source in the mountains and swelled after abundant rain. They deposited the colony's "richest Soil" during their "Inundations," yet the valued soil could be stripped away "from the same Cause." Still, this hypothetical equilibrium left unexplained the meaning of catastrophic flooding.[57] Even more surprising,

56. Catesby, *Natural History,* II, "Account," vii; Catesby to Sherard, Sherard Letters, CCLIII, 163.

57. Catesby, *Natural History,* II, "Account," iv.

Catesby seemed not only to accept the violence of the natural world but found it, from a human perspective, amusing. He remarked of turkey buzzards: "'Tis pleasant to observe their contentions in feeding." When he saw a barracuda consume another fish in three bites, he commented, "These and such like Accidents I have often been diverted with in the shallow Seas of the Bahama Islands."[58]

In contrast, Catesby was never diverted by the violence that humans exerted over nature. In this regard, he gave evenhanded criticism to human populations regardless of their origin or background. In America, for example, the blame he gave to Indians for their violence was equal to that he gave white colonists. Unlike some contemporary observers who made distinctions between "civilized" and "savage" practices, Catesby faulted both. He was disgusted that native Americans killed more animals since they had acquired guns and were drawn into the European fur trade. Indian hunters killed so much game that they took the pelts and left the carcasses to predators or to rot, but they did so with white encouragement. Catesby also maintained (like other Europeans) that Indian warfare was unusually violent. Its virulence "probably has occasioned the depopulated State of *North America* at the Arrival of the *Europeans,*" though Catesby immediately added that European vices and disease had delivered the final and debilitating blows to the native people.[59]

That humans might behave like alligators and barracudas was not a matter for resignation. People had to separate themselves from the destruction that was natural to animals, wind, and rivers and to create an order otherwise lacking in the nature around them. From Catesby's perspective, most white colonists were derelict. He repeatedly expressed a disdain for colonists' botanizing ability and lamented their lack of horticultural activity. In a 1724 letter to Sherard, he despaired that the same American tree could sport several names because of inept observation and description: "Most people here have no regard to the leaf but to the Bark and Grain of the wood only." Humans were thus implicated in Catesby's vision of America: nature in the New World was lovely, but its beautiful creatures were barely cataloged before they were reduced to carcasses.[60]

Catesby's assessment of human practices and their impact on nature followed a long tradition of asserting human superiority over the rest of the

58. Ibid., I, 6, II, 10.
59. Ibid., II, "Account," xi, xvi.
60. Catesby to Sherard, Apr. 6, 1724, Sherard Letters, CCLIII, 176.

creation—superiority in ability both to rise above matter and to order it. His own views reflected his experience in an imperial, transatlantic world even as they criticized that world. To Catesby, as to others, European empires and science were connected. An imperialist vision of nature seemed present in the Linnaean system, for instance, which organized all matter into universally recognizable kingdoms. Though it is true that earlier forms of science were connected to empire, the totalizing visions of Linnaeus (and of his contemporaries and heirs) represented a qualitative shift in expectations for science in an era of intensified European colonization. Scientific apparatus like taxonomy could serve imperialist goals, especially when it distinguished between European conquerors and aboriginal peoples. It could also masquerade as a more implicit form of imperialism, one that gathered information and specimens to service commercial needs and to justify settlement.[61]

Catesby indeed possessed an imperial vision of control over nature through ordered representation of its visible phenomena, the most distinctive portion of which had to do with the domestication of wild aspects of nature. He wanted to create within England an American garden that was the opposite of an anarchic mangrove swamp. Here he drew upon a long tradition of recreating humanity's original paradise, a garden that represented the harmony among creatures that antedated the Fall. Further, Catesby's plans registered a recent belief that paradise might best be reconstructed on an island—usually a tropical one—for which the sea provided the walls that had shut off the original paradise. In Catesby's case, the island-garden was nontropical Britain, a place he saw as site for important gardens. When he returned to England in 1726, he lived at Hoxton and worked with Thomas Fairchild, who had a nursery of American plants. In the 1730s, when he lived in London, Catesby collaborated with Christopher Gray and evidently kept his own garden on the grounds of Gray's nursery at Fulham. Catesby helped produce a 1737 broadsheet advertisement for Gray that told which American plants he sold. Catesby also worked on a gardeners' handbook that was published posthumously

---

61. See Lucile H. Brockway, *Science and Colonial Expansion: The Role of the British Royal Botanic Gardens* (New York, 1979), 61–76; Keith Thomas, *Man and the Natural World: A History of the Modern Sensibility* (New York, 1983), 17–50; Mary Louise Pratt, *Imperial Eyes: Travel Writing and Transculturation* (London, 1992), chap. 2; Worster, *Nature's Economy,* chap. 2, esp. 29–30; Miller and Reill, eds., *Visions of Empire.* On the gendered dimension of this vision, see Londa Schiebinger, *Nature's Body: Gender in the Making of Modern Science* (Boston, 1993), esp. chaps. 1, 6.

in 1763, first under the evocative title of *Hortus Britanno-Americanus* and then (in 1767) as *Hortus Europae Americanus*. These works were predicated on Catesby's assumptions in the *Natural History* and were a restatement of some of the most important ones about nature.[62]

Catesby's gardening enacted a fantasy of appropriation—it rejected a mercantilist vision of American exotica and removed all that was beautiful in America from its naturally dangerous and forbidding environment. England could become an alternative to America, a natural world that existed in *parallel* to the inconveniently distant and hurricane-prone colonies. Gardening was therefore a *para*colonial project. Indeed, Catesby's idea of a Britanno-American garden was almost postcolonial—though not in the usual sense of the destiny that could be defined by aboriginal inhabitants of ex-European empires. Catesby instead held that America itself could not be tamed, especially its tropical regions. But American products could be extracted (long an expectation of colonies) and naturalized in England, which might in the future no longer need a continued chain of connection to America. A replanted Britain would free itself from colonies and all things colonial. American flora would be denatured, or at least renatured, in a regulated landscape.[63]

Consistent with this model of appropriation, Catesby elaborated his criticism of colonists in his *Hortus Europae Americanus,* where he again lamented the ignorance of the "planters of America." His antipathy to the colonial obsession with mercantile gain paralleled this exasperation with Americans' lack of education and refinement. True civility resulted from abstract speculation about nature and from reconstruction of the physical world. Gardening, as opposed to commercial planting, represented an activity that ordered nature according to the highest, aesthetic principles. Human civility, itself a form of artifice, would be naturalized in gardens.[64]

---

62. John Prest, *The Garden of Eden: The Botanic Garden and the Re-Creation of Paradise* (New Haven, Conn., 1981), 16–17; Andrew Cunningham, "The Culture of Gardens," in Jardine, Secord, and Spary, eds., *Cultures of Natural History,* 38–56; Grove, *Green Imperialism,* introd., chap. 1, 53–54 (Britain as island); Blanche Henrey, *British Botanical and Horticultural Literature before 1800 . . .* (London, 1975), II, 275–276, facing 348 (broadsheet); Stearns, *Science in the British Colonies of America,* 323, 325; Frick and Stearns, *Mark Catesby,* 43, 68–69.

63. Sarah P. Stetson, "The Traffic in Seeds and Plants from England's Colonies in North America," *Agricultural History,* XXIII (1949), 45–56; Alan Frost, "The Antipodean Exchange: European Horticulture and Imperial Designs," in Miller and Reill, eds., *Visions of Empire,* 58–79, and cf. Lisbet Koerner, "Purposes of Linnaean Travel: A Preliminary Research Report," 117–152.

64. Mark Catesby, *Hortus Europae Americanus . . .* (London, 1767), 4.

Even during research for his *Natural History,* Catesby had betrayed an interest in assessing specimens for their potential as gardeners' materials. He had reported to Sherard of the flowering acacia that it was "a Tree not only of a fragrant scent but very ornamental and of great use of quick growth and easily raised." This view appeared with greater force in his *Hortus Europae Americanus,* in which he referred to North America—"the territory of the crown of Great Britain on the continent"—as "a forest of a thousand miles in length." Here the British colonies seemed to lack any human settlements of note and were instead a wilderness reserve of garden plants. Catesby denigrated colonists' ability to discover the properties of the trees in the forest when he claimed that, because they lived "in an infant country, little inclined to improvements, and depending on its mother country for all kinds of utensils, [natural history] cannot be expected." Instead, American trees needed to become "free denisons of our woods and gardens."[65]

Catesby's view was, needless to say, quite Europocentric, even to the point of claiming America's best climates for the mother country. In this regard, Catesby elaborated his notion that bands of climate did not express true differences between the hemispheres. He explained that even southern parts of North America had colder winters than did England. This was advantageous for the English gardener, as American "plants are so much the better adapted to the air of our more northern situation." In his *Natural History,* he had already pointed out that the magnolia could not, in America, grow north of South Carolina, whereas it was already "naturalized" in England, which lay far to the north of the Carolinas. Perhaps for this reason, the 1737 advertisement for Gray's garden at Fulham had at its center Catesby's etching of the *Magnolia grandiflora,* and Catesby began the list of trees in his *Hortus Europae Americanus* with the magnolia, for its "pre-eminence amongst the varieties in the forests of America." Even more boldly, Catesby speculated that the Carolina palmetto, a subtropical variety, could grow in England. It grew in America as far north as the thirty-fourth latitude, which was similar to the climate in Britain: "This tree, by a little protection, may be brought to endure our climate and adorn our gardens." Catesby's assertion followed a tradition of introducing tropical foliage into Europe (as Linnaeus had done with the banana), though without the artificial coaxing of greenhouses. With-

---

65. Catesby to Sherard, Jan. 17, 1723/4, Sherard Letters, CCLIII, 175; Catesby, *Hortus Europae Americanus,* i.

out truly understanding the Gulf Stream, Catesby used its properties to promote a vision of domesticated exoticism.[66]

What Catesby promoted was an inversion of mercantilism, in which products once available only from colonies were grown in the metropolis. Horticulturists would certainly make money, but Catesby seemed to regard this as different from the crass profits of overseas commerce: cultivation in Britain was superior to extraction from America. He nevertheless considered gardening as work that resembled that of metropolitan tradesmen. Catesby explained that only the "concurrent endeavours of the philosopher and artisans" would teach the useful properties of trees—their woods, fruits, and other products. Gardening connected the practical and the philosophical. The bounty of his gardening entrepreneurship acted to cement Catesby's relations with other naturalists. He sent a case of American plants to Linnaeus, a gift ordered by Isaac Lawson, physician-general of the British army stationed in Flanders and one of the Swedish naturalist's patrons. Catesby specified that he had "selected these, as being hardy and naturalized to our climate, and consequently somewhat adapted to endure your colder air." He also seized the opportunity to enclose a catalog of plants (perhaps the sheet of 1737) and said Linnaeus could "freely command any that I am possessed of." In 1748, shortly before his death, Catesby sent an inquiry via John Mitchell to see whether the plants had survived in Sweden.[67]

Still, gardening was not precisely like natural history—the former was selective, and the latter exhaustive. The content of *Hortus Europae Americanus* was different from that of the *Natural History,* even as it drew upon the earlier work. Most significantly, Catesby's interest in connections among American phenomena was not present in his descriptions of British gardening. Catesby did state that the cypress, placed in water and bearing sweet seeds, attracted "different birds," which sought safety and food. But this was an only general correlation between birds and plants, which did not replicate the more precise strategy of the *Natural History.* For example, when Catesby discussed the tulip tree, he provided no description of its peculiar function as a nesting area for orioles because of its

66. Catesby, *Hortus Europae Americanus,* ii (magnolia), 40 (palmetto); *Natural History,* II, 61. On the politics of imperial gardening see Spary, "Political, Natural, and Bodily Economies," in Jardine, Secord, and Spary, eds., *Cultures of Natural History,* 178–196 (Linnaeus's banana on 179–180).

67. Catesby, *Hortus Europae Americanus,* i; James Edward Smith, ed., *A Selection of the Correspondence of Linnaeus . . .* (London, 1821), II, 440–441, 448.

bent twigs. These trees were no longer interesting for their ancestral place within an American habitat but were desirable because of their implantation within the mother country. It is possible, however, that Catesby thought connections between American flora and European fauna would emerge in time, to be described by later generations of naturalists. His indeterminacy on this matter resembled, in fact, his rather indeterminate attitude toward habitat in general; as he had said about his illustrations, he had "adapted" his subjects to the relations most natural to them, a fine balance of art and nature that appeared again in his gardening. Catesby's hybrid landscape was in a way more artificial than was his natural history. The latter had more, and more complicated, variables; its author's guesses and silences reflected the messiness he perceived in American nature and contrasted with the tidiness of his metropolitan gardens.[68]

Gardening was further significant as a vision of a paracolonial world. It imagined and proposed to create a Britain that was not like that which had existed before the kingdom had acquired overseas colonies; nor did it become exactly like America. Instead, Britain functioned as a proper place for American flora, as if saints' bones were being translated to their most fitting site. There seemed little need, within Catesby's world, for the people who had been translated in the other direction. With revealing emphasis, Catesby gave credit to native Americans for their knowledge of American trees, in contrast to the underinformed and incurious white settlers. Thus the first settlers of Jamaica "could not possibly" have failed to notice the excellence of the island's mahogany, yet they did so. Carolina's settlers began to grow catalpa in their gardens because of its "uncommon beauty," which overcame their usual nature to be "little curious in gardening." White Virginians had the Cherokees to thank for the acacia, which was brought first from the banks of the distant Mississippi and then transplanted to the coast by Indian traders. Catesby credited other natives for knowledge of the useful products of yapoun, sweet gum, and magnolia.[69]

In this manner, Catesby's work marked the maturation of Britain's imperial natural history. In its first and primitive stage, only certain of America's natural products had received attention according to their

---

68. Catesby, *Hortus Europae Americanus*, 8, 9. Catesby did think transplantation would alter the flora themselves. He related that Bermuda cedar trees took on a different appearance when planted in Carolina, "therefore it is not to be wondered that such-like changes [will] appear in England" (36).

69. Ibid., i, 25 (whites), 3, 9, 15 (natives).

commercial promise. But in a later (indeed, belated) phase, Britons began to discover other uses for American specimens and began to welcome "these Strangers into England." Catesby put the birth of this second era at "about the year 1720" and remarked on how much had been accomplished in the few decades since that date: "A small spot of land in America has, within less than half a century, furnished England with a greater variety of trees than has been procured from all the other parts of the world for more than a thousand years past."[70]

The politics of this natural history were quite conservative. Catesby had little sense that humans themselves could wreak significant havoc in nature. Other than his diatribe against Indian hunters, Catesby did not perceive colonial damage of nature—he focused on neglect of it. His dramatic hurricanes and floods seemed unrelated to human activity (though estuarial flooding in South Carolina and Georgia was probably related to commercial rice planting there). His lack of perception that colonists might be transforming, for the worse, American nature, placed him in contrast to other naturalists; since the seventeenth century, unease over colonial settlement of new regions had drawn considerable attention. Nor was Catesby's critical view of colonies (as scenes of sloth and neglect) linked to more radical visions of their reform, like Stephen Hales's interest in reforming and curtailing slavery. Catesby's Virginia friends and family belonged to the slaveholding gentry; he himself had aspired to own a boy to assist him with his collecting. His desire to appropriate selected aspects of the New World—to put them in illustrations and garden pots—again underlined the cultural and especially class biases that led his science and his entrepreneurship.[71]

This was a sweeping vision of the material creation and of the power of naturalists to transform it. Catesby's specific plan to replant England with American flora was supported by the abstract speculations about climate, habitat, migration, and adaptation that he expressed in his *Natural History*. His views revealed the depth, variety, and ingenuity of contemporary thought on nature as a set of systems and showed science's embeddedness in the genteel and imperial cultures of eighteenth-century Britain. Given the range and creativeness of Catesby's speculations, it may seem

70. Ibid., i (philosophers and artisans), iii (recent transplantations).

71. Catesby to Sherard, Dec. 9, 1722, Sherard Letters, CCLIII, 165 (desire for a slave assistant); Frick and Stearns, *Mark Catesby*, 11–12; Chaplin, *Anxious Pursuit*, 243–247, 272–275. On Hales, see Allan and Schofield, *Stephen Hales*, 65–76.

surprising that his work did not have greater impact on other naturalists. Although his illustrations excited comment and his research invited respect, he nevertheless elicited mixed reactions from his contemporaries, reactions important in understanding the faded reputation that has descended to the twentieth century.

The market value of Catesby's *Natural History* remained high during the eighteenth century, which indicated continued demand for his work. But the high cost of his volumes in fact makes it difficult to assess their intellectual influence. His *Natural History* was clearly a luxury item, initially priced at two guineas per installment (thus twenty guineas for the full two volumes) and meant for an audience that had to be as wealthy as it was learned. People who could afford to buy the books treated them as material indications of their refinement. In late 1734, when Thomas Penn sent his first volume of Catesby to Benjamin Franklin's printing shop to have it bound, he also paid for its gilding (either of the edges of its pages or of its binding). In 1748, Pehr Kalm said the completed work's price was twenty-two to twenty-four guineas, "therefore not for a poor man to buy"; the rather poor Bartrams got their copy as a gift from Catesby himself. John Mitchell reported to Linnaeus in 1750 that Catesby had just died and his two-volume work "is already fallen in price." Nevertheless, when Franklin wanted to buy a colored edition in 1753 for the Library Company of Philadelphia, its cost of eighteen pounds exceeded his budget. By 1783, Thomas Jefferson paid ten guineas (half the original cost) for a Catesby set, which he was "very anxious" to own. Two years later, he wanted to swap this first edition for the second, indicating that used copies were already in circulation. By the nineteenth century, the price of the *Natural History* had fallen even further. The copy owned by naturalist George Edwards, who brought out an intensely edited edition of the *Natural History* after Catesby's death, was sold at Sotheby's for six pounds and five shillings in 1889.[72]

72. On the initial price, see Feduccia, ed., *Catesby's Birds of Colonial America,* 5; Smith, ed., *Correspondence of Linnaeus,* II, 451; Leonard W. Labaree et al., eds., *The Papers of Benjamin Franklin* (New Haven, Conn., 1959–), I, 371 (Penn), IV, 350, 380 (Library Co.); Pehr Kalm, *Kalm's Account of His Visit to England on His Way to America in 1748,* trans. Joseph Lucas (London, 1892), 119; Slaughter, *The Natures of John and William Bartram,* 48–50; Thomas Jefferson to Francis Eppes, Jan. 14, 1783, in Julian P. Boyd et al., eds., *The Papers of Thomas Jefferson* (Princeton, N.J., 1950–), VI, 220, Froullé to Jefferson, Oct. 7, 1785, VIII, 596; Sotheby's entry on inside front cover, Catesby, *Natural History* (with bookplate of "Geo. Edwards"), Newberry Library, Chicago.

Contemporaries who, like Jefferson, actually read their copies of Catesby judged him by two criteria: his empirical accuracy and the validity of his theoretical positions. In contrast to his twentieth-century reputation, Catesby initially received highest marks as a botanist. Naturalists and collectors praised him for his new specimens and for the accuracy of his descriptions of known plants. This was ironic, given Catesby's frustration over devoting so much time to the shipment of specimens to his patrons. But the tedium of these labors was recompensed. And he was himself concerned to establish his reputation as gatherer of the new. He tended to accompany his specimens with textual glosses as to their likelihood of being novel to a European audience. He gave one characteristic description of Carolina nuts and acorns with the qualification that he suspected Leonard Plukenet had already described many of these items; he then took care to specify that his "Small round podded Accaccia is New."[73]

Others were similarly vigilant in assessing Catesby according to his presentation of what was new (to European eyes) and to his superior presentations of what was already known. Samuel Dale thus evaluated Catesby in a 1719 letter to William Sherard; Dale reported that Catesby had about seventy Virginia specimens (half of which were new) and paintings of "Birds etc." He was worthy of Sherard's patronage and might "be very usefull for the perfecting of Naturall History." The Royal Society's review of the *Natural History,* by Cromwell Mortimer, praised Catesby for giving "the figures" of what had "never been describ'd by any Author or no good figures given of them." Mortimer further stressed Catesby's significance according to this cumulative view of knowledge by specifying which of the items pictured in the *Natural History* had already been described by Banister, Plukenet, Sloane, or others—almost the sole function of the review.[74]

Catesby's reputation for novelty and accuracy was neverthless contested. Linnaeus remained unconvinced. Dillenius insisted to Linnaeus in 1737, "Catesby is an honest, ingenuous man, who ought not to be suspected of error or fraud, as you seem inclined to do." Linnaeus received support for his suspicions from Catesby's most indignant detractor,

---

73. Catesby to Sherard, Jan. 4, 1722/3, 168 (nuts and acorns), Catesby to Sherard, Nov. 13, 1723, 170 (acacia), Sherard Letters, CCLIII.

74. Dale to Sherard, Oct. 13, 1719, Sherard Letters, CCLIII, 211; Cromwell Mortimer, "An Account of Mr. Mark Catesby's Essay towards the Natural history of Carolina, and the Bahama Islands . . . ," Register Book (Copy), XV, 180 (quotation), Royal Society.

South Carolina naturalist Alexander Garden. Garden wrote several letters to Linnaeus in which he pointed out deficiencies in Catesby's work. In his very first letter (of 1760) to the Swedish naturalist, Garden addressed himself to Catesby's fishes, in order to apprise Linnaeus "of the innacuracy and inability of this writer, in describing and delineating natural objects." Catesby had not only "forgotten to count and express the rays of the fins" but had, "which is hardly credible, left out the pectoral fins entirely, and overlooked one of the ventral ones." Garden concluded that Catesby's "sole object was to make showy figures of the productions of Nature, rather than to give correct and accurate representations." "This is rather to invent than to describe." Catesby's willingness to adapt his subjects thus compromised some of his descriptive work.[75]

Response to Catesby's theoretical material is much more difficult to recover. There are a few assessments of his principles of climatic variation. As previously discussed, Byrd gave the quickest and most vehement reply in his letter on Virginia's production of wine—which ended the exchange. Linnaeus's protégé Kalm later asked William Bartram "whether he had observed that the trees and plants decreased in size in proportion as they were brought further to the north, as Catesby pretends." Bartram answered, "The question should be more limited and then his opinion would prove more worthwhile." Here were challenges to Catesby's attempts to define laws for nonmechanical phenomena, though Bartram's assertion did not dismiss the validity of the property Catesby was beginning to define.[76]

It is clear, however, that Catesby paid a price for the hesitant manner in which he theorized. Even his most Newtonian pronouncements, as on climate, were buried in his text and overshadowed by his illustrations. Catesby's assessments were too cautious and too encrypted to be apparent to most people who read him. His English-speaking audience, especially, saw his work as an accumulation of striking portraits of nature, his text as a source of quotable anecdotes. In the eighteenth century's most

75. Smith, ed., *Correspondence of Linnaeus,* I, 300–301 (Garden), II, 102 (Dillenius). On Garden's criticism and probable envy of Catesby, see Stearns, *Science in the British Colonies of America,* 602, 605–606.

76. Adolph B. Benson, ed., *Peter Kalm's Travels in North America: The English Version of 1770* (New York, 1987), 75. Kalm also specified that Catesby had described and drawn the mockingbird, though he gave it Linnaeus's name; he also stated that the birds "stay all summer in the colonies but retire in autumn to the south" (116).

important civil history of America, William Robertson cited Catesby once in order to show Columbus's folly in assuming that birds signaled land nearby: "Catesby saw an owl at sea, when the ship was six hundred leagues from the nearest coast." By the early nineteenth century, Catesby's analytic comments were almost forgotten. Evidence for the growing view that Catesby was only an observer and illustrator came in 1819 from Abraham Rees's *Cyclopedia,* which had a good deal to say about natural history. Rees called Catesby "an eminent English naturalist" and properly stated that he was mainly a botanist, though most of the plates in his magnum opus "exhibit some subject of the animal kingdom." Rees clearly believed that Catesby's significance lay in his visual images and stated that his *Natural History* "has been allowed to be the most splendid work of its kind that had then been published in England, or even on the continent; that of Mad. Merian excepted." Even so, Catesby's importance lay in his pioneering effort rather than any lasting contribution: "Such a publication at the present day would confer little either of fame or profit on its author" because of the "want of minuteness and precision in the parts of the flowers and in the figures of the birds."[77]

Catesby's reputation as an illustrator (and purveyor of illustrative examples) made him less interesting, in the end, than naturalists who composed sustained, narrative expositions on nature. For audiences not interested in technical debates over nature, Catesby lost ground to naturalists who were, not necessarily more scientific, but certainly more readable. Early America generated a few Newtonian-style theorists, but many naturalists were guides to their country's exotic phenomena, not to an abstract nature and its universal laws. Narrative thus also served the paracolonial fantasy of European appropriation of New World exotica. Catesby's competitor in this regard was William Bartram, whose 1790 *Travels* utilized the narrative form and gave the attention to the manners and customs of native Americans that Catesby had eschewed. Bartram's writings provided a gripping and vivid narrative of American nature and by the end of the century were a significant influence on romantic writers like Coleridge and Wordsworth. Scholarship that has insisted that Catesby was eclipsed by Audubon has missed the point; it was Bartram who became the most influential purveyor of American exotica to an

---

77. William Robertson, *The History of America,* 2 vols. (London, 1778), I, note XII, 431; Abraham Rees, *The Cyclopedia; or, Universal Dictionary of Arts, Sciences, and Literature,* 1st Am. ed., rev. (Philadelphia, [1810–1824]), VII, s.v. "Catesby, Mark."

international audience, as his Florida idylls were one source for Coleridge's Xanadu.[78]

Still, a fuller understanding of Catesby's status within natural history would benefit from study of his European reputation. It was Continental scientists like Buffon and Lamarck who were publicly recognized as fashioning post-Newtonian natural history into a science. They and their lesser-known European contemporaries provide an almost unknown context for Catesby's work. Indeed, Catesby was known to European naturalists; he corresponded with several key figures, and his *Natural History* had several European editions.[79] He clearly intended to enter into Continental discourse via the French. The use of dual languages (English and French) in the *Natural History* showed an intention to be read abroad. Catesby's work followed the same bilingual model as the 1726 edition of Merian's *Metamorphosis*. That her book was his model made sense; Merian's work reached its widest audience from 1719 to 1730, just before Catesby began to publish his volumes. Each author's work had two facing title pages (one for each language), printed in red and black. Throughout the text, an illustration appeared on one page, with commentary in two languages on the facing page: for Merian, a right-hand column of text was in French while the left-hand was in Latin; for Catesby the corresponding languages were English and French. Too, the Catesby-Gray catalog of American plants was published in French and English, in the knowledge that French botanists and gardeners often relied on England for a supply of exotics. It is possible that Catesby was even slightly better known in France than in England and that his reputation lasted longer there. In the first edition of the *Encyclopédie,* for example, Catesby was cited in the entries under "oiseaux de passage" and "ornithologue," whereas the *Encyclopaedia Britannica* had no comparable coverage of this British subject. Later editions of the *Encyclopédie* inserted and kept a reference to Catesby—again in contrast to the *Britannica* on the other side of the channel.[80]

---

78. See John Livingston Lowes, *The Road to Xanadu: A Study in the Ways of the Imagination* (Princeton, N.J., 1927), 8–11, 513–516; Duncan Wu, *Wordsworth's Reading, 1770–1799* (Cambridge, 1993), 9; Wu, *Wordsworth's Reading, 1800–1815* (Cambridge, 1995), 14.

79. See Frick and Stearns, *Mark Catesby,* 86–98, 102, 105, 110–111.

80. On Merian's publication history, see Valiant, "Maria Sibylla Merian," *Eighteenth-Century Studies,* XXVI (1993), 471; Merian, *Dissertation / Dissertatio.* Gray's catalog printed in Henrey, *British Botanical and Horticultural Literature,* II, 349. For Catesby's correspondence, see Stearns, *Science in the British Colonies of America,* 326, 512. Denis Diderot and Jean Le Rond d'Alembert, eds., *Encyclopédie,* 3 vols. (Paris, 1751), s.v. "oiseaux de passage," "ornithologue."

One important debate into which Catesby's *Natural History* was drawn was the Buffonian "querelle d'Amérique." Several of Buffon's contentions about the Americas—the extremes of temperature, the calamitous events like floods and hurricanes, the hemispheric differences in animals and plants—resembled some of Catesby's observations. Catesby's opinions were, to be sure, more moderate, and he did not see an absolute hemispheric difference. But his and Buffon's inquiries clearly derived from pursuit of the same questions and from the same drive for an understanding of the planet's systemic qualities. Indeed, Buffon marshaled some of Catesby's points into service within his argument. He looked at Catesby's discussion of how American starlings wove their nests from water rushes and pointed out that European starlings did not do this; this showed "a different instinct, and therefore proves that it is a distinct species." This selective attention to Catesby's observations is in contrast to other points (avian migration, most notably) where Buffon ignored Catesby's contribution. It would have been interesting, had Catesby lived long enough, to have seen his reaction to Buffon and to the explosive dispute over his critical view of America. Kalm's 1748 note that toward the end of his life Catesby "devoted his time to reading" is evocative and frustrating, as it emphasizes that Catesby's thoughts on the maturing science of the mid-1700s never made their way into writing.[81]

In the absence of his stated opinions on Buffon, Catesby was also posthumously drawn into the controversy as evidence against the French naturalist. Oliver Goldsmith and Thomas Jefferson both ventriloquized the English naturalist to correct points Buffon had made. Goldsmith's contribution was most surprising, as his popular *History of the Earth, and Animated Nature* (1774) was perfused with Buffonian orthodoxy and had little time for lesser naturalists. Not even on points where Catesby had put forward arguments (avian migration, the environment for fish) did Goldsmith cite him. Yet at the conclusion of his rendering of the distinctiveness and inferiority of American animals, Goldsmith admitted, "Catesby adds a circumstance relative to these animals, which, if true, invalidates many of Mr. Buffon's observations." Here Goldsmith produced Catesby's assertion that the tamed wolves Indians had kept as dogs before European colonization could breed with European dogs, "which proves the dog and

81. Buffon, *Natural History, General and Particular, by the Count de Buffon,* trans. William Smellie (London, 1812), XII, 221 (starling), XIV, 393–394 (migration); Kalm, *Kalm's Visit to England,* trans. Lucas, 119.

the wolf to be of the same species." In this instance, Catesby's anecdotal thoroughness almost had power to challenge a great systematizer, even though his reluctance to base theory on merely suggestive points had diminished his intellectual authority.[82]

Jefferson was more aggressive in his attack on Buffon. He stretched Catesby's list of birds across a multiple-page table intended to disprove Buffon's contention that America lacked variety of species. Jefferson also used Catesby as an example of a European who had witnessed American animals that were not inferior to European ones: "Our grey fox is, by Catesby's account, little different in size and shape from the European fox."[83]

Catesby was perhaps more significant for Alexander von Humboldt, who revitalized the Newtonian vision of science in his program accurately to measure and map all natural phenomena capable of numerical expression. Humboldt's topographical work drew isothermic lines around the globe, a hypothesis that resembled Catesby's (and Buffon's) efforts to examine global patterns for climate. Humboldt did consult Catesby's *Natural History* before he set out for South America in 1799 (only further research among his papers could establish whether Catesby had any real effect on his theories). After Humboldt, the trail grows cold; Charles Darwin cited many earlier naturalists in his notebooks (including Buffon, Bartram, and Audubon), but not Catesby. Catesby's ornithology did not even affect Darwin's work with Galapagos birds, perhaps because Catesby had not speculated on physical adaptation or species extinction, the subjects of greatest importance for Darwin's theories.[84]

The way in which Goldsmith and Jefferson had used Catesby indicated the more common way in which he was read: as presenter of curious scenarios in natural history, rather than as a systematic natural historian.

82. Oliver Goldsmith, *An History of the Earth, and Animated Nature* (London, 1774), II, 310, 332–334 (use of Buffon), III, 322 (Catesby), V, 32–37, 318–319 (avian migration), VI, 154, 167–168, 349–350 (fish: migration and environment). See, again, Gerbi, *Dispute of the New World,* chap. 5.

83. Thomas Jefferson, *Notes on the State of Virginia,* ed. William Peden (Chapel Hill, N.C., 1954), 53, 65–70.

84. On Humboldt, see Hanno Beck, *Alexander von Humboldt,* I, *Von der Bildungsreise zur Forschungsreise, 1769–1804* (Wiesbaden, 1959), 90; Michael Dettelbach, "Humboldtian Science," in Jardine, Secord, and Spary, eds., *Cultures of Natural History,* 287–304. On Darwin, see Paul H. Barrett et al., eds., *Charles Darwin's Notebooks, 1836–1844: Geology, Transmutation of Species, Metaphysical Enquiries* (Ithaca, N.Y., 1987), 655, 656, 660.

This too was the way Robertson had used him. To a certain extent, it was of course logical for people to read Catesby's *Natural History* in this manner. His minimal use of narrative, his encrypted theorization as to climate and habitat, and his emphasis on the illustrative all conspired to make him appear even more modest in his science than he perhaps was. But, despite his intellectual diffidence, Catesby is an important register of the modes of inquiry and types of answers that guided the early science of natural history. Furthermore, the characteristics of Catesby's science—its gentlemanly confidence, its paracolonial emphasis on the English garden over and above the American wilderness, and its pitch to a luxury market—show opportunities for further examination of eighteenth-century science in its cultural context. What is apparent, above all, from Catesby's example, is that the possibility of generating laws for nonmechanical natural phenomena held considerable fascination even in the first half of the eighteenth century. This experiment with the Newtonian project was nevertheless tempered by skepticism and a suspicion that human artifice, more than impersonal (and hazardous) natural forces, gave meaning to the cosmos. This was a message that encouraged the creativity of naturalists but was critical of the character of America, which was increasingly stigmatized as the repository of nature's most colorful and lawless phenomena.

David R. Brigham

MARK CATESBY AND THE PATRONAGE OF NATURAL HISTORY IN THE FIRST HALF OF THE EIGHTEENTH CENTURY

Mark Catesby's *Natural History of Carolina, Florida, and the Bahama Islands* was published in London in ten parts plus an appendix, each containing twenty plates and related text in English and French. The book was clearly intended to be bound in two volumes, as title pages were printed for each and dated 1731 and 1743, respectively. Although these dates are typically used in catalogs and bibliographies, the publication began before and ended after these dates: the first part was issued in 1729 and the appendix in 1747. In addition the book contains dedications to Queen Caroline (vol. I) and Princess Augusta (vol. II), a list of subscribers, a preface (pp. v–xii), "A Map of Carolina, Florida, and the Bahama Islands" by sub-

I am grateful to many individuals and institutions for their help in making this essay possible. First and foremost, Amy R. W. Meyers introduced me to the topic and designated time for me to begin this project as her research associate at the Huntington Library. The Andrew W. Mellon Foundation provided a one-month fellowship to study eighteenth-century books in the Huntington Library; the McLean Contributionship Fellowship at the Library Company of Philadelphia supported an additional month's exploration of subscription publishing; and the British Academy supported one month of study in England to enable me to read manuscripts at the Royal Society, the British Library, the Natural History Museum, the Linnean Society, and the Bodleian Library at Oxford University and to study Catesby's original watercolors in the Royal Library, Windsor Castle, and the British Museum. Lebanon Valley College also provided a faculty research grant that enabled me to further my study of eighteenth-century natural history. I am especially grateful to James Green for sharing his deep knowledge of the history of the book with me while I was in residence at the Library Company. At the Omohundro Institute of Early American History and Culture, I am grateful to Gil Kelly and Fredrika Teute for their helpful editorial suggestions and for their remarkable patience. Finally, I appreciate the insightful comments I received on the manuscript from Holly Trostle Brigham.

Principal Variations in Collation of *The Natural History*

Library or Repository (First Owner)	List of Subscribers	Preface	Map	"Account of Carolina"[a]
Houghton, Harvard U. (unknown)	Vol. I, after dedication	Vol. I, after subscribers	Vol. I, after preface	Vol. I, after map
Van Pelt, U. of Pennsylvania (unknown)	Vol. I, after dedication	Vol. I, after subscribers	Vol. I, after preface	Vol. I, after map
Hunt[b] (unknown)	Vol. I, after dedication	Vol. II, after dedication	Vol. II, after "Account"	Vol. II, after preface
Winterthur Museum (unknown)	Vol. II, after dedication	Vol. I, after dedication	Vol. II, after plate 100	Vol. II, after map
Lehigh U. (Edward Harley, earl of Oxford)[c]	Missing	Vol. I, after dedication	Missing	Vol. II, after 2 extra plates[d]
Academy of Natural Sciences (Horace Walpole)[e]	Vol. I, after dedication	Missing	Vol. I, after plate 100	Vol. I, after map
Historical Society of Pennsylvania, at Library Company of Philadelphia (unknown)	Vol. II, after dedication	Vol. I, after dedication	Missing	Vol. I, after preface
Princeton U. (unknown)	Vol. I, after dedication	Vol. I, after subscribers	Vol. I, after index[f]	Vol. I, after map
Brown U. (unknown)	Vol. I, after title page	Vol. I, after subscribers	Vol. II, after appendix	Vol. II, after map

[a] Interestingly, the "Account of Carolina" often appears with vol. I, even though it was clearly issued in 1743 with the fifth part to vol. II, demonstrating the active role in the final appearance of the book played by purchasers and the bookbinders they hired to assemble the volumes. The association of "An Account of Carolina, and the Bahama Islands" with vol. II, part 5, is based on Thomas Knowlton's announcement to Samuel Brewer, Dec. 15, 1741: "Mr. Catesby . . . will very soon publish his Last part to compleat the 2 Vollm. wherein youl have a map of Caralina with a Long Disertation one [on] Birds of the East and West Indies etc with severall of the most curious plants in America" (quoted in Blanche Henrey, *No Ordinary Gardener: Thomas Knowlton, 1691–1781,* ed. A. O. Chater [London, 1986], 199). Catesby presented part 5 of vol. II to the Royal Society in 1743.

[b] Collation as recorded in Allan Stevenson, comp., *Catalogue of Botanical Books in the Collection of Rachel McMasters Miller Hunt,* 2 vols. (Pittsburgh, 1961), II, 138–139.

[c] Provenance is based on an inscription in the front of vol. I, in ink: "Richd Chiswell Esqr. / Bought at the the Sale of / Lord Oxfords Library for £19:9:6." Harley subscribed for two copies of *The Natural History,* of which this is apparently one.

[d] E. Kirkall fecit, "The Great American Aloe," published Sept. 23, 1739, dedicated to Sir Hans Sloane; and another plant specimen, not labeled.

[e] Allen T. Hazen, *A Catalogue of Horace Walpole's Library,* 3 vols. (New Haven, Conn., 1969), 160. Horace Walpole was the brother-in-law of Catesby subscriber Catharine Shorter Walpole (1682–1737).

[f] The index to the Princeton copy has an unusual placement, with the front matter to vol. I immediately following the preface and preceding the map.

scriber Henry Popple, a natural history narrative entitled "An Account of Carolina, and the Bahama Islands" (pp. i–xliv), an index in English, French, and Latin to the specimens illustrated, and a separate index to the appendix. Sets vary considerably in their level of completion and in the placement of the ancillary materials (see table). The bindings themselves also differ greatly, from the simple vellum binding on Horace Walpole's copy now at the Academy of Natural Sciences, Philadelphia, to the elaborately tooled and gilt binding on such copies as the one in the library of the Winterthur Museum.[1]

Catesby's *Natural History* was one of the most expensive publications of the eighteenth century, costing twenty-two guineas for a complete set. The large format (a folio printed on imperial paper), the abundance of engraved plates (220 in all), and the hand coloring of each plate all contributed to the beauty and cost of the production. The expense and extent of the book made it a logical candidate for publication by subscription, a quasi-contractual method of publication that ensured a base audience before the author and publisher (often the same person, as in this instance) accepted the financial risk of beginning to print. Catesby received subscriptions for 166 copies of the book from 155 subscribers (Appendix 1). The total size of the edition is unknown, though Catesby printed additional sets, some of which were still in his widow's possession upon the author's death in 1749.[2] The publication of the subscription list, an act that lent authority to the finished *Natural History* and prestige to the subscribers for their support of such a grand publication, enables the modern scholar to undertake a collective biography of the supporters of this illustrated natural history of the southern colonies and the Bahama Islands.[3]

---

1. Mark Catesby, *The Natural History of Carolina, Florida, and the Bahama Islands . . .* , 2 vols. (London, 1731–1743). The publication dates 1729–1747 are based on Catesby's recorded presentations of the completed first part and Appendix to the Royal Society, London, as noted in Raymond Phineas Stearns, *Science in the British Colonies of America* (Urbana, Ill., 1970), 319–320. A letter from Thomas Knowlton to Sir Hans Sloane, Sept. 20, 1729, confirms that Catesby was prepared to distribute copies of the first part to his subscribers by that date. Sloane MS 4050, fols. 200–201, British Library, London.

2. For sets in Catesby's widow's hands: Peter Collinson to Carl Linnaeus: "Our Ingenious Friend Mr Catesby died the 23 of December last, Etat et 70, much Lamented. His Widow to Encourage the Sale of His Works abates ½ Guinea, vizt 10s:6d on Every Book, so Eleven Books att Guinea and half comes too L17:6s:6d Sterling." Quoted in Alan Armstrong, typescript volume of Peter Collinson's correspondence.

3. For modern discussions of subscription publishing, see Sarah L. C. Clapp, "The Beginnings of Subscription Publication in the Seventeenth Century," *Modern Philology*, XXIX

Catesby's subscribers comprised a complex web of interdependent social, economic, and intellectual communities rather than a single audience with a narrow set of concerns. Their social circumstances ranged from the occasional gardener for hire to the more frequent merchant, physician, nobleman, and royal. Catesby's subscribers included people with little personal wealth as well as those with extraordinary capital, which they poured into palatial homes, spectacular gardens, and colonial investments. These elite patrons collected books, paintings, antiquities, scientific instruments, and natural history specimens. The last interest was served by some through their own labor while patronage and a vast sphere of economic and social influence connected other collectors to agents in London, the British hinterland, the European continent, and distant lands. Many subscribers received a university education at Cambridge, Oxford, and other elite institutions, including medical training at Leiden and Padua, and others gained knowledge through apprenticeships. Their correspondence demonstrates avid scientific curiosity as well as efforts to alter the course of British politics, to develop colonial enterprises around the globe, and to engage in the pressing intellectual debates of the day. Catesby's subscribers belonged to and led scientific organizations in London, Paris, and Florence as well as Philadelphia. They also joined, formed, and directed antiquarian organizations, literary societies, medical associations, a society of apothecaries, and a gardeners' company. In short,

---

(1931), 199–224; Pat Rogers, "Book Subscriptions among the Augustans," *Times Literary Supplement,* Dec. 15, 1972, 1539–1540; P. J. Wallis, "Book Subscription Lists," *Library,* 5th Ser., XXIX (1974), 255–286; F. J. G. Robinson and P. J. Wallis, *Book Subscription Lists: A Revised Guide* (Newcastle upon Tyne, 1975); Donald Farren, "Subscription: A Study of the Eighteenth-Century American Book Trade" (D.L.S. diss., Columbia University, 1982); David Foxon, *Pope and the Early Eighteenth-Century Book Trade,* ed. James McLaverty (Oxford, 1991); Hugh Amory, "Virtual Readers: The Subscribers to Fielding's *Miscellanies* (1743)," in *Studies in Bibliography,* XLVIII (Charlottesville, Va., 1995), 94–112; James Green, "The Publishing History of Olaudah Equiano's *Interesting Narrative,*" *Slavery and Abolition,* XVI (1995), 362–375.

For serial publication, see R. M. Wiles, *Serial Publication in England before 1750* (Cambridge, 1957).

For collective biography, see Lawrence Stone, "Prosopography," *Daedalus,* C (1971), 46–70; Stephen Shapin and Arnold Thackray, "Prosopography as a Research Tool in History of Science: The British Scientific Community, 1700–1900," *History of Science,* XII (1974), 1–28; Lewis Pyenson, "'Who the Guys Were': Prosopography in the History of Science," *History of Science,* XV (1977), 155–188.

Catesby's *Natural History* offers a fixed point for examining the fluid network of labor, capital, and personalities that sustained the study of natural history in the eighteenth century.

Catesby's Sponsors for Travel in the New World

Catesby traveled to Carolina in 1722 under the sponsorship of colonial governor Sir Francis Nicholson (1655–1728) and a select group of English patrons, whom Catesby later named in the prospectus and again in the preface to his *Natural History* (Appendix 2). In return for their financial support, Catesby's trip sponsors expected plant and animal specimens from the colonies and even examples of drawings made on-site from direct observation. The precise terms of reciprocation were not stated clearly upon Catesby's embarkation, and this omission later became a source of tension between the naturalist and his supporters. Although the patrons belonged to a cooperative network, their personal interests sometimes resulted in competition and tension among themselves as well. The sponsors' interests in promoting Catesby's botanizing trip included the advancement of colonial enterprise, increasing their own gardens (both scientific and ornamental), and expanding the catalog of known species of plants. His patrons belonged to an intellectual community that circulated ideas and specimens through correspondence, presentations to the Royal Society, and publications of their own. Just as the *Natural History* would later be published by subscription, so was financed the trip that enabled him to gather, observe, and draw specimens in preparation for the book.

The roots of Catesby's support stretch back to the previous decade, when he ventured independently to Virginia. His sister Elizabeth had moved with her husband, Dr. William Cocke, to Williamsburg. Between 1712 and 1719, Catesby lived in Virginia and collected plant specimens throughout the South and apparently funded this trip with his own money. Among the recipients of these collections was Samuel Dale (1659–1739), a physician and apothecary in Braintree, Essex. Dale's expertise in the medicinal value of plants extended beyond the level necessary for his practice and led him to write a *Pharmacologia* that was published in several editions. He was also an associate of John Ray (1627–1705), the most important pre-Linnaean botanist in England, and Ray credited him with providing valuable assistance in his major publications. Catesby was born near Castle Hedingham, also in Essex, and was introduced to Dale by his uncle Nicholas Jekyll, whose garden Dale visited in 1711. Catesby also knew Ray, who sparked the young man's interest in natural history.[4]

During Catesby's stay in Virginia, Dale shared specimens with William Sherard, who soon thereafter became one of Catesby's principal sponsors for his second trip abroad and, more important, his champion among naturalists and collectors. Sherard (1658–1728) acquired great wealth through his post as consul at Smyrna, where he built extensive collections of antiquities and plant specimens. His goal was to publish his vast herbarium in a *pinax,* a comprehensive study catalog of known plant species, but the project was never completed. Sherard's most lasting contributions to botany were endowing a professorship at Oxford and leaving his library and approximately twelve thousand to fourteen thousand dried plant specimens to bolster research in this discipline. When Catesby returned from Virginia in 1719, Dale said that the young naturalist would visit Sherard. Catesby would bring plant specimens, and any duplicates could be divided between Sherard and Charles Du Bois, the latter of whom also became a sponsor of Catesby's second trip to the American colonies. Dale announced that Catesby would also bring "some paintings of Birds etc which he hath drawn," indicating that, in addition to collecting specimens, drawing them from nature was already part of Catesby's field practice. Dale closed his letter with a prophetic urging: "Its pitty some incouragement can't be found for him, he may be very usefull for the perfecting of Natural History." Sherard took up this charge, as indicated in his letter to Richard Richardson (1663–1741, a Leiden-educated physician, botanist, and antiquarian):

> Mr. Catesby, a gentleman of a small fortune, who liv'd some years in Virginia with a relation, pretty well skilled in Natural History, who designs and paints in water-colors to perfection, is going over with General Nicholson, Governor of Carolina. That gentleman allows him £20 a year; and we are indeavouring to get subscriptions for him, viz. Sir Hans, Mr. Dubois, and myself, who are all that have subscrib'd to him; but I'me in hopes to get the Duke of Chandos, which will be a good help.

4. For Dale, see Edwin Lankester, ed., *The Correspondence of John Ray . . .* (London, 1848), 231, 268, 321, 328, 338, 410; Robert W. T. Gunther, ed., *Further Correspondence of John Ray* (London, 1928), 108–109, 282. For Catesby's introduction to Dale, see George F. Frick, "Mark Catesby: The Discovery of a Naturalist," Bibliographical Society of America, *Papers,* LIV (1960), 169. For Catesby and Ray, see Stearns, *Science in the British Colonies of America,* 286.

Richardson did not lend financial support to Catesby's travels but eventually did subscribe to the publication of the *Natural History*.[5]

Charles Du Bois (1656–1740) maintained an important garden at Mitcham, Surrey, that was funded by his business interests in the East India Company, which he served as treasurer. Just as Dale's education in medicine creates a logical connection to botany, so do Du Bois's commercial interests. The development of botany and gardening in Europe correlates directly to the development of colonization and trading companies. Sometimes the plants became commodities, but the collecting of exotics also conveyed symbolically the breadth of one's financial or political power. In addition, the passage of ships to distant ports was accelerated by the growth of the mercantile economy, making collecting abroad easier. Du Bois was recognized by English naturalists for the diverse origins of his collections, as when Philip Miller (1691–1771) noted an African plant in his garden, and George Edwards (1694–1773) illustrated a bustard "from Mocha in Arabia" that Du Bois had received.[6]

Also representing the connection between natural science and colonial enterprise, Sir Francis Nicholson became a leading sponsor of Catesby's journey to Carolina. Having been appointed to the governorship of Carolina in 1720, Nicholson agreed to pay Catesby a stipend of twenty pounds per year. Nicholson believed greater knowledge about Carolina's flora and fauna would advance the development of the colony now in his charge, and his support for Catesby followed a pattern established in his previous political offices. As governor of Maryland, Nicholson brought the Reverend Hugh Jones, "a pretty good Botanist," to Annapolis in 1696 and two years later funded a trip by William Vernon (d. 1706, a naturalist and fellow of Peterhouse, Cambridge) to this colonial capital. Nicholson was an active member of the Royal Society, and his sponsorship of Catesby is documented in their archives. He advanced ten pounds to Catesby in 1720 through the society, but the naturalist did not embark immediately. His hesitation frustrated Nicholson, who wrote to Sherard and Sir Hans Sloane (1660–1753) about the matter:

5. Samuel Dale to William Sherard, Oct. 15, 1719, Sherard Letters, CCLIII, 211, Royal Society, London; Sherard to Richard Richardson, Nov. 12, 1720, in Dawson Turner, ed., *Extracts from the Literary and Scientific Correspondence of Richard Richardson . . .* (Yarmouth, 1835), 157–158.

6. Philip Miller, *The Gardeners Dictionary . . .* , 3 vols. (London, 1741), III, n.p.; George Edwards, *A Natural History of Uncommon Birds . . .* , 4 vols. (London, 1743–1751), I, pl. 12.

I am very Sorry that Mr Katesby hath altered his mind of comeing hither but I desire that he will repay the Ten pounds which I advanced him to our Treasurer to be there kept till the Royall Society can find another Person to come upon the Same accot. and that Ten pounds Shall be advanced him for the first half Year at the Rate of Twenty pounds Sterl[ing] per annum while I remain Govr and this I now promise under my hand and Seal.[7]

Despite his hesitation, Catesby left for South Carolina the following spring, 1722.

Sloane was a hub of botanical activity in England in the first half of the eighteenth century, and his support ensured the assistance of numerous other patrons. Through his stature as a physician, Sloane was appointed to care for George II and to preside over the Royal College of Physicians in 1719. Just before Catesby's second journey to the colonies, Sloane had funded the botanical garden at the Society of Apothecaries in Chelsea. Patronage of this magnitude made Sloane powerful within the scientific community, as did his intellectual contributions to the Royal Society's *Philosophical Transactions* and his cabinet of specimens. Sloane's portrait (Figure 12), one of several contemporary representations of the man, pays homage to his contributions to natural history on at least two levels. He unrolls a botanical plate, a reference to his own extensive writings on botany and especially to his illustrated books on the flora and fauna of Jamaica. A sculpture of the multibreasted Artemis, a common allegorization of Nature, occupies the niche behind the seated naturalist. While the botanical plate pays tribute to Sloane the scientist, the sculpture—with its classical origins and reference to abundance—evokes a larger cultural role for Sloane as patron.[8]

Among Sloane's medical colleagues in London, Dr. Richard Mead (1673–1754) was one of the most renowned; his sponsorship of Catesby's

7. For Nicholson's patronage of Hugh Jones, see Bruce T. McCully, "Governor Francis Nicholson, Patron *Par Excellence* of Religion and Learning in Colonial America," *William and Mary Quarterly,* 3d Ser., XXXIX (1982), 324. For William Vernon, see Stearns, *Science in the British Colonies of America,* 268–271. For Nicholson's patronage of and frustration with Catesby, see Francis Nicholson to Alban Thomas, Mar. 5, 1720, Early Letters, NI 89, Royal Society; and quote from Nicholson, see Nicholson to Thomas, Nov. 6, 1721, NI 90.

8. For Sir Hans Sloane, see s.v. "Sloane, Hans," *Dictionary of National Biography,* and *Dictionary of Scientific Biography.* His writings include *Catalogus Plantarum Quae in Insula Jamaica* ... (London, 1696); and *A Voyage to the Islands Madera, Barbados, Nieves, S. Christophers, and Jamaica* ..., 2 vols. (London, 1707–1725).

12. Sir Hans Sloane, Bt. *By Stephen Slaughter, 1736. By courtesy of the National Portrait Gallery, London*

trip added to the naturalist's prestige. Mead was a prolific author of medical treatises, whose collected works filled seven volumes published shortly after his death. As a young man Mead studied in Utrecht and Leiden. Thereafter he maintained a correspondence with the Dutch botanist Hermann Boerhaave, who praised Sloane and Mead as "the most celebrated doctors in England." Catesby paid homage to Mead's contributions to botany by naming a plant for him and etching it for the appendix to the

13. *Meadia*. Catesby, *Natural History,* II, Appendix, pl. 1. Courtesy, Colonial Williamsburg Foundation

Natural History. Catesby's description of *Meadia* (Figure 13) included this explanation: "To this new Genus of Plants I have given the name of the learned Dr. *Richard Mead,* Physician to His Majesty, and *F. R. S.* in gratitude for his zealous patronage of Arts and Sciences in general, and in particular for his generous assistance towards carrying the original design of this work into execution." Mead was a consistent patron of botany, supporting not only Catesby but also Georg Dionsyius Ehret (1710–1770), who wrote:

> Some years after I came to England I became acquainted with the excellent Dr. Mead, Royal Physician, who engaged me; and I prepared for him, from time to time, paintings of rare plants, mostly with a description of them, on great folia of parchment, at one guinea apiece. The number of them reached at last 200.

Ehret's connection to Catesby is significant, too, as he contributed two plates and parts of eight more to the completed *Natural History*.[9]

Catesby's patrons also included a number of noblemen and baronets whose wealth supported gardening, among other interests. James Brydges, duke of Chandos (1673/4–1744), built vast gardens at his estate at Cannons, where the composer Handel lived under Chandos's patronage for two years. When Chandos died, his eulogy included this description: "Whom, *Science* grateful, shall revere her *friend*." Chandos was heavily invested in the Royal African Company and wrote to Sloane in 1721 about plans to send a botanist to Africa, which "will doubtless be of great Advantage, to the Company." This note implies that the advancement of colonial enterprise and not simply the love of science motivated some supporters of natural history. Catesby was mentioned as a candidate for this expedition, but Sherard opposed Catesby's participation in the plan, writing, "I cou'd wish he had held his resolutions of going to Carolina; but he's now too far engag'd with the Duke of Chandos to think of that." This proposed African venture accounts for Catesby's aforementioned hesita-

9. Hermann Boerhaave to J. B. Bassand, Oct. 21, 1731, in *Boerhaave's Correspondence,* 2 vols. (Leiden, 1962–1964), II, 293; Catesby's homage to Mead: *Natural History,* II, Appendix, 1; Mead's support of Ehret: Ehret, "A Memoir of Georg Dionysius Ehret," trans. and ed. E. S. Barton, Linnean Society of London, *Proceedings,* 1894–1895, 54; and for Ehret's contributions, see Amy Meyers, "'The Perfecting of Natural History': Mark Catesby's Drawings of American Flora and Fauna in the Royal Library, Windsor Castle," in Henrietta McBurney, *Mark Catesby's "Natural History" of America: The Watercolors from the Royal Library, Windsor Castle* (London, 1997), 24.

tion, which had resulted in Sir Francis Nicholson's frustration with him. Perhaps through Sherard's persistence, Carolina won out in the end. In his renovations at Cannons, Chandos hired Thomas Knowlton (1691–1781) as gardener and purchased fruit trees from the nurseryman Robert Furber (ca. 1674–1756), both of whom later subscribed to Catesby's *Natural History*. Knowlton also worked for James Sherard, brother of Catesby's supporter William Sherard, and for Richard Boyle, earl of Burlington. Subscriptions from gardeners and nurserymen broaden the range of social positions occupied by Catesby's supporters.[10]

Catesby's trip patrons also included Edward Harley, earl of Oxford (1689–1741), who maintained extensive gardens and whose patronage extended to key eighteenth-century British literary figures, including Alexander Pope. Catesby sent Harley a "Tub of plants" and "A Box of seed," and Harley, in turn, later subscribed to two copies of the *Natural History*.[11] In return for their support of Catesby's travels, his patrons also generally expected to receive seeds, fresh and dried plants, preserved animals, and drawings. Catesby dried plant specimens and mounted them in books, though shortages of appropriate paper occasionally made this work more difficult. Sending seeds and plants posed greater problems, since Catesby had trouble collecting the gourds in which he wanted to send them and "Makannicks" charged exorbitant prices for wooden crates. Living plants were sent in tubs, but these were the most vulnerable to the hardships of sea travel, as they were especially susceptible to weather and neglect. Catesby noted that "it's no small favour from a master to secure a Single box or parcel" on board the ship, pleading for his patrons to be reasonable in their demands. Several ship captains' names recur as carriers, so Catesby appears to have gained some reliable means of shipment. In one instance, he informed Sherard that he would ask Sir Francis Nicholson to carry

10. Brydges's eulogy: W. S., "On the Death of his Grace the Duke of Chandos," *Gentleman's Magazine, and Historical Chronicle,* XIV (1744), 452; desire to send naturalist to Africa: James Brydges, duke of Chandos, to Sir Hans Sloane, Dec. 4, 1721, British Library, Sloane MS 4046, fols. 152–153; desire to send Catesby to Carolina: William Sherard to Richard Richardson, Mar. 28, 1721, in Turner, ed., *Extracts from Richardson,* 165; Brydges's gardening activities: "Account of Payments to Tradesmen and Servants," 1722–1732, MS, 165, 219, Huntington Library, San Marino, Calif. For Knowlton's employers, see Ray Desmond, *Dictionary of British and Irish Botanists and Horticulturists, Including Plant Collectors and Botanical Artists* (London, 1977), 365.

11. For Harley's biography, see *DNB,* s.v. "Harley, Edward, Second Earl of Oxford"; for his shipments to Harley: Mark Catesby to William Sherard, Jan. 10, 1724/5, Sherard Letters, CCLIII, 184.

"what plants etc I have collected this Year." Sending animal specimens that could not be dried required glass jars, which Catesby complained were not readily available. In the most dramatic report of the complexities of sending seeds and plants, Catesby once even complained that pirates destroyed an entire shipment.[12]

As the number of sponsors grew, Catesby felt strained to meet their many demands. He asked William Sherard for clarification of the sponsors' expectations in a letter during his first summer in Carolina: "I desire to know whether Sr Hans and Mr Dubois expects distinct collections or whether what I Send them Shall be mixed with Your which Will take up less time and enable me to send the greater variety." A short time later, he reiterated the point: "I hope it is not expected that what I send should be to every one Separately but in the manner I have now Sent for indeed tis almost impracticable without half my time lost." Sloane complained about the early returns from Catesby's venture, and Catesby asked Sherard to mediate. He wondered whether Sloane would "resent" the plant specimens sent to Sherard and left it "to your discretion" whether to mention the shipment to his other powerful patron. The young naturalist later wrote to Sherard that he had sent shells and dried birds for Sloane's cabinet and hoped this would ease his dissatisfaction. Catesby continued to send dried plant specimens to Sloane, which survive today in his vast herbarium at the Natural History Museum, London, with neat annotations in Catesby's hand. These notes describe the appearance of particular plants from bud to fruit, soil and other conditions at the place of origin, and uses of the plant. For instance, next to a specimen of black poplar, which Catesby later illustrated as plate 34 of the first volume, he noted: "A kind of Asp producing in Aprile bunches of berries full of cotton In August the Trees are set with large Swelling Buds which contain the seed in Embrio These Buds are clammy (and) containing a —— Balsamick substance of a most fragrant perfume."[13]

12. Need for paper: Catesby to Sherard, Apr. 6, 1724, Sherard Letters, CCLIII, 176. Gourds and crates, difficulty sending live plants: Catesby to Sherard, Dec. 9, 1722, 165. Intention to have Nicholson escort plants: Catesby to Sherard, Mar. 19, 1723, 169. Need for jars: Catesby to Sir Hans Sloane, May 10, 1723, Sloane MS 4046, fol. 352. Pirates: Catesby to Sherard, Aug. 16, 1724, Sherard Letters, CCLIII, 178.

13. Distinct collections: Catesby to Sherard, June 20, 1722, Sherard Letters, CCLIII, 164, Dec. 9, 1722, 165, Oct. 30, 1724, 179. Shells and birds to Sloane, and plants to Sherard: Catesby to Sherard, Nov. 13, 1723, 170. Catesby's annotation to the poplar specimen: *Catesby's Florida Plants,* II, H.S. 232, 52, Sloane Herbarium, Natural History Museum, London.

Whereas Sherard was content with botanical collections, Sloane expected examples of New World flora and fauna as well as drawings from Catesby's hand. This last requirement was especially disturbing to the artist-naturalist, and he protested to Sloane:

> My Sending Collections of plants and especially Drawings to every of My Subscribers is what I did not think would be expected from me My design S[i]r (til You'l pleas to give me Your advice) to keep my Drawing intire that I may Get them Graved, in order to give a genll History of the Birds And other Animals, which to distribute Seperately would wholly frustrate that designe, And be of little value to those who would have so small fragments of the whole.

Just as Catesby asked Sherard to mediate on his behalf, he enlisted Sloane to advocate his position with Lord John Perceval (1683–1748), who sponsored Catesby's trip but did not subscribe to the *Natural History*. Catesby's correspondence with Sloane indicates a concerted effort to meet his patron's collecting needs. Shortly after his arrival in Charleston, Catesby sent shells, insects, and dried birds and requested that Sloane call upon Sherard to share seeds that had been sent separately. The next spring, Catesby added two books of dried plants, a collection of "7 kinds of wood peckers," and an additional group of shells. In the summer, Catesby added more birds and skins of mammals, including a black fox and a polecat. Catesby added more dried plants and native American artifacts in an autumn shipment. While Catesby maintained a separate correspondence with Sloane, he continued to ship plants to Sherard for distribution to his various patrons. Sherard's role as intermediary and conveyer of specimens to Catesby's other supporters is evident in this note from Sherard to Sloane:

> By the Bearer I send yr Box from Mr. Catesby, I hope 'tis in much better condition than the last yo[u] received from him. 'twas opend by the Custome house officers, but I believe nothing taken out.
>
> I have a large Gourd [filled] wth. seeds for Mr [Isaac] Rand, wch. please to give him notice of if you see him to day.[14]

14. Plants and drawings to everyone, Lord Perceval, fox and polecat: Catesby to Sloane, Aug. 15, 1724, Sloane MS 4047, fol. 212. Specimens and seeds: Catesby to Sloane, May 10, 1723, Sloane MS 4046, fol. 352. Woodpeckers and shells: Catesby to Sloane, Mar. 12, 1723/4, Sloane MS 4047, fol. 212. Plants and native American artifacts: Catesby to Sloane, Nov. 27, 1724, Sloane MS 4047, fol. 290. Sherard as intermediary: Sherard to Sloane, Feb. 7, 1723/4, Sloane MS 4047, fols. 126–127.

Rand later rewarded Catesby by subscribing to two copies of the *Natural History*.

Sherard also mediated Catesby's relationship with Charles Du Bois, as the traveler directed him to share "duplicates" with Du Bois. However, Du Bois remained a difficult sponsor. Two and a half years into his trip, Catesby wrote, "The discontent of Mr Du-Bois and the trouble he gives my Friends in recieving his Subscription is Such that I had rather be withou[t] it, I doubt Not but I have Suffered by his Complaints." Although Peter Collinson was not listed as a sponsor of the trip, Catesby felt indebted to him. Explaining this relationship to Sherard, Catesby wrote, "Mr Collinson has procured Several Subscriptions which oblidges me to send him a greater quantity than otherwise there would be occasion for." Catesby sent Collinson seeds directly and through Sherard, including one shipment of black walnut, pignut, and a variety of oaks as well as dogwood, cassena, haws, bay, and tuberose, a parallel shipment to one that he sent to Sherard. Catesby promised Collinson that shipments to him "will be as Big as what I send to the Consul which is designed for many."[15]

Catesby was also becoming indebted to colonial gardeners and collectors who assisted his travels. He asked Sherard whether he could "Spare a few common Roots such as Lillys (except the White Lilly) Martagons Daffodil or any bulbose root I shall be glad of them to Gratify Some Gentlemen at houses I frequent." The completed *Natural History* documents the many colonists who aided Catesby's travels, including Governor George Phenney of the Bahama Islands, and plantation owners, gardeners, and amateur botanists like William Byrd II. Sherard responded to Catesby's request, and he thanked him for "Your Box of Roots and seeds —all in good order except the Emonies and Renunculus's." Later, Catesby wrote to his English sponsors, in behalf of his colonial supporters, asking for information about European plants, including the viability of opium poppies and rhubarb in Carolina. Catesby also introduced Peter Collinson to Alexander Skene in Carolina, proposing that a fruitful exchange would come of their shared interest in both "useful" and "ornamental plants."[16]

15. Duplicates to Du Bois: Catesby to Sherard, Feb. 7, 1722/3, Sherard Letters, CCLIII, 167. Du Bois's discontentment: Catesby to Sherard, Jan. 10, 1724/5, 184. Collinson's patronage: Catesby to Sherard, Nov. 13, 1723, 170. Seeds to Collinson directly and through Sherard: Catesby to Peter Collinson, Jan. 5, 1722/3, Autograph Collection, Natural History Museum, London.

16. Requests for and acknowledgment of bulbs for colonial gardeners: Catesby to Sherard, June 20, 1722, Jan. 16, 1723/4, Sherard Letters, CCLIII, 164, 174. Poppies and rhubarb:

In spite of these many pressures, Catesby's productivity reached an impressive level, and the variety and number of his shipments seem to have quieted his eager supporters. Having arrived in Charleston on May 3, 1722, by June 20 he was able to send two books of dried specimens to Sherard. By the time these books were shipped, they were accompanied by "a Box of roots and seeds." Catesby sent seeds of both trees and ornamental plants, including water oak acorns, spruce pinecones, and white pinecones as well as narcissus bulbs and seed of "a kind of perriwinkle . . . [which] would makes a fine Edging for Beds." In January Catesby sent a variety of acorns and seeds, including live oak, willow oak, water oak, chestnut, hickory, and pignut, along with dogwood, cassena, and haws. The following month Catesby sent a tub of fresh plants, including erect bay, jessamy, pellitory tree, sassafras, a purple-flowering shrub, and a root that "is an excellent Stomacick." Trees and shrubs continued to be the focus of shipments to Sherard and often duplicated the species noted above. In the spring of 1724, Catesby added a number of oaks, Richland pine, swamp pine, cedar, two varieties of tupelo, maple, red bay, sweet-flowering bay, chinquapin, wild cherry, holly, and myrtle. As Catesby's travels extended, the assortment of plants he sent grew to mirror the range that would later be illustrated in his published *Natural History*. The logic behind Catesby's collecting patterns is further revealed in 1724, after two years in Carolina, when he asked Sherard which plants he should continue gathering: "As shrubs and Trees are generally of more value than hearby plants, it will I conceive be requisite to know which of those I sent are not raised from Seed that I may Send the Plants."[17]

Although profit was not the only motive for Catesby's patrons, his botanizing efforts clearly did have financial implications. He noted the arrival in 1724 of "One Dr Sinclair . . . with a patent as he says for propogating Cuchinele Nutmegs Cloves Pepper Rhubarb Opium with inumerable other Drugs and Spices, 'Tis certain he has encouragement from some as Ld Iley, and as he says Mr Walpole and other Great Men You will gues at the Man by the undertaking." Lord Islay and Lady Wal-

---

Catesby to Sherard, Aug. 16, 1724, 178. Introduction of Skene: Catesby to Collinson, Jan. 5, 1722/3, Autograph Collection, Natural History Museum.

17. First shipment: Catesby to Sherard, Dec. 9, 1722, Sherard Letters, CCLIII, 165. Acorns, pine cones, and seeds: Catesby to Sherard, Dec. 10, 1722, Jan. 4, 1722/3, 166, 168. Fresh plants: Catesby to Sherard, Feb. 7, 1722/3, 167. Pines, tupelo, etc.: Catesby to Sherard, Apr. 6, 1724, 176. Preference for trees and shrubs over herbs: Catesby to Sherard, Nov. 26, 1724, 182.

pole, though not supporters of Catesby's travels, later subscribed to the *Natural History*. Trees and shrubs, the focus of Catesby's collections, also had commercial value, as English lords and gentlemen sought to plant deer parks and avenues. The published *Natural History* also made textual reference to the fiscal significance of plants to colonial enterprise. For instance, in a section on rice, which became a staple crop in Carolina, Catesby explains the difficult harvesting process and adds, "The late Governor *Johnson* (as he told me) had procured from *Spain* a Machine which facilitates the Work with more Expedition, the Trouble and Expence ('tis hoped) will be much mitigated by his Example." Governor Robert Johnson (ca. 1676–1735) was a subscriber to Catesby's book, and this note in the prefatory essay suggests the prospective nature of their efforts to cultivate knowledge in support of prosperous colonial enterprise.[18]

Catesby's subscription was by no means definite to him and remained in a certain amount of flux throughout his journey. While his patrons in England continued to seek out additional supporters, Catesby also sought patrons in the colonies. Catesby depended upon Sherard to work in this capacity, as hinted by his note of disappointment, "Your Not Mentioning Mr Parker in neither of Your last Lrs I Suspect he refuses to Subscribe." He gave a tub of plants to a ship's captain named Clark to encourage safe passage of his other shipments, and another tub to "his Master Crawley from whome I expect a Subscription." As Catesby approached his first anniversary in Carolina, he asked, "If my Subscriptions are thought fitt to be continued another Year and that You approve of it I propose to goe to the Bahama Ilands." Alternatively, Catesby proposed a trip to Mexico with a Dr. Thomas Cooper, who also enjoyed the support of Richard Mead. While Cooper lobbied Mead directly, Catesby depended upon Sherard for news of the doctor's decision. Catesby also prevailed upon Sloane for patronage in this endeavor but does not appear to have received support for this idea. Catesby abandoned plans to botanize in Mexico, hoping that, even if his full subscription could not be renewed, Sherard might at least help "to defray My expenses" for travel in the Bahama Islands. In the same week that he wrote to Sherard, Catesby made a similar appeal to Sloane, in which he also announced his intention "to goe to the Bahama

18. Commercial venture of Sinclair: Catesby to Sherard, Nov. 26, 1724, ibid., 182. For Catesby on rice and Governor Johnson, see Catesby, "An Account of Carolina, and the Bahama Islands," *Natural History,* II, xvii.

Islands to make a further progess in what I am about." "This will add another Year to my continuance in America." Catesby proceeded to the Bahama Islands, where he visited Providence as well as *Ilathera, Andros,
Abbacco* and other neighbouring Islands." He continued to collect plants
but made a special effort to gather "many Submarine productions, as
Shells, Corallines, Fruitices Marini, Sponges, Astroites, *etc.*," he noted in
the preface to the *Natural History*. Sloane's support of Catesby's travels in
the Bahamas is implied in this further note on the specimens he collected
there: "These I imparted to my curious Friends, more particularly (as I had
the greatest Obligations) to that great Naturallist and promoter of Science
Sir *Hans Sloane,* Bart. to whose goodness I attribute much of the Success I
had in this Undertaking."[19]

   The 12 trip sponsors formed a base upon which Catesby would build
the larger subscription of 155 names for the publication of his *Natural History*. However, 4 of those trip sponsors did not become subscribers to the
book: they were James Brydges, duke of Chandos, John Perceval, Viscount
Perceval and later earl of Egmont (1683–1748), Sir George Markham
(1666–1736), and William Sherard. The reasons why they limited their
support to Catesby's botanizing and drawing trip remain somewhat unknown, though Sherard's death before publication began accounts for his
absence from the book subscription list. Moreover, Catesby's difficulty
meeting the expectations of each trip sponsor for specimens and drawings,
a recurring theme in his letters from the colonies to Sloane and Sherard,
may explain the departure of Perceval from Catesby's subscribers. Other
problematic trip sponsors, most notably Charles Du Bois, did renew their
support when Catesby initiated the publication of the illustrated volumes.

Subscription Publishing

   Catesby was back in London in 1726 and beginning to act on his plans
to have his drawings engraved, "in order to give a genll History of the
Birds And other Animals" of North America, as he put it to Sloane in

19. Regarding Mr. Parker: Catesby to Sherard, Nov. 13, 1723, Sherard Letters, CCLIII,
170. Subscriber prospect: Catesby to Sherard, Feb. 7, 1722/3, 167. Continuation of subscriptions: Catesby to Sherard, Jan. 16, 1723/4, 174. Proposed trip with Dr. Cooper: Catesby to
Sherard, Aug. 16, 1724, Oct. 30, 1724, 178, 179; Catesby to Sloane, Aug. 15, 1724, Sloane MS
4047, fol. 212. Bahamas: Catesby to Sherard, Jan. 10, 1724/5, Sherard Letters, CCLIII, 184;
Catesby to Sloane, Jan. 5, 1724/5, Sloane MS 4047, fol. 307. For Catesby on his collections in
the Bahamas, see Preface, *Natural History,* I, x.

1724. Catesby hoped to commission an engraver in Amsterdam or Paris, but found the cost of such an arrangement to be prohibitive. Instead Catesby hired artist Joseph Goupy (ca. 1698–ca. 1782) to teach him the art of etching. Catesby later recognized Goupy's contribution both in the preface to the *Natural History* and by including him among the subscribers. Coming to terms with such expenses must have been a contributing factor in Catesby's decision to publish by subscription, which was a means of moderating financial risk. By the time Catesby endeavored to issue his *Natural History* by subscription, the practice was already more than a century old and had been used to produce literary, religious, historical, and scientific volumes. Collective undertakings called subscriptions were also used to erect buildings, provide insurance against loss by fire, and gather capital to commence business in the colonial trades. This last use of subscriptions is especially noteworthy, since Catesby's efforts promoted both a publishing venture and the business interests of his patrons. More-over, as demonstrated in the preceding discussion of Catesby's research trip, his travels were also supported by subscription.[20]

Ephraim Chambers's *Cyclopaedia* explains the practice for contemporary readers:

SUBSCRIPTION, in the commerce of books, signifies an engagement to take a certain number of copies of a book going to be printed; and a reciprocal obligation of the bookseller or publisher, to deliver the said copies, on certain terms. The usual conditions of these *subscriptions* are, on the part of the bookseller, to afford the books cheaper to a sub-scriber than to another, by one third or one fourth of the price; and, on the part of the latter, to advance half the money in hand, and to pay the rest on the delivery of the copies: an agreement equally advantageous to the one and the other; as the bookseller is hereby furnished with money to carry on works, which would otherwise be above his stock; and the subscriber, receives as it were, interest for his money, by the moderate price the book stands him in.[21]

20. Catesby to Sloane, Aug. 15, 1724, Sloane MS 4047, fol. 212. Catesby on Goupy: Preface, *Natural History,* I, xi.

21. E[phraim] Chambers, *Cyclopaedia; or, An Universal Dictionary of Arts and Sciences,* 2 vols. (London, 1738), II, s.v. "Subscription. . . ." The first book published by subscription, according to Sarah L. C. Clapp, was John Minsheu's *Ductur in Lingues,* in 1617. See "Beginnings of Subscription Publication," *Modern Philology,* XXIX (1931), 200–202, 205, for other early uses of the word "subscription."

This description makes clear that subscription publishing was a business practice, involving reciprocal benefits and obligations for the publisher and subscriber. The process of subscription publishing usually began with the author's issuing a prospectus, which advertised the contents of an intended work. It also explained the terms on which the book could be purchased, including when payment was due and to whom a customer should address his or her wish to subscribe.

As Chambers explains, a subscriber might choose to purchase a book in this manner to obtain a discount, but this was not the only reason. Indeed, Catesby's subscribers were not offered a reduced price for their promise to purchase his book. The decision to subscribe to a publication was also a way to patronize a worthy project. Since the list of subscribers' names was often published in the front matter, the act of subscribing could also be a public statement of patronage. In that way, a subscriber might identify himself or herself as a person of culture, as having particular religious or political conviction, or with any number of other associations that a book might carry. In this instance, Catesby's subscribers attached themselves to the scientific, artistic, commercial, and colonial aspects of his *Natural History*.

Catesby's Prospectus to Publish by Subscription and in Parts

About 1729, Catesby issued a one-page prospectus, which began "PRO-POSALS, For PRINTING AN ESSAY TOWARDS A NATURAL HISTORY OF FLORIDA, CAROLINA and the BAHAMA ISLANDS." The proposal described the contents of the book, noting that it would encompass an ambitiously broad natural history of the American colonies, including the "BIRDS, BEASTS, FISHES, SERPENTS, INSECTS and PLANTS" as well as notes on climate, soil, and agriculture. Numerous illustrations would enrich the usefulness of the study, including figures of specimens and maps of the region. Noting his unique qualifications for creating such a book, the prospectus told of Catesby's three years of travels in Carolina and Florida, starting in 1722, and his subsequent stay of nine months in the Bahamas. As noted, Catesby had also traveled to Virginia in the previous decade, which prompted his later, more systematic study of the southern colonies.[22]

22. [Mark Catesby], "Proposals, for Printing an Essay towards a Natural History . . . ," n.d., ca. 1729, bound with Catesby's *Natural History* at the Humanities Research Center, University of Texas at Austin.

The assigned date, about 1729, for the proposal is based first upon the fact that Catesby

The names of 12 men who had already "assisted and encouraged" Catesby's "Undertaking" were listed, along with their noble titles, university degrees, and affiliations in institutions of learning (Appendix 2). The group included some of England's wealthiest men; collectors of natural history specimens, books, and antiquities; professionals in medicine and related fields; cultivators of ornamental and botanical gardens; and promoters of colonial enterprise. When Catesby published the final list of subscribers, it would include 155 names of men and women (Appendix 1) whose interests largely mirrored those identified for the first 12.[23]

Catesby emphasized the importance of the plates that would adorn his spectacular publication, noting "the Want of which hath caused so great Uncertainty in the Knowledge of what the Antients have described barely by words." Because Catesby decided to etch the plates himself, the book would be published in parts and delivered to subscribers as each section was completed. Catesby "intended to publish every Four Months TWENTY PLATES, with their Descriptions, and printed on the same Paper as these PROPOSALS." At this pace, the book would have been completed in three years and four months, with an additional four months devoted to the appendix. In fact, Catesby began producing segments of his book in 1729 and issued the final planned part in 1743. Twenty additional plates were published as an appendix in 1747, making the total span of the publication eighteen years. The price for each installment was set at one guinea, and a finer edition on imperial paper "put in their Natural Colours from the ORIGINAL PAINTINGS" was offered at two guineas per part. The nature of the difference between these two versions is somewhat ambiguous. One difference was the size of the paper. The difference in coloring was probably in the degree of care taken to assure proper coloring, although it may also be interpreted to be between a black-and-white set and a hand-

---

described his address as follows: "at the AUTHOR's at Mr. *Bacon's* late Mr. *Fairchild's,* in *Hoxton.*" Nurseryman Thomas Fairchild died in 1729, making the issuance of the proposal before that date impossible. The prospective nature of the document suggests that the proposal was printed at the beginning of the lengthy publication process.

23. Ibid. I have located two versions of the subscription list. One version lists 154 names, including both individuals and institutions, the other 155 names. Examples of the shorter list appear in the Catesby sets at the Huntington Library, the Academy of Natural Sciences, Philadelphia, the University of Pennsylvania, Princeton University, and the Houghton Library at Harvard University. The longer list is bound with the sets at the John Carter Brown Library at Brown University, Winterthur Museum, and the Historical Society of Pennsylvania, on deposit at the Library Company of Philadelphia.

colored set. It was common practice in the period to offer a special edition on large paper, to which noble patrons were expected to subscribe. None of the ten copies of the *Natural History* inspected in preparation for this essay varies from another substantially in size or coloring, and there are no known black-and-white copies. However, when the first part of Catesby's book was shipped to John Bartram, he was informed that it "is in a more contracted manner, and smaller paper." Although the present location of this set of plates is unknown, this note suggests that Catesby did indeed produce at least a few copies of the less expensive version of the book.[24]

The terms of acquiring the book were simply stated and protected the subscriber from common shortcomings of books published in this manner: "The Encouragers of this Work are only desired to give their Names and Places of Abode to the Author and his Friends, or at the Places here under-named: no Money being desired to be paid 'till each Set is deliver'd; that so there be no Ground to suspect any Fraud, as happens too often in the common way of Subscription." The risk was thus placed squarely on the author, who was also the publisher of this book. The risk was considerable, and approximately one-third of his 155 subscribers died before Catesby completed the last part of his book in 1747. Whether the next generation of the family purchased the remaining parts is unknown; in some instances the identity of a particular subscriber is ambiguous. This was the case of "*The Right Hon. the Earl* of DERBY." The nineteenth earl of Derby died in 1735/6, and his successor in 1776; since Catesby began collecting subscriptions before 1735/6 and continued after that date, the subscriber could be either man. It was common practice to list noble sub-

---

24. Ibid. The financial difficulty presented by publishing illustrated natural histories is suggested in a letter from William Sherard to Richard Richardson, Nov. 20, 1720: Micheli "is poor, and desires me to get him subscriptions for graving his plates, having got but ten patrons in Italy: each plate costs him forty-two giuolios, which is a guinea of our money. . . . I believe I must subscribe for more than two of them myself, which are as many as I am design'd." In Turner, ed., *Extracts from Richardson*.

On the smaller version to Bartram, see Collinson to John Bartram, Feb. 25, 1740/1, in Edmund Berkeley and Dorothy Smith Berkeley, eds., *The Correspondence of John Bartram, 1734–1777* (Gainesville, Fla., 1992), 152.

There are slight variations in paper size among existing Catesby sets, though these appear to result from the fact that each set was bound by the owner and sometimes bound again and, consequently, trimmed in different ways. Coloring variations include the amount of transparent versus opaque body color, and differences in the finer strokes that convey details of feather markings on the throat of "The Humming-Bird," pl. 65 in vol. I, for instance.

scribers by their title, without their given name, but this practice served Catesby inasmuch as the next lord in line might have been expected to assume his predecessor's obligations.[25]

Catesby's ability to publish the book without collecting money in advance was facilitated by a loan from Peter Collinson. In an annotation to his copy of the *Natural History,* Collinson wrote, "This copy of this work is very valuable; as it was highly finished by this ingenious author, who, in gratitude, made me this present for the considerable sums of money I lent him without interest, to enable him to publish it for the benefit of himself and family: else, through necessity, it must have fallen prey to the booksellers." Collinson's copy of Catesby's *Natural History* is made more extraordinary by twenty-two extra illustrations, original drawings by William Bartram, George Edwards, and Georg Dionysius Ehret.[26]

The final piece of information on the prospectus was where to place an order for the book. Subscriptions were being accepted by William Innys and by the author at Stephen Bacon's in Hoxton. Innys was often involved in the production and distribution of scientific books. When Eleazar Albin issued his ornithology in 1738, Innys and Richard Manby printed the book and were listed as "Printers to the Royal Society." This learned society was of immeasurable importance to Catesby, as its network supplied him with contacts in England and abroad, and its rolls produced numerous buyers for his book. Mr. Bacon, by contrast, ran a commercial nursery from which Catesby operated, a relationship that hints at an important link between the scientific study of botany and the importation and cultivation of plants for a wider range of uses, including commercial profit, ornament, medicine, and manufacture.[27]

Gathering a Subscription

Although the prospectus suggests the beginning of the process of collecting names for Catesby's publishing project, the further development of the list is more difficult to reconstruct. Contemporary correspondence suggests some of the methods by which Catesby built the rolls.

25. Ibid. The earl of Derby is identified by *Burke's Peerage.*

26. [Catesby], "Proposals." Collinson's loan and special copy of the *Natural History,* quoted in Turner, ed., *Extracts from Richardson,* 401 n. 7.

27. [Catesby], "Proposals"; Eleazar Albin, *A Natural History of Birds,* 3 vols. (London, 1738).

Communities of subscribers become evident, which revolved around economic, social, and intellectual interests. Catesby was not alone in his effort to sell copies and distribute the book. The book, either in its text or illustrations, appealed variously to aesthetic concerns, to scientific curiosity, or to economic ties to the colonies or the commodities they produced for readers. Alternatively, the act of patronizing a distinguished book was a public act that might have satisfied the needs of gentlemen and noblemen, whose libraries were full of monuments to similar acts of largess.

Catesby's subscriptions were gathered over time, as internal evidence in the published list indicates. It includes the names of subscribers who were deceased before the book was completed, including Sir Francis Nicholson, who died in 1728, even before the first part was issued. At the other extreme, Martin Folkes is recognized as the president of the Royal Society, an office he did not hold until 1741. As such, the list was probably not printed until the end of the project, probably in 1743 with the tenth part, which Catesby had intended to be the end of the book. Furthermore, at least two versions of the list were published. The sole difference between these two lists is that one includes the name of Lord Islay. On the copy of the subscription list in the John Carter Brown Library, Islay's name is printed darker and was clearly added to a sheet that had already been printed with the names of the others. It is not clear whether he was a late subscriber or his name was inadvertently omitted from the first printing.[28]

Catesby's diligent collecting during his second trip to the American colonies in the 1720s surely contributed to his success in recruiting subscribers to his publishing venture. He managed to send seeds for his friends, including Samuel Dale, Isaac Rand (d. 1743, director of the botanical garden of the Apothecaries Company), and Thomas Fairchild (1667–1729, the nurseryman), though these men did not have the capital to sponsor his trip. Catesby also noted sending "Ceder Berries" to Cromwell Mortimer (ca. 1700–1752), a Leiden-educated physician and close associate of Sloane. Whereas Fairchild died in 1729, just about the time Catesby was gathering subscriptions, Rand and Mortimer both became subscribers to the *Natural History,* and Mortimer chronicled the issuance of the parts in the *Philosophical Transactions* of the Royal Society.[29]

28. On Nicholson, see *DAB,* s.v. "Nicholson, Francis." On Folkes, see *DNB,* s.v. "Folkes, Martin."

29. Seeds to Dale, Rand, and Fairchild: Catesby to Sherard, May 10, 1723, 1724/5, Nov.

Catesby's subscribers came from both London and the provinces. Richard Richardson, a physician and plant collector in North Bierly, Yorkshire, demonstrates the roles played by patrons in the hinterland who were asked to gather subscriptions among their friends. Recruiting financing for his publication, John Morton wrote in 1704, asking Richardson for help in gathering subscriptions "from the Gentlemen and Noblemen of Northamptonshire." As his book would include "a brief account of the principal houses of Northamptonshire," Morton suggested that Richardson might appeal to his neighbors' vanity. The author also requested their names and titles for inclusion in the book, further indicating that public recognition was a motive for subscribing. Both the author and subscriber benefited from associating themselves with one another's work and reputation: In the case of Richardson, his distance from London accorded him a special place of prestige within the British learned community, earning him favors and deference from other naturalists and authors. A letter from Thomas Hearne, written February 8, 1712/3, indicates that Richardson could be counted on to perform this task among his neighbors in northern England: "Your note of subscribers . . . is a new Testimony of your Kindness to me, and of your Readiness to promote our English Antiquities."[30]

Richardson was also a subscriber to Catesby's *Natural History,* whose work he learned of from other subscribers. William Sherard informed Richardson in 1720 that Catesby was traveling with Sir Francis Nicholson to Carolina. Two years later, Sherard reported to Richardson that "two quires of dry'd plants" sent by Catesby had arrived from Carolina and that forty previously unknown specimens were among them.[31]

Sherard died in 1728, before Catesby began publishing his drawings of the flora and fauna he recorded, but the gardener Thomas Knowlton

---

13, 1723, Oct. 30, 1724, Sherard Letters, CCLIII, 170, 171, 179; Catesby to Sloane, Nov. 15, 1723, Sloane MS 4047, fol. 90.

Mortimer biography: *DNB,* s.v. "Mortimer, Cromwell." Mortimer's accounts of Catesby's *Natural History:* Royal Society, Classified Papers, 1660–1740 . . . , Dec. 31, 1730, Dec. 16, 1731, June 14, 1733, Jan. 23, 1734, June 3, 1736, June 9, 1737, Jan. 31, 1739.

30. John Morton to Richard Richardson, Nov. 9, 1704, in Turner, ed., *Extracts from Richardson,* 85–86; Thomas Hearne to Richardson, Feb. 8, 1712/3, Richardson Correspondence, Radcliffe Trust, c. 2, fol. 89, Bodleian Library, Oxford University.

31. Sherard to Richardson, Nov. 12, 1720, Oct. 13, 1722, in Turner, ed., *Extracts from Richardson,* 158, 188.

took up his cause with Richardson in subsequent years. Knowlton wrote in 1729:

> I have had the pleasure of hearing of your wellfair, both by Mr. Brewer and Sir Walter Hawksworth, whom I have got to become a subscriber to Mr. Catesby's *History of Carolina,* which I presume both you and the good Dr. Stanhope are incoragers of.—My self have become one some time since; and likewise have got him three more from his lordship, who was very willing, from my recommendation of the person and performances.—I likewise shall procure him some more, when I wait upon Esquire Willeby, who, I am sure, will be one, which will not be long.

Catesby eventually realized subscriptions from Knowlton, Hawksworth, Richardson, and Willoughby. Knowlton was also gardener to Richard Boyle, earl of Burlington (1695–1753), who subscribed to three copies of the *Natural History.* When Catesby issued the second part of the book, Knowlton reported that Boyle declared it "was the best done he ever see any thing of that Kind." In short, noble subscribers might have impressed Catesby's audience to a greater degree than gardeners did, but men such as Knowlton were clearly of great importance to the success of gathering the subscription.[32]

Catesby identified himself in the imprint as the publisher and listed three other booksellers from whom the *Natural History* could be purchased. William Innys, whom the proposal (ca. 1729) identified as collecting subscriptions, was listed in volume I in partnership with Richard Manby. In the second volume Manby was still a source for the book but at his own address on Ludgate-Hill. In addition, the book could be obtained through "Mr. HAUKSBEE, at the *Royal Society* House." Typically, in the eighteenth century, several booksellers were listed in the imprint as offering a book for sale, indicating a coordinated publishing effort. In the back of volume I of J. T. Desaguliers's *Course of Experimental Philosophy* (1734) is bound an advertisement that identifies "*BOOKS printed for* J. SENEX, W. INNYS *and* R. MANBY, *and* J. OSBORN *and* T. LONGMAN." These books were primarily concentrated in various branches of science, including mathe-

---

32. Thomas Knowlton to Richardson, Oct. 29, 1729, ibid., 302–303. Knowlton similarly wrote to Sloane, "My old aquance Mr Catesby has sent me down a part of his fine History of Carolina haveing become a subscriber to it and hope shall procure him some more" (Thomas Knowlton to Sir Hans Sloane, Sept. 20, 1729, Sloane MS 4050, fols. 200–201). Boyle's comments: Knowlton to Samuel Brewer, Nov. 17, 1729, in Blanche Henrey, *No Ordinary Gardener: Thomas Knowlton, 1691–1781,* ed. A. O. Chater (London, 1986), 125.

matics, physics, medicine, and natural history. Senex, Innys, and Manby were all subscribers to Catesby's *Natural History,* demonstrating that their support for him was part of a concentration of their publishing efforts in science. The second volume of Desaguliers's *Experimental Philosophy* carried a similar advertisement for books printed for Innys, Longman, and Senex.[33]

Booksellers also actively supported the *Natural History* through subscriptions. Purchasing books in this manner enabled them to distribute books for which they did not bear the financial burden of publishing. Ten of Catesby's subscribers were booksellers, including Innys and Manby, usually listed in the following manner: "Mr. Brindley for ——." This does not appear to have been a common designation in subscription lists, but it conveys the idea that the book is not intended for their own library. Instead, it is meant for resale, perhaps to a specific buyer recognized before making the subscription. Bookseller-subscribers also facilitated the distribution of the book outside London. One such subscriber, Benjamin Smithhurst, lived in Plymouth, as noted in the subscription list to Bishop Burnet's *History of His Own Time.* According to Thomas Knowlton, Richard Richardson was a late subscriber, purchasing the first eight parts in 1737/8 from an unidentified bookseller. Knowlton suggested further that, had Richardson purchased the book directly from Catesby, he might have received the gift of "some forain seeds as they come to hand." The gardener's comments are significant, because they demonstrate the continuing work of generating sales of the parts of the *Natural History,* the role of booksellers in distributing the book, and the additional gifts that one might receive as a reward for subscribing.[34]

These booksellers were also active in publishing, sometimes producing books that complemented Catesby's. Benjamin Stichall, a subscriber to the first edition, was one of the undertakers (a contemporary term for a publisher) of the second edition of Catesby's *Natural History,* which was issued in 1754, five years after the author's death. In 1729, Robert Willock issued an introduction to the botanical lectures of John Martyn, a topic directly related to Catesby's. Willock later published an explanation of sugar production, just as Catesby's book included notes on the commer-

33. Catesby, *Natural History,* imprint from title pages to vols. I, II; J. T. Desaguliers, *A Course of Experimental Philosophy,* 2 vols. (London, 1734–1744).

34. Gilbert Burnet, *Bishop Burnet's History of His Own Time* (London, 1724). Richardson's purchase from a bookseller: Knowlton to Samuel Brewer, Feb. 7, 1737/8, quoted in Henrey, *No Ordinary Gardener,* ed. Chater, 169.

cial applications of New World plants, such as his essay on the production of pitch and tar. Willock was also the publisher in 1753 of a group of papers presented at the Royal Society but omitted from the *Philosophical Transactions*. Other bookseller-subscribers focused their attention on different parts of the market, such as Edward Wickstead, whose efforts seem to have been concentrated in religious books.[35]

Multiple subscriptions were an effective way for patrons to facilitate a worthy project and to single themselves out as particularly generous benefactors. Five subscribers lavished their support upon Catesby by pledging to buy sixteen copies of his work. Sir Hans Sloane led the group with a subscription for five books. Sloane also helped to distribute the book, as suggested by Johann Ammann's expression of gratitude for the receipt of part of the *Natural History* in 1737. William Innys purchased four books, which he probably intended for resale; still, this commitment set him apart from the other booksellers in the imprint and the subscription list. Richard Boyle, earl of Burlington, an avid collector of plants and books, subscribed for three copies, as did his fellow nobleman, Charles Lennox, duke of Richmond (1701–1750). Catesby paid tribute to this latter patron by etching a "Java Hare" in the duke's possession for plate 18 of the appendix: "This was in the possession of his Grace the Duke of RICH-MOND, who was pleased to think it worth a place in this collection." Finally, Isaac Rand, the director of Chelsea Physic Garden and himself the beneficiary of Sloane's patronage, pledged for two sets of the *Natural History*. Rand later bequeathed fifty shillings per year to the Physic Garden to replenish specimens in the collection there.[36]

Although this is an incomplete picture of how subscriptions were gathered, it is highly suggestive. A set of avid supporters, including Sloane, Sherard, and Knowlton, prevailed upon their friends and correspondents to support a worthy project. The shared concern might have been botany, gardening, or the cultivation of prestige, as it was among these subscrib-

---

35. John Martyn, *The First Lecture of a Course of Botany* . . . (London, 1729); *The Art of Making Sugar* . . . (London, 1752); and *Several Papers, Most of Which Were Read before the Royal Society, in the Year 1752, and Were Not Printed in the Last Volume of the Philosophical Transactions* (London, 1753). Other books published by Catesby's subscriber-booksellers were identified with the Eighteenth-Century Short-Title Catalog database. I appreciate the assistance of Holly Phelps at the Library Company of Philadelphia in conducting these searches.

36. "A List of the Encouragers of This Work," Catesby, *Natural History;* Johann Ammann to Sloane, Aug. 6, 1737, Sloane MS 4055, fol. 155; *DNB*, s.v. "Rand, Isaac." I am grateful to Peter McCracken for the transcript of Ammann's letter to Sloane.

ers, or it might have been ornithology, art, or colonial enterprise, as we might surmise from the composition of the completed list of buyers.

The Scientific Community

The Royal Society was critical to establishing Catesby's scientific audience. Catesby became a member in 1732/3, about the time he completed the first volume of his *Natural History*. Records of his election to this learned society acclaim his contributions to the study of the natural world, describing him as

> a Gentleman well Skill'd in Botany and Natural History who travel'd for Several years in Various parts of America where he Collected Materials for a Natural History of Carolina and the Bahama Islands which Curious and Magnificient Work he has presented to the Royal Society.

In fact, the Royal Society itself was listed as a subscriber to Catesby's book. The subscription list also named Sloane, who was president of the society from 1727 to 1741; Martin Folkes, president from 1741 to 1753; and Cromwell Mortimer, secretary of the society from 1730 to 1752. Additionally, at least fifty-seven of Catesby's subscribers, including those just named, were members of this body.[37]

A number of Catesby's subscribers maintained cabinets of natural history specimens that included plants, birds, mammals, reptiles, and shells. Ralph Thoresby noted in his diary in 1723, during a visit to London, that he was distracted from his religious duties by a visit to Sloane's "invaluable museum of natural and artificial curiosities, antiquities, deities, lamps, urns, Roman and Egyptian." Sloane's cabinet was one of the greatest assembled in eighteenth-century England, and Catesby drew specimens there and deposited specimens that were sent to him in Sloane's keeping. When George Edwards published his ornithology, he often noted that his drawings were based upon live and mounted birds, and specimens preserved in spirits in the collections of people who were also subscribers to Catesby's *Natural History*. Entries by Edwards such as these are typical: "This Bird I drew at Sir *Hans Sloane*'s, where it lived some Years"; and "I saw this Bird alive in the Park of the Right Honourable the Earl of *Bur-*

---

37. Catesby's election to the Royal Society, quoted in Raymond Phineas Stearns, "Colonial Fellows of the Royal Society of London, 1661–1788," *WMQ*, 3d Ser., III (1946), 221. Members of the Royal Society: *The Record of the Royal Society of London . . .* , 4th ed. (London, 1940).

lington, at his House at *Chiswick,* near *London,* where I made this Design."
Additionally, Edwards drew specimens in the collections of the Royal
Society, Sir Charles Wager, Mrs. Sidney Cannon (who was midwife to the
princess of Wales), Peter Collinson, Charles Du Bois, Richard Mead, and
Charles Lennox, duke of Richmond, all of whom subscribed to Catesby's
Natural History.[38]

Catesby's correspondence with his English patrons suggests that, while
sponsorship of collecting expeditions was an important way to build a
cabinet, exchange was another. In this regard, collectors with country
houses or who lived in the provinces had an advantage over naturalists
living in London. Richard Richardson is an excellent example. His residence in Yorkshire gave him access to flora and fauna that were not
available in the environs of London. Additionally, his northern location
made him a point of contact for Scottish, Irish, and Welsh collectors.
Sherard and Sloane supplied him with English and Continental volumes
on natural history, ranging from Konrad von Gesner to Sloane's own
studies of Jamaica. Sloane also invited Richardson to samples of anything
growing in the Chelsea Physic Garden, which was started and endowed
with his patronage. In spite of these apparently grand gestures, Sloane was
still able to write sincerely, "I am ranging my curiosities where every day I
find my obligations to you and wish I could retaliate them." Sherard also
benefited from trade with Richardson. He reciprocated, in part, by offering to share plants he collected during a trip to Leiden, where Richardson
had been a fellow student of Hermann Boerhaave under the tutelage of
Paul Hermann.[39]

Despite the interdependence of collectors, their relationships were not
always cordial. One senses this in Catesby's timidity in making Sherard
aware of his shipments to Collinson and in his request to keep his receipt
of plants secret from Sloane. Competitiveness among collectors is also
evident in Catesby's putting the English collector Collinson in correspon-

38. Ralph Thoresby, *The Diary of Ralph Thoresby, F.R.S.* (London, 1830), 374–375. See
Catesby, *Natural History,* II, Appendix, 19, for instance, which illustrates two fish in Sloane's
cabinet, one deposited by Catesby and the other received by Sloane from New England. The
specimen collected by Catesby was sent from Gibraltar, perhaps by Catesby's brother, who,
according to Edwards, was a military officer there. Edwards, *A Natural History of Uncommon
Birds,* the King of the Vultures, I, pl. 2, and Great Horned Owl, II, pl. 60.

39. Debt to Richardson: Sloane to Richardson, Aug. 7, 1733, Richardson Correspondence, c. 8, fols. 91–92. Offer to collect specimens in Holland: Sherard to Richardson, July
14, 1727, c. 6, fol. 78. Richardson's studies abroad: *DNB,* s.v. "Richardson, Richard."

dence with the Carolinian Alexander Skene, advising, "I earnestly intreat You will burn or concell this Letter and the purport of it for reasons you easily conceive." Sherard complained to Richardson that Sloane was unwilling to reciprocate the favor of sharing his collections, and Sloane responded by declaring that Sherard's charges were unwarranted.[40]

In the same way that provincial collectors were sought after by urban ones, knowledgeable naturalists in North America enjoyed special favors from English collectors. They also bore the burden of supplying an entire community of eager collectors. John Bartram (1699–1777), who earned a place in Catesby's subscription list by supplying plant and animal specimens, is an excellent case in point. Peter Collinson recruited Robert James Petre, Baron Petre (1713–1742), to pay Bartram ten guineas to "Make an Excursion on the Banks of the Schuylkill" in 1735/6 and later raised an additional five guineas each from Charles Lennox, duke of Richmond, and Philip Miller. Both noblemen were also subscribers to Catesby's *Natural History,* Lennox for two copies. Edward Howard, duke of Norfolk (1686–1777), later subscribed to Bartram's collections; his wife, Mary Howard, duchess of Norfolk (d. 1773), was also an avid supporter of gardening and a subscriber of Catesby's.[41]

Collinson informed Bartram over time of the desires of his patrons, which included flora, fauna, and fossils, and urged him to travel in New York, New England, and the Middle Atlantic. Bartram's English patrons returned his favors by crediting an account through which he purchased textiles, hardware, and other valuable English imports. They also sent gifts of books, including Miller's *Gardeners Dictionary,* Johann Friedrich Gronovius's *Flora Virginica,* and Sloane's *History of Jamaica.* Collinson also introduced Bartram to Catesby, who prevailed upon him for shipments of American plants. In general, Catesby wrote, "my taste is agreeable with yours . . . those plants that are specious in their appearance, or use in physic, or otherwise." Sometimes he specified plants he had missed during his own travels, such as the chamaerhodendron, or rhododendron maximum, which Bartram supplied and Catesby illustrated in his appendix, plate 17. Catesby promised Bartram a copy of his *Natural History,* which he

40. Secrecy and competitiveness: Catesby to Sherard, June 20, 1722, Nov. 13, 1723, Sherard Letters, CCLIII, 164, 170. Introduction to Skene: Catesby to Peter Collinson, Jan. 5, 1722/3, Autograph Collection, Natural History Museum.

41. Schuylkill trip: Collinson to John Bartram, Mar. 12, 1735/6, and n.d. [1737], in Berkeley and Berkeley, eds., *Correspondence of Bartram,* 23, 36. Additional patrons: Collinson to Bartram, Oct. 20, 1740, ibid., 146.

explained was worth twenty guineas. Bartram's subscription, therefore, was paid in kind with plants and descriptions of American plants that Catesby sometimes incorporated in the completed book. A number of the plates in the second volume and the appendix demonstrate the importance of the cooperative relationship established among Catesby, Bartram, and Collinson. For example, the following entry clearly articulates the mutual benefits enjoyed by these three botanists:

> This curious *Helleborine* was sent from *Pensilvania* by Mr. *John Bertram*, who by his Industry and Inclination to the Searches into Nature, has discovered and sent over a great many new Productions both Animal and Vegetable. This Plant flowered in Mr. *Collinson's* Garden in *April*, 1738.

This passage shows that their collaboration contributed a plate to Catesby's book that would not have been possible otherwise, while Catesby's prose added prestige to Collinson as a gardener and Bartram as a collector.[42]

Subscribers and Colonial Interest

Notably, the word "subscription," upon which Catesby's travels and publication depended, was also used in contemporary business practice to refer to investment in trading companies. More than this formal connection, natural history and colonial enterprise were closely linked. Discovering the natural stores of a locality previously unexploited by world markets was an important step in making colonial trade profitable. As such, the flora and fauna as well as native practices with herbal medicine were among the categories of exploration with which naturalists like Catesby were charged. At least two dozen of Catesby's subscribers had substantial interests in the American colonies, including those in regions visited during his two journeys to North America. They included former and present colonial proprietors, governors, and founders as well as people whose wealth was built upon investment in trading companies that spanned Africa, North America, and Asia. Others were merchants, including woolen draper Peter Collinson and John Hanbury.[43]

In addition to the merchants who plied their trade with the colonies,

---

42. Catesby to Bartram, May 20, 1740, ibid., 132, and Bartram to Collinson, [Apr. 1, 1739], 117; Catesby, *Natural History*, II, 72.

43. Subscription as a commercial term: Chambers, *Cyclopaedia*, II, s.v. "Subscription."

Catesby's subscribers also included men with political power and capital investment in North America. For instance, two of the proprietors of the Carolina colony, Sir John Colleton (1669–1754) and John Carteret, earl of Granville (1690–1763), were subscribers. Granville is especially noteworthy, since he was the only one of eight proprietors who refused to part with his share of the Carolina colony when the proprietary government was overthrown in 1719. Interestingly, Catesby paid homage to Colleton at least twice in the text to the plates, noting that the laurel tree and the pseudo-acacia were growing in his gardens at Exmouth in Devonshire. This is noteworthy as an indication of one symbolic function of gardens: domestication of colonial plants as a demonstration of control over colonial holdings. Catesby's subscribers also included the proprietors of Maryland and Pennsylvania, Charles Calvert, Baron Baltimore (1699–1751), and Thomas Penn (1702–1775). Catesby paid tribute to the former subscriber by illustrating "The Baltimore-Bird" and by writing, "It is said to have its Name from the Lord *Baltimore*'s Coat of Arms, which are Paly of six Topaz and Diamond, a Bend, counterchang'd; his Lordship being a Proprietor in those Countries." This description of American fauna adds another layer to the symbolic claiming of the New World through its natural stores by describing the bird's incorporation into Baltimore's heraldic device. Of further note, John Bartram first saw Catesby's then incomplete book in 1737 at the house of Thomas Penn, whom Peter Collinson arranged for Bartram to meet:

> Dress thy self Neatly in thy Best Habits and wait on him for them for I have in a pticular manner Recommended thee to Him—
>
> I have Desired Him to show thee the Natural History of South Carolina in Eight Books, finely Colour'd to the Life so forget not to Ask that favour—first inquire his most Leisure Time and then wait on Him—

Collinson was cultivating the budding naturalist's talents as a collector and artist while educating him on the proper performance of deference toward the proprietor.[44]

Catesby's patrons also encompassed the colonial governors charged

44. Edward McCrady, *The History of South Carolina under the Proprietary Government, 1670–1719* (New York, 1901), 679. For plants growing in Colleton's gardens: Catesby, *Natural History*, II, 61, and Appendix, 20; for the "Baltimore-Bird," I, 48. For Bartram's introduction to Penn: Collinson to Bartram, Sept. 8, 1737, in Berkeley and Berkeley, eds., *Correspondence of Bartram*, 64.

with managing the reaches of the British Empire in North America. As noted in the discussion of Catesby's trip to Carolina in 1722, his funding began with the pledge of £20 from Sir Francis Nicholson, governor of South Carolina from 1720 to 1725. It is significant that Nicholson commenced his term as governor with the commission of a naturalist, Catesby, to explore its natural stores; identification of these resources would guide him in making the colony flourish. Nicholson was a generous promoter of cultural activities in the American colonies, including patronage of the church, education (including the gift of a library to the College of William and Mary), natural history, and cartography. Robert Johnson, governor of Carolina from 1717 until 1719 and governor of South Carolina from 1731 until 1735, was also a subscriber. Catesby listed among Governor Johnson's contributions to the colony the acquisition of a device for harvesting rice and recipes for pickling sturgeon and preparing caviar. The personal alliance between these two governors of Carolina is evident in the provision of Nicholson's will requesting the purchase of "Mourning Rings of a guinea value" for "the Hon. Collonel Robert Johnson and his present wife." Another associate of these two colonists, James Edward Oglethorpe, was the founder of the Georgia colony in 1732, a scheme supported by Sir Hans Sloane and numerous other subscribers as well as a grant of £10,000 from Parliament. Demonstrating the importance that Oglethorpe placed on projects like Catesby's, he ordered the establishment of a public garden. By 1734 one visitor to the Georgia colony was able to observe:

> There is laid out near the Town, by Order of the Trustees, a Garden for making Experiments for the Improving Botany and Agriculture; it contains 10 acres and lies upon the River; and it is cleared and brought into such Order that there is already a fine Nursery of Oranges, Olives, white Mulberries, Figs, Peaches, and many curious herbs; besides which there are Cabbages, Peas, and other European Pulse and Plants which all thrive.

Catesby also enjoyed a subscription from Woodes Rogers, who rented the Bahama Islands and was appointed governor by the proprietors in 1717.[45]

45. For Nicholson: McCully, "Governor Francis Nicholson," *WMQ*, 3d Ser., XXXIX (1982), 310–333; *DAB*, s.v. "Johnson, Robert"; Catesby on Johnson: *Natural History*, II, "Account," xvii, xxxiv; Nicholson's will: "South Carolina Gleanings in England," *South Car-*

14. Map of Asia. *Cartouche. John Senex,* Modern Geography; or, All the Known Countries in the World . . . *(London, 1708–1725). The Library Company of Philadelphia*

The relationship between botanical collections and colonization was expressed allegorically in contemporary print sources. Cartographers produced maps that aided in staking colonial claims. Their maps, like Catesby's *Natural History,* were at once artistic and scientific accomplishments. Two of Catesby's subscribers, Henry Popple and John Senex, were notable mapmakers in the first half of the eighteenth century in England. Both men were members of the Royal Society, demonstrating a contemporary scientific understanding of their work. Senex's maps were collected in his *Modern Geography* and begin with representations of the solar system and the world. The next maps depict the four continents, of which *Asia* and *North America* are illustrated here (Figures 14, 15). These maps included both the contours of the land masses they represented and elaborate cartouches that linked the land with a native figure and

olina Historical and Genealogical Magazine, V (1904), 223. On Oglethorpe's plans for Georgia: *DNB,* s.v. "Oglethorpe, James Edward"; Sloane as a supporter of the colony: E. St. John Brooks, *Sir Hans Sloane: The Great Collector and His Circle* (London, 1954), 99; contemporary account of public garden at Savannah: Baron von Reck, quoted in Bertha Sheppard Hart, "The First Garden of Georgia," *Georgia Historical Quarterly,* XIX (1935), 327. For Rogers: *DNB,* s.v. "Rogers, Woodes."

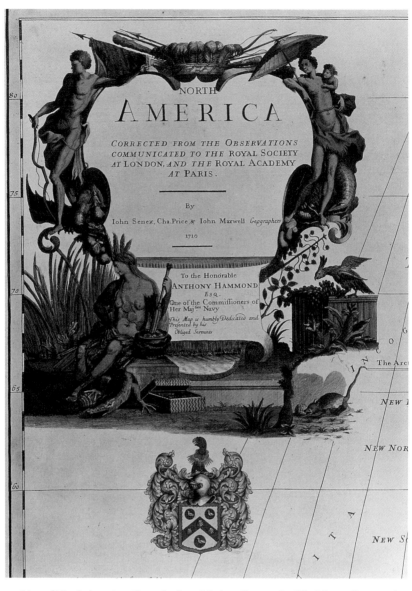

NORTH
AMERICA

CORRECTED FROM THE OBSERVATIONS
COMMUNICATED TO THE ROYAL SOCIETY
AT LONDON, AND THE ROYAL ACADEMY
AT PARIS.

By

Iohn Senex, Cha. Price, & Iohn Maxwell *Geographers*

1710

To the Honorable
ANTHONY HAMMOND
Esq.
One of the Commissioners of
Her Maj:ᵗⁱᵉˢ Navy

*This Map is humbly Dedicated and
Presented by his
Obliged Servants*

The Arc

NEW

NEW NOR

NEW S

15. Map of North America. *Cartouche.* Senex, Modern Geography. *The Library Company of Philadelphia*

examples of the flora and fauna that originated there. These maps also bore dedications to patrons, as *Asia* was in honor of Sir George Markham (1666–1736), a sponsor of Catesby's second trip to Carolina and the Bahamas.[46]

Illustrations in eighteenth-century books about gardening and related fields also made symbolic links between colonial enterprise and natural history. For instance, the frontispiece (Figure 16) to John Hill's *British Herbal* related the gathering of plants from around the world to the advancement of medical knowledge in England. The plate, engraved by H. Roberts, is called *The Genius of Health Receiving the Tributes of Europe Asia Africa and America and Delivering Them to the British Reader.* This idealization of botanical collecting hinged upon the efforts of naturalists like Catesby under the sponsorship of those whose financial interests were vested in the successful production of colonial resources. More important, this image depended upon the assumption of the central place of England in the building of an empire. That an angel, albeit a pagan Genius of Health, delivers the world's produce adds an element of divine inevitability to England's dominant position in global enterprise and botanical endeavor. Of course, Catesby's subscribers included numerous physicians, apothecaries, and keepers of herbal gardens, who shared a medical interest in botany. The two communities—colonial investors and medical professionals— were not separate, however, as is exemplified by Sloane, a physician and naturalist who became wealthy through investments in quinine bark and sugar.[47]

Catesby's subscribers also included merchants like Peter Collinson, John Hanbury, and George Clifford (1685–1760), whose occupations more immediately identify their stake in colonial resources. Their fortunes often were expended in large part to satisfy their botanical curiosity, which, in turn, expressed their commercial ventures. George Clifford, for instance, made his fortune through the Dutch India Company and expressed his global financial interests symbolically by having his gardens laid out according to the four continents from which they originated. Moreover, by supporting Catesby and having their names published as

46. Henry Popple designed the map published in Catesby's *Natural History*. He also published *A Map of the British Empire in America . . .* (London, 1733). John Senex, *Modern Geography; or, All the Known Countries in the World . . .* (London, 1708–1725).

47. John Hill, *The British Herbal . . .* (London, 1756).

The Genius of Health recieving the tributes of Europe Asia Africa and America and delivering them to the British Reader.

16. *The Genius of Health.* . . . By H. Roberts. Frontispiece to John Hill, *The British Herbal* . . . (London, 1756). This item is reproduced by permission of *The Huntington Library, San Marino, California*

subscribers to his *Natural History,* these merchants, investors, governors, and proprietors advertised their interests in colonial enterprise.[48]

Gardening Interests of Catesby's Subscribers

Catesby's travels and his *Natural History of Carolina* introduced dozens of species of new plants into England, and many of his patrons were attracted to the publication for this reason. Through text and image the book was clearly useful in identifying plants to be sought by English and European gardeners and also helped to indicate whether the plants could be grown outside North America. Gardening also brought people into Catesby's subscription list from diverse occupations and classes: gardeners and nurserymen, alongside physicians, professors, and merchants, as well as noblemen and royals. Catesby's entries for individual plants were dotted with notations of whether they were viable in English soil and climate and whether examples were then flourishing in English gardens. These notations include references both to the gardens of his patrons and to the commercial nursery of Mr. Fairchild, where Catesby was apparently employed. In his entry on the willow oak, for instance, Catesby wrote, "Most of these Oaks are growing at Mr. *Fairchild*'s." Peter Collinson was frequently recognized for the successes in his garden at Peckham, in Surrey. Hinting at Collinson's famous patronage of John Bartram, Catesby credited Collinson with introducing the martagon from Pennsylvania and noted that in his "curious Garden it flow'red in Perfection." Notes on the viability of American plants on English soil hinted at another type of viability: the economic potential of imported plants as valuable and renewable commodities. In both the subscription list and the body of the text, Catesby advertised his own as well as his friends' and supporters' intellectual and commercial stakes in domesticating American plants.[49]

The Society of Gardeners issued a catalog of plants available for sale in the nurseries in and around London. Their ranks included Thomas Fairchild, who employed Catesby but did not subscribe, as well as three subscribers: Robert Furber, Philip Miller, and Christopher Gray (1693/4–1764). Gray was frequently noted in *The Natural History* for successfully

48. Allan Stevenson, comp., *Catalogue of Botanical Books in the Collection of Rachel McMasters Miller Hunt,* 2 vols. (Pittsburgh, 1961), II, pt 1., lx.

49. For Fairchild's nursery, see Conway Zirkle, "Some Forgotten Records of Hybridization and Sex in Plants," *Journal of Heredity,* XXIII (1932), 435–437. For examples of Catesby's mention of Fairchild, see *Natural History,* I, 22, II, 56.

cultivating the plants illustrated by Catesby, such as the notice of catalpa trees "having stood out several Winters, and produced plentifully their beautiful Flowers, without any Protection, except the first Year." Entries like this one at once proclaimed the viability of ornamental American plants in English gardens and advertised Christopher Gray's commercial nursery "at *Fulham*" as a ready source. Eight of Catesby's subscribers (and the brother of a ninth) were singled out in the preface of the Society's *Catalogus Plantarum* as having cultivated distinguished gardens. Furber maintained a commercial nursery in Kensington and published several catalogs and books on gardening. His *Short Introduction to Gardening* was published with funding from 388 subscribers, 22 of whom also subscribed to Catesby's book. Furber's gardening book focused upon ornamental gardening, explaining, for example, the types of trees that produce fruit each month and listing flowers that are suitable for edging versus potting. The clear intention of Furber's book indicates one possible application for Catesby's, since they shared at least a part of their readership.[50]

Gardens associated with medical practice were also grown by Catesby's subscribers. Philip Miller was in charge of the Chelsea Physic Garden, which is still situated in Chelsea and was endowed by Sir Hans Sloane. With the botanical garden at Oxford, Chelsea was among the most important herbal gardens in England. Upon the stipulation of Sloane, Chelsea and the herbarium at the Royal Society were interconnected. Each year, Miller was charged with adding fifty specimens to the cabinet of the Royal Society, and the catalog of these plants was duly published in the *Philosophical Transactions*. Miller increased the collections at Chelsea through English and foreign sources, including a correspondence with Richard Richardson. For instance, Miller sent Richardson "seeds which I lately recieved from Carthagena" and asked in return for "some Northern and Welsh plants." Miller was also one of four subscribers of annual support for John Bartram's botanizing efforts in North America; the other three supporters of Bartram were noblemen: Robert Petre, Baron Petre, Charles Lennox,

---

50. Society of Gardeners, *Catalogus Plantarum . . . A Catalogue of Trees, Shrubs, Plants, and Flowers, Both Exotic and Domestic, Which Are Propagated for Sale in the Gardens near London* (London, 1730). For recognition of Christopher Gray, see Catesby, *Natural History,* I, 49, 53, 55, 57, 66, II, 78, Appendix, 4. For the quote on the catalpa trees growing at Fulham, see I, 49.

For Furber: John H. Harvey, "The Nurseries on Milne's Land Use Map," London and Middlesex Archaeological Society, *Transactions,* XXIV (1973), 185; Robert Furber, *A Short Introduction to Gardening . . .* (London, 1733).

duke of Richmond, and Edward Howard, duke of Norfolk. Baron Petre, the duke of Richmond, and the duchess of Norfolk were all subscribers to Catesby's *Natural History*. These relationships demonstrate the interdependency of botanical circles in the period, a point further underscored by Peter Collinson's role in arranging for Bartram's subscriptions. Catesby's subscribers also included Richard Walker (1679–1764), professor of moral philosophy at Cambridge, who established the botanical garden there. Walker began the garden during his tenure at Cambridge and bequeathed his property and garden to the university. A proposal in the *Gentleman's Magazine* the year after Walker's death requested subscriptions to sustain the garden and described its current state:

> Besides a small stove, a large and commodious green-house has been erected; a great part of the ground laid out; and the curator, with two men under him, and all other expences have been paid.[51]

Catesby listed subscriptions from a number of royal and noble gardeners, including Queen Caroline (1683–1737) and Augusta, princess of Wales (d. 1772). These royal patrons lent their prestige to the publication, and Catesby paid homage to them by dedicating the first volume to Caroline and the second to Augusta. Robert James Petre, Baron Petre, amassed one of England's most remarkable ornamental gardens in his short life. Collinson estimated his holdings at ten thousand American plants, twenty thousand European ones, and a number of Asian exotics. Petre had an aesthetic sensibility, setting light and dark greens in contrast and using color in "Mixtures [that] are perfectly picturesque and have a Delightfull Effect." His gardens produced a symbolic expression of English dominion over the rest of the globe. In their density, his plantings transported visitors with impressions of "American thickets." Through the garden's yield, "one would think South America was really There to see a Servant come in Every Day with Tenn or a Dozen pine apples."[52]

Peter Collinson also accumulated one of the great collections of plants

51. Philip Miller to Richardson, June 18, 1734, Richardson Correspondence, c. 9, fols. 13–14. For Bartram's subscribers, see Collinson to Bartram, Oct. 20, 1740, in Berkeley and Berkeley, eds., *Correspondence of Bartram,* 146. For Walker's garden at Cambridge, see *DNB*, s.v. "Walker, Richard"; "A Proposal for an Annual Subscription for the Support of the Botanic Garden at Cambridge," *Gentleman's Magazine,* XXXV (1765), 200.

52. Collinson to Bartram, Sept. 1, 1741, in Berkeley and Berkeley, eds., *Correspondence of Bartram,* 167.

in eighteenth-century England, a fact of which he was keenly aware. In the preface to a manuscript published posthumously as the *Hortus Collinsonianus,* he wrote,

> I often stand with wonder and amazement when I view the inconceivable variety of flowers, shrubs, and trees, now in our gardens, and what there were forty years ago; in that time what quantities from all North America have annually been collected by my means and procuring . . . very few gardens, if any, excell mine at Mill Hill, for the rare exotics which are my delight.[53]

The catalog is dotted with references to the sources of the exotics he prized so dearly, including Catesby and many of his subscribers: John Bartram, Christopher Gray, Thomas Knowlton, Philip Miller, John James Dillenius, Sir Charles Wager, Charles Lennox, duke of Richmond, Robert James Petre, Baron Petre, and Johann Ammann, a professor of botany in Saint Petersburg.

A number of subscribers maintained gardens on the Continent, including both botanical and ornamental gardeners in Holland who supplied many specimens to English collectors. The mercantile and colonizing histories of the Netherlands provide an important parallel to the economic factors that contributed to English natural history. The garden of George Clifford, a Catesby subscriber, is a case in point. Clifford was a wealthy merchant, whose gardens were cataloged by Linnaeus and published as the *Hortus Cliffortianus* in 1737. The importance of this volume was described by Johann Friedrich Gronovius (1690–1760), a German-born professor and botanist at Leiden, as "one of the most curious book[s] that ever is printed." Gronovius recognized the significance of Linnaeus's new method of classification, which the Swedish naturalist made famous in the *Species Plantarum.* Gronovius wrote further that Linnaeus directed his colleagues at Leiden in meetings: "We examined one time the minerals, another day flowers of plants, and so insects and fishes. We are now come so far, that by his tables we could tell this fish, plant or minerall belongs to such a genus, and so we came to the species, however no one of us hath seen it before." Gronovius was recommending the book to Richard Richardson in this letter but noted that the *Hortus Cliffortianus* could only be obtained as a gift from Clifford. The German physician

53. L. W. Dillwyn, ed., *Hortus Collinsonianus: An Account of the Plants Cultivated by the Late Peter Collinson, Esq., F.R.S.* (Swansea, 1843), preface, vii.

suggested to his English friend that a present of petrifactions to Clifford might be enough to secure the return gift of this important new book.[54]

Subscribers as Authors

Many of Catesby's subscribers were not only gardeners and investors but also authors themselves, some of them extremely prolific. The bibliography of essays and books by Catesby's subscribers includes more than five hundred titles and ranges in subject from natural history to gardening, medicine, physics, religion, politics, travels, antiquities, and law. One subscriber, Martin Bladen (1680–1746), was even a gentleman playwright. When they published by subscription, their supporters overlapped with Catesby's.[55] For example, Sir Hans Sloane's books on the flora and fauna of Jamaica were important models for Catesby's own work. Under the patronage of Christopher Monck, second duke of Albemarle, Sloane traveled to Jamaica, where he served as the duke's physician. During his stay there he made extensive observations of the flora and fauna and collected eight hundred plant specimens. From his studies, Sloane published a *Catalogus Plantarum Quae in Insula Jamaica* . . . (1696) and a two-volume natural history called *A Voyage to the Islands Madera, Barbados, Nieves, S. Christophers, and Jamaica* (1707–1725). Although this latter book is probably the most frequently cited source in the *Natural History,* it was by no means a template for Catesby's book. Sloane's long descriptions and narrative stand in marked contrast to Catesby's succinct text. Also, Sloane's linear, black-and-white engraved specimens contrast sharply with Catesby's aesthetically striking hand-colored plates.[56]

In addition, Philip Miller, who was in charge of the botanical garden of the Apothecaries Company, published *The Gardeners Dictionary* (1731) as well as subsequent editions of this book and other guides for gardeners.

54. Johann Friedrich Gronovius to Richardson, July 22, 1738, Richardson Correspondence, c. 10, fols. 31–32. Gronovius uses the word "curious" in the eighteenth-century sense: that is, to describe an intellectual project that inspires considerable thought or curiosity.

55. Bladen biography: David Erskine Baker, Isaac Reed, and Stephen Jones, *Biographia Dramatica; or, A Companion to the Playhouse* . . . , 3 vols. (London, 1812), I, pt. 1, 43.

56. Sloane's travels: s.v. "Sloane, Hans," *DNB,* and *DSB.* Sloane, *Catalogus Plantarum Quae in Insula Jamaica;* and *A Voyage to the Islands Madera* (commonly referred to as *The History of Jamaica*).

Among Miller's subscribers was Mark Catesby (for a copy in large paper) as well as twenty-nine other people whose names supported both books.[57]

Another important author-subscriber is George Edwards, who was Catesby's protégé in ornithology. Between 1743 and 1764, he published seven volumes comprising his *Natural History of Uncommon Birds* and *Gleanings of Natural History*. Many of his specimens were supplied by Catesby, and others were collected by Catesby's brother in Gibraltar. Edwards's deference to Catesby demonstrates the level of his debt: "I should not have presumed to re-publish any thing that was directly the same with what has been published by Mr. *Catesby,* because I know myself not capable to add any Amendations to what he has done." At least twenty-three subscribers to Edwards's publications had previously patronized Catesby's *Natural History*. Catesby, too, was among the subscribers to Edwards's first volume of *Birds*.[58]

John James Dillenius (1687–1747) was a German botanist hired and imported by William Sherard to work on the latter's *pinax*. He was the first to hold the professorship of botany endowed by Sherard at Oxford. Although the *pinax* never reached the press, Dillenius did publish a history of mushrooms and *Hortus Elthamensis,* a catalog of the plants growing in the gardens of James Sherard, brother of Catesby's sponsor, William. The latter volume credits a number of plants growing at James Sherard's estate, Eltham, to Catesby's successes in collecting. For example, Dillenius wrote, "This plant is born without cultivation in the rocks of Providence, an island in the Bay of the Bahamas, whence Mark Catesby brought back seeds. Plants born from these seeds bore flowers and fruit in the third year after planting in the Eltham garden in July 1728 and in subsequent years, for the plant is perennial, and it becomes branchy; looking like a tree, it grows fewer branches, which come forth in a much higher part of the plant."[59]

---

57. Miller, *The Gardeners Dictionary* (London, 1731).

58. George Edwards, *A Natural History of Uncommon Birds* (vols. II–IV omit *Uncommon* from the title); Edwards, *Gleanings of Natural History . . .*, 3 vols. (London, 1758–1764). These volumes are typically numbered consecutively, with the *Gleanings* comprising vols. V–VII. The quote is taken from I, 24.

59. "Sponte autem nascitur haec planta in rupibus Providentiae, sinus Bahamensis insula, unde semina attulit Marc. Catesby, ex quibus natae plantae tertio post sationem anno in Horto Elthamensi flores et fructus tulere Julio mense, Anno 1728, et sequentibus annis; perennis enim planta est, et sublignosa fit, specie arborea, ramis licet paucioribus, et in superiore tantum parte enascentibus, praedita." Johann Jakob Dillenius, *Hortus Elthamensis . . .*, 2 vols. (London, 1732), I, 2.

In addition to prefatory acknowledgments and bibliographic citations, botanists paid tribute to their admiration of a colleague by naming a plant in his honor. Catesby was honored in this way by Gronovius, whose *Flora Virginica* was based on the collections made by John Clayton. Catesby illustrated *Catesbaea* (Figure 17) as the last plate to the second volume of his *Natural History*, an especially auspicious place until he added the appendix. Although the plant had been named by Gronovius, Catesby felt compelled to feign a degree of humility rather than answer to charges of self-celebration:

> N.B. It is not without Reluctance, that I here exhibit a Plant with my own Name annexed to it; but the Regard and Obligations I owe to my learned Friend Dr. *J. F. Gronovius* of *Leyden,* who was pleased some Years since to honour me, tho' undeservedly, with the Title of this Genus, obliges me not to suppress it.

Thus it is an act of deference rather than hubris that propels Catesby to include his namesake at the conclusion of his monumental study.[60]

In short, authors comprised a scholarly community, who shared information and patrons. The travels of Catesby and other naturalists supplied numerous gardens, which in turn were exchanged among collectors in England and on the Continent. These fed catalogs and, later, studies in plant classification. The correspondence among these collectors and gardeners documents a thriving international community, deeply interdependent. Their publications cite one another's articles and books as well as the generosity they received in the form of specimen sharing and patronage.

Catesby's Subscribers as Book Collectors

Catesby's subscribers were avid book buyers, and the libraries they accumulated were among the most important ones of their day. Natural history, gardening, and medicine were frequent themes in their holdings, but they ranged the full span of material, intellectual, and spiritual inquiry. They reflected shared economic desires as well as reflections upon the plenitude of natural productions and the wonders of ancient civilizations that were being excavated. In some instances, the sheer number of volumes suggests that the mere act of acquisition was itself the source of satisfaction.

60. Catesby, *Natural History,* II, 100.

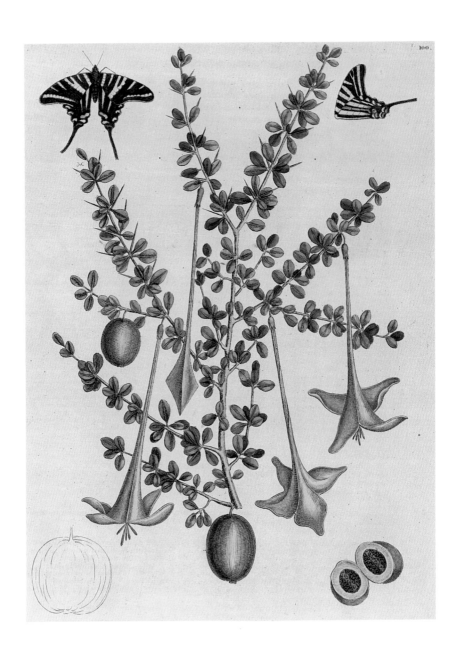

17. *Catesbaea.* Mark Catesby, *The Natural History of Carolina, Florida, and the Bahama Islands . . .* (London, 1731–1747), II, pl. 100. Courtesy, Colonial Williamsburg Foundation

Richard Mead's library of more than 100,000 volumes brought in excess of £5,000 pounds when it was auctioned in 1754 shortly after his death. The library spanned many disciplines, including natural history and medicine but also history, religion, art, and literature. Catesby's *Natural History* yielded £20 9s. 6d., which is nearly 2 guineas per part (the price originally charged by the author) and was among the highest prices paid for any books in his collection. Mead's library also contained a number of volumes written by Catesby's other subscribers, including Johann Ammann, John James Dillenius, Sir Hans Sloane, Samuel Dale, Adrian Van Royen, George Edwards, Philip Miller, and James Douglas. All of these works are in the fields of botany or medicine. Additionally, Mead collected seminal works by earlier naturalists, including Pliny, Gesner, and Gaspard Bauhin. For perspective on the value of Catesby's book, Dillenius's *Historia Muscorum,* a lavishly illustrated quarto volume brought £1 9s.; Sloane's two-volume folio *History of Jamaica* sold for £6 10s., and Edwards's four-volume, handcolored *History of Birds* £9 5s. Only a handful of the thousands of books in Mead's library sold for more than £20, most of them multivolume sets such as the ninety-three-volume *Acta Eruditorum* with supplements (£23). A number of other subscribers left impressive libraries: Edward Harley, earl of Oxford, owned 50,000 books at his death, and Sir Hans Sloane possessed nearly the same number. Among Catesby's American subscribers, William Byrd II surely accumulated the most impressive library, which numbered 3,486 volumes, according to Thomas Jefferson.[61]

Many of Catesby's subscribers were frequent consumers of books through subscription. For instance, P. J. Wallis identifies Sir Hans Sloane as the buyer of 125 books published by subscription between 1699 and 1757, and Martin Folkes of 52 books between 1717 and 1757. Sloane was one of the most prominent physicians of his day, an accomplished naturalist in his own right, president of the Royal Society and the Royal College of Physicians, and, upon his death, founder of the British Library and British Museum. Folkes was an antiquarian, who served as president of the Society of Antiquaries and succeeded Sloane as president of the Royal Society. The books supported by these erudite men spanned many disci-

61. Samuel Baker, *Bibliotheca Meadiana, sive Catalogus Librorum Richardi Mead, M.D.* (London, 1754). The copy of this catalog at the Library Company of Philadelphia is annotated with prices realized at the auction. Harley's library is estimated at fifty thousand printed books and Sloane's library between forty thousand and fifty thousand books in William Young Fletcher, *English Book Collectors* (London, 1902), 145, 151–152. Byrd's library is the subject of Kevin J. Hayes, *The Library of William Byrd of Westover* (Madison, Wis., 1997).

plines, including history, religion, mathematics, architecture, literature, medicine, and natural history.[62]

For the frequency and depth of their patronage, the most generous patrons were recognized as the dedicatees of books. A number of Catesby's subscribers were honored in this way. Sir Hans Sloane was so honored, including in Philip Miller's *Gardeners and Florists Dictionary* (1724) and *The Gardeners Dictionary* (1731) and George Edwards's *Natural History of Birds* (vol. II, 1747). Sloane was also the dedicatee of Joseph Miller's *Botanicum Officinale* (1722) for his consistent patronage of botany, and especially for his "late noble Present of the PHYSICK-GARDEN at *Chelsea* to the *Apothecaries Company*." The Society of Gardeners dedicated its *Catalogus Plantarum* (1730) to Thomas Herbert, earl of Pembroke. Sir Richard Boyle, earl of Burlington, was the dedicatee of Francis Drake's *Eboracum* (1736), along with thirty-eight other titles between 1707 and 1751. John Hill dedicated his *Eden* (1757) to John Stuart, earl of Bute. Catesby's subscriber Lady Walpole was similarly honored by John Cowell in *The Curious and Profitable Gardener* (1730).[63]

Catesby's subscribers included men with substantially lesser means, whose subscribing habits were more tightly focused. Thomas Knowlton, gardener to the earl of Burlington, subscribed to at least thirteen other books on natural history, history, and gardening. The histories that Knowlton purchased were mostly devoted to particular locales in England—Yorkshire, York, Kingston-upon-Hull, and London—a genre of writing that often encompassed geographical and natural observations that would have aided Knowlton's interest in collecting and growing plants. Knowlton was not single-minded, however; his subscriptions also included *Miscellaneous Poems and Translations,* published in 1740, by Henry Travers.[64]

62. Wallis, "Book Subscription Lists," *Library,* 5th Ser., XXIX (1974), 279–284.

63. Philip Miller, *The Gardeners and Florists Dictionary* (London, 1724) and *The Gardeners Dictionary* (1731); Edwards, *A Natural History of Birds,* II; Joseph Miller, *Botanicum Officinale; or, A Compendious Herbal* (London, 1722); Society of Gardeners, *Catalogus Plantarum . . . A Catalogue of Trees, Shrubs, Plants, and Flowers;* Francis Drake, *Eboracum; or, The History and Antiquities of the City of York* (London, 1736); John Hill, *Eden; or, A Compleat Body of Gardening* (London, 1757); John Cowell, *The Curious and Profitable Gardener* (London, 1730).

On Burlington as frequent dedicatee: John Harris, *The Palladian Revival: Lord Burlington, His Villa and Garden at Chiswick* (New Haven, Conn., 1994), 269. On Lady Walpole as dedicatee to Cowell's *Curious and Profitable Gardener:* Stevenson, comp., *Catalogue of Botanical Books,* II, pt. 2, 128.

64. Henrey, *No Ordinary Gardener,* ed. Chater, 293–294.

Catesby's subscribers often appeared as the most generous patrons of books celebrated as important publishing events. For instance, 26 of Catesby's supporters are listed as agreeing to purchase 80 copies of Alexander Pope's *Odyssey of Homer,* published in five volumes in 1725. Five of these bibliophiles accounted for the purchase of 50 books. Pope's subscription list included 573 names for 827 copies of the book. The subscribers who overlapped with Catesby's made up just 4 percent of the buyers but purchased nearly 10 percent of the copies subscribed.[65]

Bishop Gilbert Burnet's history of the reigns of British monarchs after the Restoration was another major publishing event that attracted many of Catesby's subscribers. At least 56 names are listed in both Catesby's "List of Encouragers" and among the subscribers to this history. Burnet's book was an enormous success. The first volume attracted 1,218 subscribers, and the second 2,067, with many names appearing in both lists. Many of those subscribers in common with Catesby's were royals, nobles, baronets, and men with military titles.[66]

Subscription publishing defined a set of mutual rewards and obligations that extended far beyond the exchange of money for books. The list of the 12 distinguished sponsors of Catesby's botanizing trip to Carolina and the Bahamas lent the authority of the English nobility, the most important learned society, colonial government, and the medical establishment to his intended publication. The direct assistance of these original supporters and the prestige attached to their names and titles helped Catesby to expand the list to include further support from a total of 155 subscribers in each of those categories as well as in the worlds of mercantile exchange, horticultural commerce, botany, and publishing. Catesby even netted subscriptions from the royal families of three European countries. In addition to the books they added to their libraries, Catesby's subscribers benefited through their association with the beauty, learning, and luxuriousness of the publication. They announced themselves as natural aristocrats and as leaders in their fields of study and trade. Catesby reinforced their leading roles not only by listing his "Encouragers" but also in textual references to their contributions in the preface, natural history narrative, notes to the plates, and identification with the names of plants. The book reflects an economic system in which plants and the products made from them were important commodities, stemming from the expanding empires built in

65. Alexander Pope, trans., *The Odyssey of Homer,* 5 vols. (London, 1725–1726).
66. Burnet, *History of His Own Time.*

the seventeenth and eighteenth centuries by Britain and other European monarchies; a social system in which gardeners, authors, and scientists depended upon the patronage of noblemen, wealthy merchants, gentlemen, and each other; and a cultural system in which art, science, and gardening were overlapping fields of exploration in which beauty, knowledge, order, and vastness were prized in themselves and as symbols of power and authority. Catesby's book was a record of the natural stores of the American colonies, an engine for converting them into intellectual and economic capital, and a validation of those who held the power necessary to make those conversions.

Subscribers to Mark Catesby's *Natural History of Carolina*

This appendix is based on the subscription list in the copy of Catesby's *Natural History* at the John Carter Brown Library, Brown University, Providence, Rhode Island. The names are given exactly as they appear in the original, followed in parentheses in expanded form along with birth and death dates.

A List of the Encouragers of This Work.

A

John Amman, *M.D. Prof. Bot. Petrop.* (Johann Ammann, 1707–1742)
William Archer, *Esq;* (Died 1739)

B

The Right Hon. the Lord BALTIMORE. (Charles Calvert, Baron Baltimore, 1699–1751)
The Right Hon. the Lord BATEMAN. (William Bateman, Viscount Bateman, died 1744)
Richard Bateman, *Esq;* (Died 1762)
Mr. John Bertram *of* Pensilvania. (John Bartram, 1699–1777)
The Hon. William Bird, *Esq; of* Virginia. (William Byrd II, 1674–1744)
Stephen Biss, *Esq;* (Died 1746)
The Hon. Martin Bladen, *Esq;* (1680–1746)
His HIGHNESS the Duke of BOURBON. (Louis-Henri, duke of Bourbon, 1692–1740)
Capt. J. Brewse.
Mrs. Bridgeman. (Sarah Bridgman, died 1786)
Mr. Brindley *for——* (John Brindley, died 1758)
Brook Bridges, *Esq;*
Mr. Elias Brownsword. (Ca. 1708–1781)
The Right Hon. the Earl of BUCCHAN. (Probably David Erskine, died 1745)
The Rt. Hon. the Earl of BURLINGTON, 3 *Books.* (Richard Boyle, earl of Burlington, 1695–1753)
Peter Burwell, *Esq;*
The Right Hon. the Earl of BUTE. (John Stuart, Earl of Bute, 1713–1792)

C

Colin Campbel, *Esq;*
John Campbel, *Esq;*
Mrs. Canon. (Mrs. Sidney Cannon or Kennon, died 1754)
William Car, *Esq;*
Sir William Carew, *Bart.* (1689–1744)
The Right Hon. the Lord CARTERET. (John Carteret, earl of Granville, 1690–1763)
Jacob de Castro Sarmento, *M.D.* (1692–1762)
The Hon. the Lord JAMES CAVENDISH. (Died 1741)
The Hon. Lieut. Gen. Charles Churchill. (Died 1745)
George Clifford, *Esq;* (1685–1760)
Sir John Colliton, *Bart.* (John Colleton, 1669–1754)

John Colliton, *Esq;*

Mr. James Collinson. (Died 1762)

Mr. Peter Collinson. (1693/4–1768)

The Hon. Lieut. Gen. Columbine. (Francis Columbine, died 1746)

Sir William Courtenay, *Bart.* (William Courtenay, 1675/6–1735; or his son William
    Courtenay, 1709/10–1762)

Mr. Thomas Cox *for* —— (Died 1754)

D

Mr. Samuel Dale, *M.L.* (1659?–1739)

The Right Hon. the Earl of DERBY. (James Stanley, earl of Derby, 1664–1735/6; or his
    cousin, Edward Stanley, earl of Derby, 1689–1776)

His Grace the Duke of DEVONSHIRE. (William Cavendish, duke of Devonshire, 1698–1755)

John James Dillenius, *M.D. B. Pr. Ox.* (Johann Jakob Dillenius, 1687–1747)

James Douglas, *M.D.* (1675–1742)

Charles Dubois, *Esq;* (Charles Du Bois, 1656–1740)

Ebenezar Dubois, *Esq;* (Died 1747)

Godefrydus Dubois, *Phil. & M.D. & Prof.* (1700–1747)

E

The Right Hon. the Lord EDGCOMB. (Richard Edgcumbe, 1680–1758)

Mr. George Edwards. (1694–1773)

Mr. Thomas Esson, *Esq;*

Kingsmil Eyre, *Esq;* (Died 1743)

F

Martin Folkes, *Esq; Presid. of the* ROYAL SOCIETY. (1690–1754)

The Hon. Sir Thomas Frankland, *Bart.* (Died 1747)

Mr. Robert Furber. (Ca. 1674–1756)

G

Gardiners Company.

Mr. Fletcher Giles for ——

Sir Henry Goodrick, *Bart.* (Sir Henry Goodricke, 1677–1738)

Mr. Joseph Gopy. (Joseph Goupy, ca. 1698–ca. 1782)

Mrs. Gray.

Mr. Christopher Gray. (1693/4–1764)

John Green, *Esq;*

John Frederick Gronovius, *M.D. Civitatis Leydensis Senator.* (1690–1760)

H

Joh. Henric Hampe, *M.D. Nassov. Med. Principissae Walliae* (Ca. 1697–1777)

Mr. John Hanbury. (Died 1758)

        Hare, *Esq;*

            Harnage, *Esq;*

Sir Walter Hawksworth, *Bart.* (Sir Walter Hawkesworth, died 1735)

Mr. Thomas Haughton. (Died 1733)

Richard Hazard, *Esq;* (Died 1784)

Mrs. Holloway, *of* Virginia. (Elizabeth Catesby Cocke Holloway, died 1755)

The Hon. General Honywood. (Sir Philip Honywood, died 1752)

Silas Hooper, *Esq;*

Sir James How, *Bart.* (Sir James Howe, ca. 1670–1735/6)

Mr. Joseph Hurlock. (Ca. 1714–1793)

Alexander Hume, *Esq; of* Carolina.

J. Aug. Hugo. *Med. Reg. Hanov.* (August Johann von Hugo, 1686–1760)

I

John Jeoliff, *Esq;*

Mr. William Innis *for* —— 4 *Books.* (William Innys, died 1756)

The Hon. and Rev. Mr. George Ingram. (Died 1763)

The Right Hon. the Earl of Iley. (Archibald Campbell, viscount of Islay and later duke of
    Argyll, 1682–1761)

The Rt. Hon. the Lord Viscount IRWIN. (Arthur Ingram, Viscount Irvine, 1689–1736; or his
    brother Henry Ingram, Viscount Irvine, 1691–1761)

James Justice, *Esq; of* Edinburg. (1698–1763)

The Hon. Rob. Johnson, *Gov. of* S. Carolina. (Robert Johnson, ca. 1676–1735)

K

Abel Kettelby, *Esq;* (Abel Kettleby, died 1744)

Robert Kettleby, *Serjeant at Law.* (Robert Kettleby, died 1743)

The Hon. Lieut. General Kirk. (Percy Kirke, 1684–1741)

John Knight, *Esq;*

Mr. Thomas Knowlton. (1691–1781)

L

Stephen Labass, *Esq;*

Madam L'Ambrosia.

Isaac Lawson, *M.D.* (Died 1747)

Mr. James Leak. (James Leake, died 1737)

His Grace the Duke of LEEDS. (Thomas Osborne, duke of Leeds, 1713–1789)

Smart Lethieulier, *Esq;* (Smart Lethieullier, 1701–1760)

His HIGH. Prince LIECHTENSTEIN *at* Vienna.

The Hon. Lumbly Lloyd, *D.D.*

Guy Lloyd, *Esq;*

The Right Hon. the Lord LOVEL. (Thomas Coke, Baron Lovel and later earl of Leicester,
    1697–1759)

M

The Right Hon. the Earl of MACCLESFIELD. (Thomas Parker, earl of Macclesfield, ca. 1666–
    1732)

The Rev. Dr. Thomas Manningham, *Prebend. of* Westm (1684–1750)

Mr. Richard Manby *for* —— (Died 1769)

Richard Mead, *M.D. Med. Reg.* (1673–1754)

Mr. Joseph Miller. (Died 1748)

Mr. Phillip Miller. (1691–1771)

His Grace the Duke of MONTAGU. (John Montagu, duke of Montagu, ca. 1688–1749)

Cromwell Mortimer, *M.D. R.S. Secr.* (Ca. 1700–1752)

John Morley, *Esq;* (1655–1732)

N

Mr. De Narischkin, *Envoy extraordinary from her IMPERIAL MAJESTY of* RUSSIA. (Semen Kirillovich Narischkin, 1710–1775)

Sir Michael Newton, *Knight of the* Bath. (Ca. 1695–1743)

Roger North, *Esq;* (1651–1734)

The Hon. Lieut. Gen. F. Nicholson, *Gov. of* S. Carolina. (Sir Francis Nicholson, 1655–1728)

Her Grace the Dutchess of NORFOLK. (Died 1773)

O

The Hon. Major General Ogilthorp. (James Edward Oglethorpe, 1696–1785)

The Right Hon. the Earl of OXFORD, 2 books. (Edward Harley, earl of Oxford, 1689–1741)

P

Adrian Paats, *J.U.D. Societatis Indiae Orientalis in Statione Rotterodam. Moderator.*

Thomas Pen, *Esq; Proprietor of* Pensilvania. (Thomas Penn, 1702–1775)

The Right Hon. the Earl of PEMBROKE. (Thomas Herbert, earl of Pembroke, 1656–1732/3; or his son Henry Herbert, earl of Pembroke, 1693–1749/50)

Thomas Pellet, *M.D.* (Ca. 1671–1744)

The Right Hon. the Lord PETRE. (Robert James Petre, Baron Petre, 1713–1742)

Richard Plumpton, *Esq;* (Died 1746)

Henry Popple, *Esq;* (Died 1743)

Her ROYAL HIGHNESS the PRINCESS of WALES. (Augusta, princess of Wales, died 1772)

Q

Her late MAJESTY QUEEN CAROLINA. (Caroline, queen of Great Britain, 1683–1737)

Her MAJESTY the QUEEN of SWEDEN. (Ulrika Eleonora, queen of Sweden, 1688–1741)

R

Mr. Isaac Rand, 2 *Books.* (Died 1743)

Sir John Randolph *of* Virginia. (Sir John Randolph, ca. 1693–1736/7)

His Grace the Duke of RICHMOND. 2 *Books.* (Charles Lennox, duke of Richmond, 1701–1750)

Richard Richardson, *M.D. F.R.S.* (1663–1741)

Joseph Richardson, *Esq;*

Henry Rolle, *Esq;* (1708–1750)

Adrianus Van Royen, *Med. & Bot. Prof. in Acad. Lugd. Bat.* (1704–1779)

Woods Rogers, *Esq; Governor of the* Bahama Islands. (Woodes Rogers, died 1732)

The Right Rev. Dr. Rundel, *Bishop of* DERRY. (Thomas Rundle, ca. 1688–1743)

S

Thomas Scawen, *Esq;* (Died 1730)

Mr. John Senex. (Died 1740)

Sir Hans Sloane, *Bart. the late President of the* ROYAL SOCIETY, *and* COLLEDGE *of* PHYSICIANS, 5 *Books.* (1660–1753)

The Hon. Alex. Skene, *of* S. Carolina. (Alexander Skene)

Mr. Godfrey Smith.

Mr. Benjamin Smithhurst *for* ——

The ROYAL SOCIETY.

Mr. Van Spekelson.

Alexander Stewart, *M.D.* (Died 1742)

       Stanhope, *M.D.* (Probably John Stanhope, M.D.)

Thomas Stack, *M.D.* (Died 1756)

Jo. Geo. Steigertahl, *M.D.* (Johann George Steigertahl, born ca. 1667)

Nicolaus Stumphius, *M.D.*

Mr. Benjamin Stichall *for* ——

T

George Lewis Teissier, *M.D.* (Died 1742)

Henry Trelawney, *Esq;*

W

The Right Hon. Sir Charles Wager, *first LORD of the* ADMIRALTY. (1666–1743)

The Right Hon. the Lady Walpole. (Catharine Shorter Walpole, Lady Walpole, 1682–1737)

Mr. Aaron Ward *for* —— (Died 1747)

Mr. Edward Wicksteed *for* —— (Died 1758)

Mr. Robert Willock *for* ——

The Hon. —— Willoughby, *Esq;* (Perhaps Thomas Willoughby, 1694–1742)

The Right Hon. the Earl of WILLMINGTON. (Spencer Compton, earl of Wilmington, ca.
    1673–1743)

Benj. Whitaker, *Esq; of* Virginia

Dr. Walker, *Master of* Trinity Colledge, Cambridge. (Richard Walker, 1679–1764)

APPENDIX 2
Sponsors of Catesby's Trip to Carolina, Florida, and the Bahama Islands, 1722–1726

Each sponsor is listed first in exactly the manner he is named in Catesby's "Proposals, for Printing an Essay towards a Natural History of Florida, Carolina, and the Bahama Islands." Following in parentheses is the expanded name as it is commonly spelled, with birth and death dates.

His Grace JAMES *Duke* of *Chandois.* (James Brydges, duke of Chandos, 1673/4–1744)

The Right Honourable EDWARD *Earl* of *Oxford.* (Edward Harley, earl of Oxford, 1689–1741)

The Right Honourable THOMAS *Earl* of *Macclesfield.* (Thomas Parker, earl of Macclesfield, ca. 1666–1732)

The Right Honble JOHN Lord PERCIVAL. (John Perceval, Viscount Perceval and later earl of Egmont, 1683–1748)

Sir Geroge MARKHAM, Bar^t F.R.S. (1666–1736)

Sir HENRY GOODRICK, Bar^t. (Sir Henry Goodricke, 1677–1738)

Sir HANS SLOAN, Bart *President* of the *Royal Society,* and of the *College of Physicians.* (Sir Hans Sloane, 1660–1753)

The Honble Colonel FRANCIS NICHOLSON, *Governour of South Carolina.* (1655–1728)

RICHARD MEAD, M.D. & F.R.S. (1673–1754)

CHARLES DU BOYS, Esq; F.R.S. (Charles Du Bois, 1656–1740)

JOHN KNIGHT, Esq; F.R.S.

WILLIAM SHERARD, L.L.D. & F.R.S. (1659–1728)

Therese O'Malley

MARK CATESBY AND THE
CULTURE OF GARDENS

I n the study of early America, we know little of the real substance of
colonial garden practice. Mark Catesby's work, however, can shed
new light on the overlapping roles of botany, horticulture, and
collecting within that world of gardening. Two principal aims of
this essay are to establish a context for understanding early American
gardens in the culture of the early eighteenth century and to understand
the writings of and about Mark Catesby within this context. The great
problem is that only traces of gardens from this period survive. Therefore,
we must join the extremely limited information to the more abundant
evidence and scholarly literature concerning European gardens of the
same time. Only when gathered into a larger transatlantic context are the
fragments meaningful. From Catesby's botanical efforts in England and in
the colonies emerges a sense of what distinguishes garden theory and
practice in the eighteenth century from other times.

Catesby and Eighteenth-Century Garden History

Mark Catesby lived during a dynamic period in the history of European
landscape and garden design. Within this period in England, a transition
in the aesthetics of gardens coincided with a transformation from classical
design (derived from the Renaissance) to a modern sensibility that continues into the contemporary world.[1] In garden design this meant a shift

The author would like to thank Amy Meyers for making available documentary material she
has accumulated on the history of natural history illustration.

1. For a useful bibliographic essay on British and American garden history literature, see
Peter Martin, *The Pleasure Gardens of Virginia: From Jamestown to Jefferson* (Princeton, N.J., 1991),

from geometric regularity and architectonic design to irregular, asymmetrical plans that evoked the nondesigned landscape. A garden aesthetic that valued the least obvious artifice, the imitation of an unimproved landscape, and the cult of rusticity is often discussed in terms of the development of the natural style.[2]

However, the shaping of landscape taste also resulted from the increasing desire for new plants and from the interest in sponsoring expeditions, collecting, and publishing among the most powerful political and cultural elite.[3] It was, in part, to "bring home," or to simulate the experience of the artist/naturalist/explorer, that the re-creation of more natural environments in the garden or landscape would become in the eighteenth century the preferred mode of display or design. The new, naturalistic style of eighteenth-century garden design was greatly influenced by several factors, including the arrival of imported exotic plants, empiricism in the botanical sciences, the impact of exploration, and the increasing cultural significance of natural history. Furthermore, the botanic garden, which emphasized the scientific aspects of plants, became increasingly more popular in the eighteenth century. It was as innovative and expressive of a new garden aesthetic as the English landscape garden, although the latter has received the greater attention of historians. A study of Mark Catesby's work—his writing, gardening, collecting, and drawing—provides an opportunity for a deeper understanding of the world of gardening in his lifetime.

225–231; worth noting also is David R. Coffin, *The English Garden: Meditation and Memorial* (Princeton, N.J., 1994). On the cult of rusticity, see Ann Bermingham, *Landscape and Ideology: The English Rustic Tradition, 1740–1860* (Berkeley, Calif., 1986).

2. The development of the "natural" garden of the eighteenth century, however, has resulted in simplistic dichotomies in the description of garden styles that persist into this century. Whether a garden is regular or irregular, formal or informal, geometric or natural, symmetrical or asymmetrical are fundamental modalities that are difficult to escape in criticism, historical writing, and discussion of garden design. Clearly, these dualities hardly describe the subtlety and complexity of most sophisticated design. Still, these are taxonomic labels by which gardens have been categorized for three hundred years. See Mark Laird, *The Formal Garden: Traditions of Art and Nature* (London, 1992), 6–9, and his introduction for a discussion of the use and misuse of these terms in garden history.

3. Douglas Chambers, *The Planters of the English Landscape Garden: Botany, Trees, and the Georgics* (New Haven, Conn., 1993). Chambers discusses the impact of new planting materials, mostly American, on the development of the English landscape garden between 1650 and 1750. See also Mark Laird's book, *The Flowering of the Landscape Garden: English Pleasure Grounds, 1720–1800* (Philadelphia, 1999), for an extensive history of plant material in the garden during this period.

The history of the eighteenth-century English garden has been dominated by the categories of the picturesque and sublime, philosophical categories that pervaded all forms of literary and visual arts. Early American gardens of the same period have been dismissed, largely, as purely utilitarian until quite late in the eighteenth century. Thereafter they are often labeled *retardataire* in relation to European garden practice. A more accurate history would stress that the art and science of garden making on both sides of the ocean were influenced by transatlantic gardening culture. Interest in plant material was shared by collectors in England and America, and its successful pursuit was fully interdependent and collaborative. A better understanding of the American garden is therefore essential to building a comprehensive history of the European garden during this period of interaction. As Catesby was intricately linked with botanical collectors and their gardens in both England and America, it is possible to see how, by his agency, American gardens provided living laboratories for experiments in naturalizing plants, studios for artistic depictions, and venues for the distribution of seeds and plants locally and internationally. The gardens with which Catesby was associated were transfer depots for a vast network of intellectual and material exchange that served a burgeoning culture of gardeners, botanists, politicians, and artists.

To understand Catesby better, it is useful to reevaluate the typical categorization that distinguishes among the designed landscape, the non-designed cultivated landscape, and the "unimproved," uncultivated landscape also called "wilderness."[4] Catesby was deeply invested in all three

---

4. These three aspects of the broad term "landscape" have been discussed in terms of the three natures by scholars such as John Dixon Hunt; see his "Gard'ning Can Speak Proper English," in Michael Leslie and Timothy Raylor, eds., *Culture and Cultivation in Early Modern England: Writing and the Land* (London, 1992), 197. Also see Claudia Lazzaro, *The Italian Renaissance Garden* . . . (New Haven, Conn., 1990) 9–10. "Wilderness" is a complex word and has been the subject of much scholarly attention. Here it is important to distinguish between two senses. First, in this section of the essay it pertains to uncultivated land (to European eyes), seemingly unchanged by human intervention. The second use refers to a part of a designed garden or landscape that is an ornamental woodlands (also known as a grove or bosquet). The "wilderness" as a garden type, either carved out of an existing woodland or made by dense planting of trees, existed as early as the Renaissance and served as a contrast to the geometric and architectonic parts of the garden. With the availability of exotic trees from the New World in the seventeenth and eighteenth centuries, the plant material could be specifically chosen from various wilderness regions (such as North America) to create a specific "wilderness" garden. Such specificity in plant material did not exist in the earlier ornamental woodlands of the Renaissance and baroque periods. The later wilderness gar-

realms of landscape. He was obviously concerned with new ornamental plants for designed landscapes and gardens. He also investigated plant use and methods of agriculture of both European colonists and native Americans. As a naturalist/artist Catesby explored in the Carolinas and Georgia the natural "unimproved" landscape of the American colonies and described it in his *Natural History,* which provided new material for the use and delectation of his colleagues and sponsors. Often, in the study of landscape, these various aspects are approached independently. However, I would like to argue that the three landscapes each informed and shaped the perception of the others. They should be understood as aspects of a single, central interest in the natural world that pervaded the life's work of Catesby. His *Natural History of Carolina, Florida, and the Bahama Islands* (1731–1743) and *Hortus Britanno-Americanus; or, A Curious Collection of Trees and Shrubs* (1763) provide valuable information about his landscape interest in Europe as well as in colonial America. These works also attest to the active transatlantic context of the garden culture in which he worked. Much of that information is given in terms of what garden an imported plant has been successfully grown or naturalized in or where it came from originally. Although we have only brief mention of the gardens with which he had contact and the nature of that contact, from this evidence we can begin to discern Catesby's garden-related activities and his contributions to the changing world of gardens and their meanings.

Catesby's Garden Contacts

Catesby lived in a period referred to by Linnaeus as "The Golden Age of Botany." Richard Pulteney, in his 1790 *Progress of Botany in England,* wrote, "At the same period of time, lived RAY, MORISON, PLUNKENET, PETIVER, SLOANE, and SHERARD, under whose countenance, and culture, the knowledge of nature received the most rapid and substantial improvement, which it had ever experienced."[5] Joseph and Nesta Ewan have

---

dens were also distinguished from their predecessors by a requirement for appropriate growing conditions peculiar to the plants that reflected a sensitivity to the relationship between environment and the culture of North American plants. See Mark Laird, "Approaches to Planting in the Late Eighteenth Century: Some Imperfect Ideas on the Origins of the American Garden," *Journal of Garden History,* XI (1991), 167–168.

5. Richard Pulteney, *Historical and Biographical Sketches of the Progress of Botany in England . . . ,* 2 vols. (London, 1790), II, 65.

described that botanical world and how Catesby and his contemporaries, born in an era when medieval conceptions of the natural world were still loaded with theology and superstition, became leaders in the revolutionary development of empirical sciences.[6] In order to carry out Francis Bacon's philosophy of experimentation and direct observation, botanists, naturalists, and garden enthusiasts such as Catesby helped establish, stock, and maintain gardens of living plants that would support empirical study.

Before he began his travels, Catesby was associated with several important horticultural collections and botanic gardens in England. As a young man he probably began his career as a gardener and botanist at the botanic gardens of his uncle Nicholas Jekyll and of Samuel Dale of Braintree.[7] After Catesby began traveling, he continued his connection with many of the most notable botanical collections in England, including those he mentions in his writings: Peter Collinson's at Peckham, Thomas Fairchild's nursery at Hoxton (Figure 18), and Sir Charles Wager's at Parson's Green. Christopher Gray's nursery at Fulham received special mention in the preface to the *Hortus Britanno-Americanus,* where "Mr. Gray has for many years made it his business to raise and cultivate the plants of America (from whence he has annually fresh supplies) in order to furnish the Curious with what they want."[8] In 1737, Christopher Gray in collaboration with Catesby published in English and French a catalog of American plants "that would endure the climate of England" (Figure 19). Catesby also contributed many of the American species in the garden of James Sherard at Eltham.

The subscribers to Catesby's *Natural History*—called "the encouragers"—included as well very prominent people in the world of horticultural and sylvicultural exchange. Robert Furber, owner of Kensington Nurseries, which specialized in American plants, ran one of the most fashionable commercial nurseries of the day. Furber is well known for producing the first illustrated catalog of his botanical collection, which included

---

6. Joseph Ewan and Nesta Ewan, *John Banister and His Natural History of Virginia, 1678–1692* (Urbana, Ill., 1970), 4–5. For example, Hans Sloane still believed that every country produced plants especially suited to the cure of its diseases.

7. George Frederick Frick and Raymond Phineas Stearns, *Mark Catesby: The Colonial Audubon* (Urbana, Ill., 1961), 7–10.

8. Mark Catesby, *Hortus Britanno-Americanus* ... (London, 1763), preface. This is the same book as the author's *Hortus Europae Americanus* ... (London, 1767), which carries a new title page.

18. *The City Gardener*. . . . By Thomas Fairchild (London, 1722), title page. This item is reproduced by permission of *The Huntington Library, San Marino, California*

19. *Magnolia Altissima.* Plate by Mark Catesby, after drawing by Georg Dionysius Ehret, in Christopher Gray, *A Catalogue of American Trees and Shrubs That Will Endure the Climate of England* (London, 1737). Collection of Rachel Lambert Mellon, Oak Spring Garden Library, Upperville, Virginia

twenty-five American plants (Figure 20).[9] Mrs. Bridgeman, another en-courager, was married to the leading garden designer, Charles Bridgeman. Lord Burlington and the earl of Bute were also encouragers and members of a powerful and innovative cultural elite.

When he first arrived in the colonies in 1712, Catesby was received by Governor Alexander Spotswood and Dr. William Cocke of Williamsburg, Catesby's brother-in-law, and thus into the social and political center of the British colonies. He also was closely tied to Francis Nicholson and James Oglethorpe, two governors and leaders in the planning of new towns in the colonies. Among the American gardens Catesby mentioned

9. Furber counted among his clients Henry Hoare of Stourhead, which is a landscape considered by many the supreme achievement of the English landscape garden style. John Harvey, "The Nurseries on Milne's Land Use Map," London and Middlesex Archeological Society, *Transactions,* XXIV (1973), 177–198. These prints could be seen in the homes of colonial leaders, including John Custis in Virginia (Martin, *The Pleasure Gardens of Virginia,* 62–63).

20. *November.* From Robert Furber, *Twelve Months of Flowers* (1730). Courtesy of National Gallery of Art

21. *A Seat on the Ashley River* (Plantation of William Bull). By Charles Fraser. 1802. Courtesy of Gibbes Museum of Art / Carolina Art Association

in the *Natural History* was Colonel William Bull's plantation in South Carolina on the Ashley River (Figure 21). Colonel Bull was the first native-born American to receive a Doctor of Medicine degree from Leiden, site of one of the greatest botanic gardens in Europe.[10] Catesby also mentioned the plantation and garden of Mr. Spatches, Providence, Bahamas. We know he was consulted by William Byrd II, a subscriber to the *Natural History,* on the design of his garden at Westover (Figure 22). Byrd wrote: "After dinner I . . . walked about the garden all the evening, and Mr. Catesby directed how I should mend my garden and put it into a better fashion than it is at present."[11] These useful references place Catesby within a

10. Richard Beale Davis, *Intellectual Life in the Colonial South, 1585–1763,* 3 vols. (Knoxville, Tenn., 1978), II, 860. William Bull's *Reminiscences* records that the oak trees were planted by a visitor, Mark Catesby, who came to Carolina in 1722. The author was appointed to assist General Oglethorpe in settling Georgia. Quoted in Charles Fraser, *A Charleston Sketchbook, 1796–1806* . . . (Rutland, Vt., 1959), 26.

11. Louis B. Wright and Marion Tinling, eds., *The Secret Diary of William Byrd of Westover, 1709–1712* (Richmond, Va., 1940), 540. Frick and Stearns, *Mark Catesby,* 92, report that Byrd was "engaged in planting a colony of Switzers upon the Roanoke," referring to the English landscape gardener and writer Stephen Switzer, whose garden treatise *Ichnographia Rustica* (London, 1718) was known among colonial landowners. He is credited with formulating the "ferme ornée," or ornamented farm, a landscape that blended the "pleasurable with the profitable."

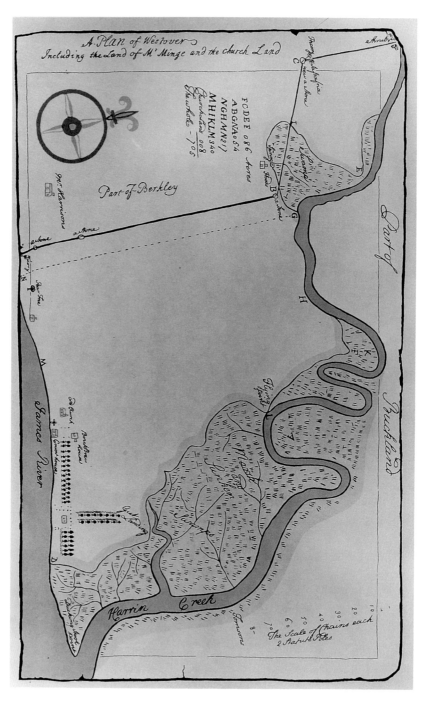

22. Westover, Estate of William Byrd. *1701. Virginia Historical Society, Richmond, Virginia*

sophisticated, albeit small, group of gardeners and garden makers. He would continue his contact with botanists in the colonies throughout his lifetime. John Bartram's garden on the Schuylkill River in Philadelphia was one of the most active botanic gardens in the British colonies (Figure 23). Begun about 1729, the gardens comprised an unprecedented collection of American plants gathered from all regions of the continent for study, experimentation, and export. Although Catesby never visited this garden, he and Bartram did carry on an exchange of materials and information that bound them together in common pursuit well into the century. With John Clayton, author of *Flora Virginica* (1739–1743), and John Custis of Williamsburg, Catesby continued to exchange plants and seeds despite the difficulties of shipping and corresponding across the Atlantic.[12]

Catesby and Horticultural Exchange

In addition to his publications, Catesby's actual participation in the international exchange and his cultivation of plants were important contributions to the history of the garden and botanical studies. There are three aspects of the movement of plants between the Old and New Worlds in which Catesby was party: the importation of North American plants into Europe, the naturalizing of imported plants in the colonies, and the movement of plants within the colonies.

In the well-established history of the transfer of North American plants to Europe, Mark Catesby was responsible for a significant share of the activity in the early eighteenth century. Catesby himself (in the preface to *Hortus Britanno-Americanus*) asserted that, in the half-century in which he was active, more plants were imported into England from the British colonies in North America than during the previous one thousand years from all other parts of the world.[13] Whether or not he knew the history of imported plants, it is unquestionable that this was a particularly productive period of botanical discovery and exchange: There *was* an exponentially increasing number of plants introduced into Europe between 1500 and 1900. The designed landscape and the rise of ornamental horticulture depended on these introductions and in turn stimulated the demand for

---

12. For a fuller discussion of Catesby's contacts in the botanical world, see Frick and Stearns, *Mark Catesby,* 86–97.

13. Catesby, *Hortus Britanno-Americanus,* preface, iii.

23. *A Draught of John Bartram's House and Garden as It Appears from the River.* By John or William Bartram. 1758. ©Private Collection

them.[14] Tremendous effort was expended in this period to bring exotics into the country in order to satisfy the increasing taste for them on the part of individual collectors such as Samuel Dale and Peter Collinson, scientific societies such as the Royal Society, the Company of Gardeners, and the Temple Coffee House Botany Society as well as commercial nurseries such as Robert Furber's and Thomas Fairchild's. Catesby had close ties with all these people and institutions and shared their interests.[15]

Although the understanding of nature was a goal of the Enlightenment context in which Catesby worked, naturalization—rather than strictly scientific study—was key to the enterprise of plant exchange; and Catesby was deeply committed to domesticating the flora of North America into English gardens. The success or failure of his endeavors was often expressed in *The Natural History,* where he provided the original location of each plant in America and where it was grown in England. For example, in the plate of the yellow lady's slipper (Figure 24), he wrote: "They grow on the sandy Banks of Rivers in *Carolina, Virginia,* and *Pensilvania,* from which last Place they were introduced to the Garden of Mr. *Peter Collinson* at *Peckham,* where they flowered in Perfection." Catesby's preface to the *Natural History* asserts that it will take notice of those plants "that will bear our English Climate, which I have experienced from what I have growing at Mr. *Bacon's,* successor of the late Mr. *Fairchild,* at *Hoxton,* where many have withstood the Rigour of several Winters, without Protection, while other Plants, tho' from the same Country, have perished for Want of it." The *Natural History* is rich in similar references to the various gardens in which the illustrated plants had been successfully grown in England as well as in the colonies.[16]

14. P. J. Jarvis, "Plant Introductions to England and Their Role in Horticultural and Sylvicultural Innovation, 1500–1900," in H. S. A. Fox and R. A. Butlin, eds., *Change in the Countryside: Essays on Rural England, 1500–1900* (London, 1979), 145–164.

15. Through its sponsorship of publications, expeditions, and research, the Royal Society (chartered in 1662) was responsible for much of the early natural history knowledge of the Americas. For a history of the society, see Michael Hunter, *Establishing the New Science: The Experience of the Early Royal Society* (Woodbridge, 1989). For a history of American botanical exploration before Catesby, see Ewan and Ewan, *John Banister and His Natural History of Virginia.*

16. Frick and Stearns, *Mark Catesby,* 27; Mark Catesby, *The Natural History of Carolina, Florida, and the Bahama Islands . . . ,* 2 vols. (London, 1731–1743), II, 73.

Gardens mentioned in *The Natural History* are as follows. In England: Thomas Fairchild's (subsequently Mr. Bacon's) at Hoxton; Peter Collinson's at Peckham; Christopher Gray's at Fulham; Catesby's own garden at Fulham; Sir John Colleton's at Exmouth, Devonshire; Sir Charles Wager's at Parsons Green; Mr. Plathwair's at Derham. In America: Colonel Bull's on the Ashley River; Mr. Waring's on the Ashley River; John Bartram's in Pennsylvania.

24. The Yellow Lady's Slipper and the Black Squirrel. *Mark Catesby*, The Natural History of Carolina, Florida, and the Bahama Islands . . . *(London, 1731–1747), II, pl. 73. Courtesy, Colonial Williamsburg Foundation*

Even at the end of his career, the stated purpose of Catesby's posthumous publication, *Hortus Britanno-Americanus,* was the adaptation of British North American produce to the soil and climate of England. Catesby's preface justified the treatise as for the "benefit of their country . . . of our woods, and for ornaments to our garden." In it he described eighty-five plants, including

> a plentiful variety of trees and shrubs, that may be usefully employed to inrich and adorn our woods by their valuable timber and delightful shade; or to embellish and perfume our gardens with the elegance of their appearance and the fragrancy of their odours; in both which respects they greatly excel our home productions of the like kind.[17]

Naturalizing American plants, thus recreating colonial environments, was a literal incorporation of the colonies into the mother country. It can be understood as part of the colonialist projects of appropriation and possession and could only benefit England. The exotics imported from the colonies were often planted in "American gardens" in the form of a "shrubbery" or "wilderness" to emulate the natural landscape in which the plants were originally discovered. Thomas Fairchild's *City Gardener* in 1722 recommended using newly imported material planted in "Wilderness-Work rather than in Grass Platts." Also, Philip Miller in his *Gardeners Dictionary* described the "wilderness" as a garden type in which the American trees and shrubs were displayed in a serpentine design. Thus, these "wilderness" gardens were laid out in a manner visually symbolic of the American natural habitats, if not true environmental recreations.[18]

Less often discussed in the history of botanical exchange is a second issue, the effort on the part of colonists and, specifically, individuals such as Catesby to naturalize imported plants *in* the colonies.[19] Why were plants

---

17. Catesby, *Hortus Britanno-Americanus,* preface, i.

18. Fairchild quoted in Penelope Hobhouse, *Gardening through the Ages: An Illustrated History of Plants and Their Influence on Garden Styles—from Ancient Egypt to the Present Day* (New York, 1992), 206–207; Mark Laird, "Approaches to Planting in the Late Eighteenth Century," *Journal of Garden History,* XI (1991), 159. Laird has traced the origins of this feature back from its heyday in the early nineteenth century to the first plantations of American exotics in the 1740s. For a history of the "wilderness" in English gardens, see Laird, *The Flowering of the Landscape Garden.*

19. Those who do discuss naturalizing plants include Joseph Ewan, "Traffic in Seeds and Plants between Continental North America, England, and the Continent during the Six-

sent to the colonies? The colonies provided varied environmental conditions not available in England in which to experiment with new plants for
food, medicine, timber, or ornamentals. If they were successful, it would
be possible to found plantations and botanic gardens that would support
new products. The hope was that plants that were exotic and delicate in
England, such as Asian and Mediterranean imports, might thrive in the
vastly varied climates available in the colonies. The colonies at large therefore became an extensive botanic garden for Europe in which to pursue
experimentation and naturalization.[20]

The collector's mentality that prevailed in England was shared by many
of the colonists who kept close ties with European trends and fashions.
We know that William Byrd II had Asian and Mediterranean exotics in his
garden at Westover on the James River in Virginia. For example, his
collection of pomegranates (introduced into Europe from southeast Asia
in the Middle Ages) was well known. What material was sent *to* the Americas might be estimated by the correspondence between colonists and
European counterparts. In 1725, John Custis of Virginia wrote to Robert
Cary, merchant and agent for Custis in London, about his garden in
Williamsburg:

> I have a pretty little garden in which I take more satisfaction than in
> anything in this world and have a collection of tolerable good flowers
> and greens from England; but have had great losses in their coming
> in. . . . I had 100 roots of fine double Dutch tulips sent me from one
> [Jones,] a gardiner at Battersy but the ship came in so late that most of
> them split themselves.[21]

---

teenth and Seventeenth Centuries," in XIIe Congres international d'histoire des sciences
(Paris, 1968), *Actes,* VIII (1971), 47–49; Sarah P. Stetson, "The Traffic in Seeds and Plants
from England's Colonies in North America," *Agricultural History,* XXIII (1949), 45–56. On
the importation of exotics into British North America, see also Joyce E. Chaplin, *An Anxious
Pursuit: Agricultural Innovation and Modernity in the Lower South, 1730–1815* (Chapel Hill, N.C.,
1993), 161. For a discussion of plants introduced into New England in the seventeenth
century, see Michela Sullivan-Fowler and Norman Gevitz, "Angelica Roots to Defend the
Heart, Coltsfoot for the Measles: Indigenous and Naturalized Remedies in a 1696 *Vade
Mecum,"* in Peter Benes and Jane Montague Benes, eds., *Plants and People,* Dublin Seminar for
New England Folklife, 1995 (Boston, 1996), 66–77.

20. For the theme of America and the edenic ideal and as a botanic garden, see Therese
O'Malley, "Art and Science in American Landscape Architecture: The National Mall, Washington, D.C., 1791–1852" (Ph.D. diss., University of Pennsylvania, 1989).

21. John Custis to Robert Cary, in E. G. Swem, ed., *Brothers of the Spade: Correspondence of*

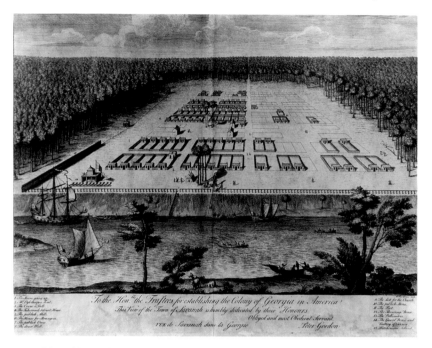

25. *A View of Savannah.* By Pierre Fourdrinier. 1734. Courtesy of the Library of Congress

Another example of the colonial garden as a botanical laboratory in the service of Britain is seen in the planning of Savannah, Georgia, by James Oglethorpe in 1733 (Figure 25). Savannah was to be the main settlement of the new colony of Georgia, an area first explored by Catesby. His *Natural History* makes clear that Catesby shared with the trustees of the colony a mutual interest in the establishment of the Trustees Garden, which was a botanic garden and nursery. The garden was part of the initial development of the new town, set aside as part of a concerted effort to naturalize exotics and ensure a future for silk and wine production. As described by Francis Moore in 1735:

> There is near town ... a garden belonging to the Trustees, consisting of Ten Acres. ...
>
> Besides the mulberry trees, there are in some of the quarters of the coldest part of the garden all kinds of fruit trees usual in England, such as apples, pears etc. In other quarters are olives, figs, vines, pomegranate and such fruits as are natural to the warmest part of Europe. At the

Peter Collinson, of London, and of John Custis, of Williamsburg, Virginia, 1734–46 (Barre, Mass., 1957), 21–22.

bottom of the hill, well sheltered from the north wind and in the warmest part of the garden, there was a collection of West India plants and trees, some coffee, some cocoa-nuts, Palma-Christi [castor bean], and several West India physical plants.[22]

Mulberry trees and grapevine cuttings were sent in large tubs and planted in this public garden until private vineyards would be ready for them.[23] The backing of the botanic garden in Savannah came from the leading English botanists and collectors of the period, with the name of Sir Hans Sloane, author of a catalog on the plants of Jamaica in 1696, heading the subscription list for the "improvement of Botany in Georgia." The Apothecaries Society, which ran the Chelsea Physic Garden (Figure 26), also contributed to this fund, as did the earl of Derby, the duke of Richmond, the Bank of England, Lord Petre, and Mr. Du Bois. Several of these same people were either sponsors of Catesby's expeditions or subscribers to his publications. James Oglethorpe was later sponsored by Catesby for membership in the Royal Society.

Catesby solicited plants from abroad while he was in the colonies. William Sherard in his correspondence records many requests from Catesby. For example, his plea for anemones and ranunculuses was answered, and the flowers, he reported, were planted by him in the garden of a "Dr. of Physicks" in Charleston.[24] His struggles with cultivating imported plants also appear in his correspondence with Sherard, in which several questions suggest the pressing issues and range of choices with which he had to contend:

> I have put into the ground some seeds of *Coloquintida* which ripen early here and have made a great increase but now ... to cure them we are at a loss . . . whether or not it would be worth to export th[e]m to England? . . . Whether opium might not be made here if we had the true poppy from Turky and knew their method of making it? whether Rhubarb if it could be procured would agree with this clymate? of Worm seed?[25]

22. Quoted in Alice G. B. Lockwood, *Gardens of Colony and State* (New York, 1931–1934), I, 270–272.

23. Bertha Sheppard Hart, "The First Garden of Georgia," *Georgia Historical Quarterly,* XIX (1935), 328.

24. Mark Catesby to William Sherard from Charles Town, Apr. 6, 1724, Sherard Letters, CCLIII, 176, Royal Society, London.

25. Ibid., Aug. 16, 1724, 178.

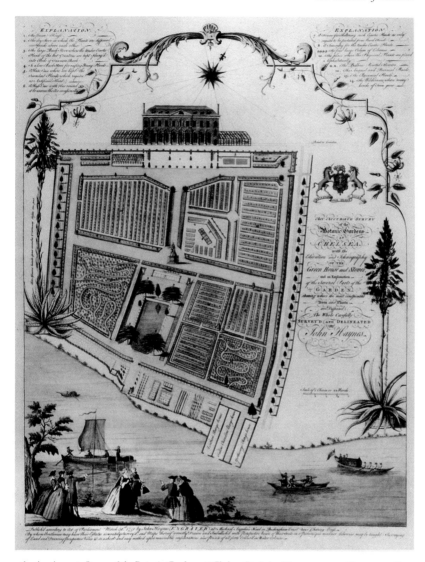

26. *An Accurate Survey of the Botanic Gardens at Chelsea.* By John Haynes. 1751. Courtesy of the Royal Society. (Cf. Figure 40)

Thus Catesby was concerned with the broadest spectrum of imported plants. *Coloquintida* is the source of quinine and cinchonine, cures for fevers that afflicted so many colonists and explorers. It was a monopoly of the Spanish, who procured this precious powder from their colonies in South America. Opium poppies and rhubarb were known from the Old World and represent those useful plants with which Catesby and his colonial colleagues could experiment.

27. The Catalpa Tree and the Bastard Baltimore. *Catesby,* Natural History, *I, pl. 49. Courtesy, Colonial Williamsburg Foundation*

After he returned to England, Catesby continued to send plants to the colonies. His correspondence with his family in Virginia indicates that he sent seeds of English plants to his niece Elizabeth Cocke Jones and her husband, Thomas Jones, who had been a companion to Catesby on his collecting trips in the colonies.

In addition to the importation and exportation of plants between England and the colonies, Catesby was also instrumental in the movement of New World plants *within* the colonies. This third area of botanical exchange has received the least scholarly notice. In his *Natural History* Catesby described his efforts to introduce the catalpa tree (Figure 27) to the inhabited parts of Carolina from the remoter parts of the country:

> And tho' the inhabitants are little curious in Gard'ning, yet the uncommon Beauty of the Tree has induc'd them to propagate it; and 'tis become an Ornament to many of their Gardens, and probably will be the same to ours in *England*.[26]

Throughout, his writings and correspondence illustrate the movement of plants within the colonies: Catesby reports on the introduction of plumeria (Figure 28) to the mainland of America from Barbados and others of the Sugar Islands, where it "is planted and in great esteem for its odour and ornament."[27] The planting of "unusual plants" in colonial gardens is a frequent theme:

> In *Virginia* I found one of these Dogwood Trees with flowers of a rose-colour, which was luckily blown down, and many of the Branches had taken Root, which I transplanted into a Garden. That with the white Flower Mr. *Fairchild* has in his garden. [Figure 29][28]

The story of the elusive peach-colored dogwood, which he planted in John Custis's and the Cocke-Jones gardens in Williamsburg as well as in a garden in England, is perhaps only the best-known example of how native plants were introduced in colonial and English gardens simultaneously.[29] This movement of plants and seeds within the colonies was not a minor part of Catesby's activity. To John James (Johann Jakob) Dillenius, the English botanist, Catesby wrote:

> I am as I always was of the opinion that the American Ceders as they are vulgarly called are not specifically different. In Virginia and Caroline

26. Catesby, *Natural History,* I, 49.

27. Ibid., I, 92.

28. Ibid., I, 27.

29. Quoted in Martin, *The Pleasure Gardens of Virginia,* 59. "Mr. Catesby Gives His Humble service and is und'r Great Concerne for fear the Race of that Curious peach colour'd Dogwood is Lost, without [that is, unless] you have One in your Garden. He says most of them that He had Transplanted from the Mother Tree into Mr. Jones Garden was Destroyed by Fire, but He Thinks One or Two was saved and He brought and planted in your Garden. There is many flowers when In Decaye in particular the White thorn with us will Turn Redish but He Says this open'd of a Red Colour att First." Peter Collinson to John Custis, January 1737.

28. *Plumeria Flore Roseo Odoratissimo.* Catesby, *Natural History,* II, pl. 92. Courtesy, Colonial
Williamsburg Foundation

my transplanting hundreds of them from the Woods into gardens gave
me an appertunity of observing them critically, and I am satisfied that
their Juniper and Cypress like leaves is caused in certy from the difference of soil the climate, and as Mr. Collinson agrees with me, that the
leaves of these trees grow more compact and like those of Cypress in
New England the Northern parts, and more open and divided in Carolina and to the . . . south, and No wonder is seeds brought from
another world should produce even a greater variation since they differ
so much not only on the same continent but in the same field, and

29. The Dogwood Tree and the Mock-Bird. *Catesby,* Natural History, *I, pl. 27. Courtesy, Colonial Williamsburg Foundation*

often on the same tree is to be seen all the differences (except that of colour) which hath been observed.[30]

The importance of "observing them critically" underscores Catesby's empirical approach to his work, which grew out of the method of Ray and Sherard. Only by planting and replanting within varied contexts could he achieve the goals of experimentation: to introduce and naturalize new plants. The different landscapes in which he moved became experimental gardens whenever it was possible. Whether it was his niece's yard or the woods of Virginia, he considered the natural world a living laboratory in which he could experiment with new plants and then observe, describe, and depict those plants in various states of culture. The understanding of plant geography and the role of environmental, climatic, or geological conditions in relation to vegetation resulted from naturalists/artists such as Catesby who saw newly explored areas for themselves and applied this experience to their practice of the cultivation and study of plants.

The Anglo-American Enterprise

The transfer of plants between the Old and the New World became an important aspect of Catesby's work specifically and British imperialism of the eighteenth century generally.[31] What was the purpose of this enterprise of collecting, naturalizing, and publishing botanical discoveries, and why was it a national pursuit? In the preface of the *Natural History,* Catesby addresses the reasons for this work: they were aesthetic, scientific, or economic. His text offers insights into the perceived value of each plant in just those terms, whether it was as ornamental or medicinal, or for dye-stuffs or fibers. Sometimes, the search for new food or flavoring motivated the study of new plants. For example, in the *Natural History,* Catesby commented on one plant introduction that was not particularly success-ful, vanilla (Figure 30):

30. Johann Jakob Dillenius, n.d., Sherard MSS, CCII, fol. 17, Dillenius Correspondence, Department of Plant Sciences, Oxford University.

31. Chaplin, *An Anxious Pursuit,* 158–165. W. J. T. Mitchell posed a relationship between landscape and imperialism in his essay "The Imperial Landscape," in which he wrote: "At minimum we need to explore the possibility that the representation of landscape is not only a matter of internal politics and national or class ideology but also an international, global phenomenon, ultimately bound up with the discourses of imperialism." Imperialism is not a "one-way phenomenon but a complicated process of exchange, mutual transformation, and ambivalence." *Landscape and Power* (Chicago, 1994), 9.

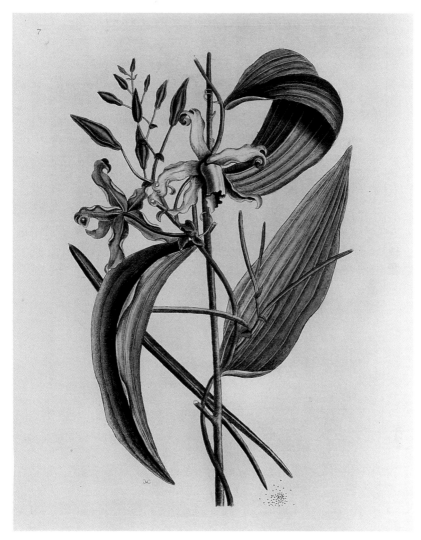

30. The Vanelloe. *Catesby,* Natural History, *II, Appendix, pl. 7. Courtesy, Colonial Williamsburg Foundation*

This perfume is so little agreeable to an *English* palate, that it is rarely made use of any more in our *American* Plantations than at home, and therefore not cultivated by us.[32]

In the *Natural History* appendix, Catesby described the extensive "Cacao-walks," planted by the Spaniards in Jamaica, and argued for their economic value (Figure 31):

32. Catesby, *Natural History,* II, Appendix, 7.

31. The Cacao Tree. *Catesby*, Natural History, *II, Appendix, pl. 6. Courtesy, Colonial Williamsburg Foundation*

Whatever infatuation continues to possess our countrymen in the neglect of it, 'tis certain that the balance of trade, in this branch, is considerably against us; the *Spaniards*, and of late the *French*, supplying not only us, and our northern Colonies, but all *Europe* with this valuable commodity, I cannot but think it serves the consideration of the legislature; for were a method found to encourage its cultivation, our Sugar-islands (being as well adapted to the growth of it as any part of *America*) might not only supply our home-consumption, but come in for a share of exportation to foreign markets.[33]

33. Ibid., II, Appendix, 6,

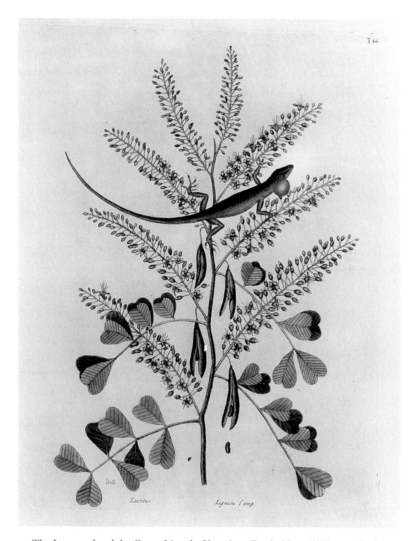

32. The Logwood and the Green Lizard of Jamaica. *Catesby,* Natural History, *II, pl. 66.*
Courtesy, Colonial Williamsburg Foundation

The breakdown of monopolies of certain plants and the development of an infrastructure for trade were important motivations for the successful experimentation with both native and nonnative materials. That Catesby brought political and economic concerns to his work is suggested by his discussion of the logwood (*Lignum capechianum*) (Figure 32). He found this tree, a valuable source of black and violet dyes, growing on the island of Providence in the Bahamas from seeds collected from the Bay of Honduras:

The bloody Disputes which this useful Tree has occasioned between the *Spaniards* and *English* are too well known to say much of here, only I could wish that the Inhabitants of our Southern Plantations could be induced to propagate it, as well for their own Advantage, as that we may be supplied by them, when wholly deprived of getting it from the *Spaniards* as we have hitherto done either by Force or Stealth.[34]

Therefore, a fundamental impetus behind movement of and experimentation in plants as well as concomitant sponsorship of gardens, both domestic and colonial, was to make Britain independent of other nations. In order to break those monopolies held by foreign powers, to be able to harvest seeds at optimal times, and to avoid the pitfalls of sea transportation, it was critical to have gardens of essential plants under British control. The founding of colonial botanic gardens was vital because it allowed for the acclimatizing of plants that would ultimately render the colonies self-sufficient. Such regional self-sufficiency would secure resources of food and wood for ships as they sailed around the world in imperial pursuits, providing sources of supplies for crews and naval materials.[35]

The Botanic Garden

In order to understand the significance of Catesby's experimental garden activities, it is useful to understand the history of botanical gardening

---

34. Ibid., II, 66. "Logwood," called *Lignum campechianum* by Catesby, seems to be *Haematoxylum campechianum* L. described by Hans Sloane in his *History of Jamaica,* II, 189. If so, it might be the same as "bloodwood," *Haemetoxylum,* a source for black and violet dyes (Marguerite Duval, *The King's Garden,* trans. Annette Tomarken and Claudine Cowen [Charlottesville, Va., 1982], 85). See also Jonathan D. Sauer, "Changing Perception and Exploitation of New World Plants in Europe, 1492–1800," in Fredi Chiappelli, ed., *First Images of America: The Impact of the New World on the Old* (Berkeley, Calif., 1976), 818. "Cargoes of related dyewoods, brasilette and logwood, were carried from Central America and Mexico by Spanish ships in the sixteenth and seventeenth centuries. Late in the seventeenth century, English buccaneers in the Bay of Campeche learned the value of logwood, quit burning prize Spanish cargoes of it, and began seeking stockpiles of it ashore. Finally they settled down along the coasts of Campeche and Belize to cut the wood themselves."

35. Alan Frost, "The Antipodean Exchange: European Horticulture and Imperial Designs," in David Philip Miller and Peter Hanns Reill, eds., *Visions of Empire: Voyages, Botany, and Representations of Nature* (Cambridge, 1996), 74; Ian McPhail, comp., *Hortus Botanicus: The Botanic Garden and the Book . . .* (Meriden, Conn., 1972), 6. "Botanic gardens are phenomena of the culture of nations and, as such, reflect dominant national interest in their patterns of growth."

to which he was heir. In relation to the European continent, England was late in the development of the botanic garden, that is, gardens in which the systematic collection of living plants is associated with botanical teaching and research. Italy had the first botanic gardens in the mid-sixteenth century at Pisa, Padua, Florence, and Bologna. The Dutch, French, Germans, and Swedish established their botanic gardens within the next few decades. These "mother" gardens were soon followed with important tropical botanic gardens in their respective colonies that served as suppliers supporting the collections at home. With the exception of the Oxford Botanic Garden founded in 1621, powerful Continental gardens dominated the world of botany until the eighteenth century. The Chelsea Physic Garden was founded in 1722, but Kew not until 1760.[36] Pulteney explains England's late development of botanical and horticultural interests: "The growing commerce of the nation, the more frequent intercourse with *Holland,* where immense collections from the *Dutch* colonies had been made, rendered these gratifications more easily attainable than before; and, from all these happy coincidences, science in general reaped great benefit." By the first decades of the eighteenth century, many private gardens in England had notable botanical collections, and their owners and advisers were participating in an international exchange and competition for more plant material. The establishment of botanic gardens in the colonies therefore received the endorsement and support of private and public interests.[37]

Unlike "paper" museums, *Wunderkammern* (cabinets of curiosities), and natural history collections, botanic gardens in this period served as living cabinets of wonders.[38] There was a constant tension in the botanic garden

36. The Chelsea Physic Garden was first founded as a place to demonstrate medicinal plants by the Company of Apothecaries in 1673. It was not until Sir Hans Sloane revitalized it in the next century that it achieved the status of a major botanic garden. He gave the freehold of the ground to the company in 1721 with the condition that the company deliver annually fifty new plants to the Royal Society until the number should amount to two thousand, all specifically different from each other. Pulteney, *Progress of Botany,* II, 101.

37. Ibid., 105. See W. T. Stearn, "Sources of Information about Botanic Gardens and Herbaria," *Biological Journal of the Linnean Society,* III (1971), 225–233; Lucia Tongiorgi Tomasi, *Giardino dei Semplici* (Pisa, 1991), and "Projects for Botanical and Other Gardens: A Sixteenth-Century Manual," *Journal of Garden History,* III (1983), 1–34.

38. John Tradescant, James Petiver, and Hans Sloane had well-known natural history cabinets. See John Dixon Hunt's chapter "On Cabinets of Curiosity," in *Garden and Grove: The Italian Renaissance Garden in the English Imagination, 1600–1750* (Philadelphia, 1996), 78–82, for a discussion of the congruities of cabinets and gardens. See also Paula Findlen, *Possessing*

between the abstract taxonomic arrangement of specimens and the re-creation of habitats in which plants were found. A history of the various botanic gardens in both Europe and in the colonies illustrates this garden type emerging as the site of debates and changing theories in the natural sciences, ranging from a belief in the fixity of species to the newer study of environmental determinism and early evolutionary thought.

Gardens and Botanical Illustration

The empirical basis of botanical sciences was promulgated in the seventeenth century by John Ray and J. P. de Tournefourt. Because it was based on the experience of direct observation of plants, it increased the dependency on both gardens and illustration. As historians have shown, in modern botanical study there were critical connections between the study of plants (either living or dried in herbaria), botanic gardens, and the publication of illustrated catalogs that acted as indexes or guides to collections. Catesby's publications, indeed, grew out of a historical link between gardens and illustration, except that he selected models not only from plants in gardens or herbaria but from a "garden" the extent of the British colonies.[39]

The value placed on direct study of living plants is attested to by Dr. Cadwallader Colden, surveyor general of the Province of New York, who wrote to Peter Collinson regarding his daughter Jane and her botanical education: "As she cannot have the opportunity of seeing plants in a Botanical Garden I think the next best is to see the best cuts or pictures of them for which purpose I would try for her Tournefort's *Institutiones Herbariae* and Morison's *Historia Plantarum*." Colden thus conveys the preference for seeing live plants in a garden as well as the need for books in the absence of

---

Nature: Museums, Collecting, and Scientific Culture in Early Modern Italy (Berkeley, Calif., 1994), who wrote: "Through the possession of objects [natural or artificial], one physically acquired knowledge, and through their display, one symbolically acquired the honor and reputation that all men of learning cultivated" (3).

39. John Gerard, *Catalogus Arborum, Fruticum, ac Plantarum tam Indigenarum, quam Exoticarum in Horto Johannis Gerardi . . . Nascentium,* 2d ed. (London, 1599). Gerard was the first gardener to produce a complete catalog to the contents of this garden. See Anita Guerrini, *Natural History and the New World, 1524–1770: An Annotated Bibliography of Printed Materials in the Library of the American Philosophical Society* (Philadelphia, 1986), 6; Stearn, "Sources of Information about Botanic Gardens and Herbaria," *Biological Journal of the Linnean Society,* III (1971), 25–233; Tomasi, *Giardino dei Semplici,* and "Projects for Botanical and Other Gardens," *Journal of Garden History,* III (1983), 1–34.

living plants. However, he also suggests a hierarchy of preference, the live experience being the better. The need for gardens and experimental plantations was appreciated from the earliest days of colonization.[40]

In addition to the political and economic motivations discussed above, the scientific and artistic advantages for students of botany were significant. Having trained from his earliest professional days either in or near botanic gardens in England, Catesby had a deep understanding of this advantage. He discussed the benefit of direct botanical contact over herbaria, horti sicci, or treatises in his *Natural History* (Figure 33). The "Bison Americanus" is depicted with "Pseudo Acacia hispida floribus roseis," accompanied by Catesby's description of his method of representing plants:

> And as for Plants, it is easy to conceive how imperfect the Figures must be which are drawn from dried Specimens, in comparison of those taken from living Plants, as all those are which I have exhibited.
>
> From these Observations it may be inferred, that however accurately human art may be exercised in the representation of Animals, it falls far more short of that inimitable perfection so visible in Nature itself, than when attended with the circumspection and advantages I was blessed with in the compiling of my History, and which I flatter myself are in some measure conspicuous therein.[41]

Catesby's disillusionment with study from dried species led to his search for better methods with which to understand and classify plants. As drawing was not sufficient, observation in situ was recognized as essential, either through exploration in its original context or in a botanic garden in cultivation. The next best thing to viewing live plants was to study drawings made from live specimens, preferably drawn to actual size.[42] Although Catesby discusses his interest in verisimilitude, the plate of the bison and pseudo-acacia shows enormous distortion of size between the plant depicted and the buffalo accompanying it. (The relation of plant to animal is a complex issue in his illustrations and is addressed by

40. H. W. Rickett and Elizabeth C. Hall, eds., *Botanic Manuscript of Jane Colden, 1724–1766* ([New York], 1963), preface. On other early colonial garden histories, see Peter Benes, "Horticultural Importers and Nurserymen in Boston, 1719–1770," in Benes and Benes, eds., *Plants and People*, 38–55.

41. Catesby, *Natural History*, II, Appendix, 20.

42. Catesby makes this claim in his preface for the *Hortus Britanno-Americanus*, iii: "They are nevertheless represented in their natural size, which necessarily gives a more perfect idea than if they had been contrasted to a smaller scale."

33. *Bison Americanus* and Rose Acacia. *Catesby,* Natural History, *II, Appendix, pl. 20. (Cf. Figure 47). Courtesy, Colonial Williamsburg Foundation*

Amy R. W. Meyers, below.) The claim of naturalists/artists of working directly from live species had a long tradition in natural history illustration, dating from the Renaissance. As the value of empirical study became more and more valued in the seventeenth and eighteenth centuries, there seemed to be increasing claims by artists of their contact with live specimens while producing the natural history illustration: this in spite of the evidence to the contrary. Although we know it was necessary for Catesby to rely on dried specimens and earlier field sketches to complete his publications, the value of study from the living plant was unequivocal.

After returning to England, Catesby studied American plants growing in gardens such as Peter Collinson's when preparing the illustrations for his publications. Part of the history of that process of making images involves the continued reliance upon his American colleagues and their proximity to the living plants. Catesby in his *Natural History* and *Hortus Britanno-Americanus* comments upon vigor or lack of vigor in plants due to a new context in which they grew, suggesting his awareness of the instability and constant change in a live plant's appearance and behavior depending on its nurture. A letter to John Bartram from Peter Collinson in 1739 indicates something of the character of the exchange among these botanical pioneers:

> Pray remember for Fr[ien]d Catesby Flowers of the Papaw. He thanks thee very kindly for the Fruite and come they either Dry or in spirits they will lose their Colour—so pray Describe It as well as thee Can, that he may be qualified to paint it and what colour is the Fruite when Ripe and its Time of Flowering and Time when the Fruite is Ripe. [Figure 34][43]

There is one further congruity between botanic gardens and Catesby's conception of his *Natural History* illustrations that should be mentioned. From the sixteenth century on, menageries, collections of live animals, were found alongside botanic gardens. Although never as prominent an activity as gardening in this era, collections of exotic animals in zoos were known.[44] For example, Cosimo I had a botanic garden that specialized in Mexican plants with a menagerie of live animals from America and Africa.

43. Edmund Berkeley and Dorothy Smith Berkeley, eds., *The Correspondence of John Bartram, 1734–1777* (Gainesville, Fla., 1992), 108; William Darlington, ed., *Memorials of John Bartram and Humphry Marshall* (1849), rpt. in Joseph Ewan, ed., *Classica Botanica America* (New York, 1967), 124, 134.

44. Guerini, *Natural History and the New World*, 7.

34. Papaw *(Anona Fructu Lutescente, Laevi, Scrotum Arietis Referente)*. Catesby, Natural History, *II, pl. 85. Courtesy, Colonial Williamsburg Foundation*

A view of the Botanical Garden at Leiden (Figure 35) illustrates this association by the inclusion of fish, reptiles, and mammals in the bottom range of the image, beneath the precisely arranged *pulvilli,* or order beds, in which the plant collection is displayed. By the eighteenth century, as the sciences of botany and zoology became more and more specialized and academic divisions spread apart, fewer unions of living plants and animals

35. The Botanical Garden at Leiden. *In Peter Overadt,* Hortorium Viridariorumque . . . Formae *(1655). Print courtesy of Sterling Morton Library, The Morton Arboretum, Lisle, Ill.*

were found in gardens. However, their cohabitation can still be seen in many of Catesby's drawings, reflecting their alliance in the natural world but also his own worldview of environmental relationships between flora and fauna.[45]

Scholars have written about early colonists' attempts to appropriate and exploit the physical space and natural resources of the colonies. Chandos Brown has shown how intellectuals undertook to systematize knowledge, in the service of the marketplace and the emerging English state.[46] Mark Catesby can be seen as sharing the same drive to capture both physically and intellectually the explosion of natural history information in the early eighteenth century. In his life's work, Catesby engaged in systematic trans-

45. See Amy R. W. Meyers, "Environmental Interchange and Colonial Expansion in the Americas," below. See also Meyers, "Sketches from the Wilderness: Changing Conceptions of Nature in American Natural History Illustration, 1660–1889" (Ph.D. diss., Yale University, 1985).

46. Chandos Michael Brown, "Scientific Inquiry": "The British Colonies," in Jacob Ernest Cooke, ed., *Encyclopedia of the North American Colonies* (New York, 1993), III, 165.

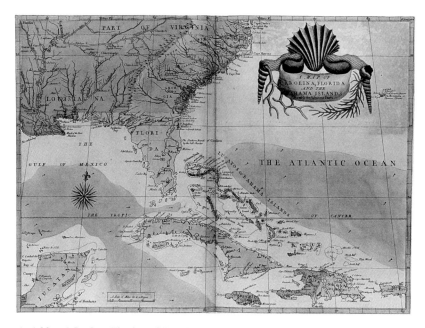

36. *A Map of Carolina, Florida, and the Bahama Islands.* Catesby, *Natural History,* II, Appendix.
Courtesy, Colonial Williamsburg Foundation

formations of the physical world into manageable and ordered representations: maps, treatises, and gardens. First, his exploration and surveying
of Carolina, Florida, and the Bahama Islands resulted in a map of the
region for the *Natural History* (Figure 36).[47] Second, he produced guide-
books to the natural wonders of the New World with his *Natural History*
and *Hortus Britanno-Americanus* that served as catalogs to the collection of
the New World as a botanic garden without walls. And, finally—the subject in which this essay is most concerned—he organized the world of new
plants through systematic collecting, moving, and naturalizing plants in
gardens. Through his scientific approach to knowledge, his works contributed to a new era for natural history and to the development of networks that tied together colonies and mother country.[48]

47. Although Catesby was no cartographer and this map was not original to him, it "was a
good representation of the better English ideas about the geography of North America in
the 1730's and early 1740's" (Frick and Stearns, *Mark Catesby,* 71–72). Many have written
about maps as "spatial ideograms." In reference to early America, see Wayne Franklin,
Discoverers, Explorers, Settlers: The Diligent Writers of Early America (Chicago, 1979).

48. These ideas on systematic collecting are discussed in relation to Joseph Banks by John
Gascoigne, "The Ordering of Nature and the Ordering of Empire: A Commentary," in

Mark Catesby's interests in collecting, describing, and experimenting met in the garden, whether it was highly contrived and artificial as in a botanic garden such as Hoxton or in the woods of Virginia. There he could bring together the curiosities of the natural world. Catesby's illustrations, writings, and innovative career are explicit records of the links between art and science in the development of natural history and transatlantic garden culture in the eighteenth century.

Miller and Reill, eds., *Visions of Empire,* 108–109. On a new era, see Davis, *Intellectual Life in the Colonial South,* II, 844–864.

Mark Laird

FROM CALLICARPA TO CATALPA: THE IMPACT OF MARK CATESBY'S PLANT INTRODUCTIONS ON ENGLISH GARDENS OF THE EIGHTEENTH CENTURY

The introduction of North American plants to eighteenth-century English gardens provoked a collecting frenzy that came close to the mania for tulips in seventeenth-century Europe. Contributing to this consumer boom, Mark Catesby's *Natural History of Carolina, Florida, and the Bahama Islands* stimulated consumers to try out America's gloriously illustrated exotics in the new shrubberies of the English landscape garden. However, the cultivation of North American shrubs and trees (some specifically introduced by Catesby) was beset with difficulties. This essay looks at the successes and failures of the experimental process through the prism of a dozen such species whose cultivation in Britain harks back to Catesby's collecting endeavors.

The Catesby plants thus illuminate a complex story of importation, germination, and acclimatization. Their life histories reflect different aspects of culture and cultivation in eighteenth-century England: the merchant ships that brought exotics from Charleston or Philadelphia to London, the nursery trade that turned expensive luxuries into affordable commodities, and the American shrubs themselves that inspired the graduated display of the "theatrical" shrubbery.

Those tiered displays of plants, like the theaters of conservatory pots before them, allowed a collection of rare or beautiful species to be artistically and scientifically organized. Gathered from different parts of the globe and arranged in six or seven graduated rows, they formed a con-

I am grateful to the late John Harvey for his thoughtful comments on this essay and for supplying much help with plant identifications. I would also like to thank Amy Meyers and Therese O'Malley for their support in sending me valuable research materials.

spectus, as though the Garden of Eden had been reassembled in neatly classified ranks. In time, this regular arrangement would give way to modulated picturesque compositions, as gardeners discovered how to exploit the successful plants and turn to advantage the irregularities that came from "errors in classification" and in conformity with changing aesthetics. For the whole of the eighteenth century, however, the theatrical shrubbery remained an experimental stage for ornamental planting. Mark Catesby's plants were the dramatis personae.[1]

In *The English Gardener* of 1829, William Cobbett described the ideal shrubbery—the ornamental plantation that had dominated the pleasure grounds of the landscape garden for eighty years since its first appearance around 1750:

> Shrubberies should be so planted, if they be of any considerable depth, as for the tallest trees to be at the back, and the lowest in front; if one could have one's will, one would go, by slow degrees, from a dwarf Kalmia to a Catalpa.... Such a slope, however, would require the depth of a mile; and therefore, that is out of the question.[2]

One hundred years before, Batty Langley, promoting the use of decorative shrubs around "wilderness quarters," had first given form to the "perfect Slope of beautiful Flowers"—a modest three rows, compared to Cobbett's

---

1. For background reading on this horticultural revolution—its inspiration in classical texts, scientific advances in botany, and the need to replant England's deafforested landscape—see Douglas Chambers, *The Planters of the English Landscape Garden: Botany, Trees, and the Georgics* (New Haven, Conn., 1993). For the role that Bishop Henry Compton, John Banister, Mark Catesby, Peter Collinson, and John Bartram played in the introduction of plants from North America, see Richard Gorer, *The Growth of Gardens* (London, 1978). For the history of the nursery trade—how nurserymen like Christopher Gray and Nathaniel Powell helped make exotics accessible and affordable during the eighteenth century—see John Harvey, *Early Gardening Catalogues* ... (London, 1972); Harvey, *Early Nurserymen: With Reprints of Documents and Lists* (London, 1974). And for a wider discussion of the theatrical shrubbery and shrub mania, see Mark Laird, "Ornamental Planting and Horticulture in English Pleasure Grounds, 1700–1830," in John Dixon Hunt, ed., *Garden History: Issues, Approaches, Methods,* Dumbarton Oaks Colloquium on the History of Landscape Architecture, XIII (Washington, D.C., 1992), 243–277. The introductory chapter to Laird's book, *The Flowering of the Landscape Garden: English Pleasure Grounds, 1720–1800* (Philadelphia, 1999), discusses the place of the exotic shrubbery and flower garden in eighteenth-century society and expands on the themes of this essay.

2. William Cobbett, *The English Gardener* (1829), ed. Anthony Huxley (Oxford, 1980), 224. The dwarf kalmia is *Kalmia angustifolia* L.

several hundred ranks. In the intervening century, as the shrubbery evolved from the wilderness, many new links were added to the "chain of vegetable existence." Indeed, during the mid-eighteenth century, plant importation from eastern North America gained such momentum that Peter Collinson could suggest to John Bartram, his plant hunter in Philadelphia, that "after this Rate England must be turned up side down and America transplanted Heither."[3] At the beginning of this horticultural revolution, Mark Catesby—importer and illustrator of North American exotics—stands as a towering figure. Indeed, it is to him (whether directly or indirectly) that we owe the introduction of the *Kalmia* and *Catalpa* of Cobbett's mile-deep shrubbery.

Since its publication in 1789, William Aiton's *Hortus Kewensis* has remained the first authority on when and how plants came into English gardens. In the three volumes, the name of Mark Catesby is connected with a number of significant species: *Amorpha fruticosa* L., *Callicarpa americana* L., *Calycanthus floridus* L., *Catalpa bignonioides* Walt., *Fraxinus americana* L., *Ilex cassine* L., and *Wisteria frutescens* (L.) Poir.[4] Later research, however, has elaborated on Aiton's work and revealed some shortcomings. In a few cases it turns out that Catesby's importation was not, strictly speaking, the original introduction. At the same time, it seems likely that he was responsible for plant introductions not recognized by Aiton, notably *Ptelea tri-*

3. Batty Langley, *New Principles of Gardening* . . . (London, 1728), 182; Mrs. Hofland, *A Descriptive Account of the Mansion and Gardens of White-Knights, Seat of His Grace the Duke of Marlborough* (London, 1819), 51 ("chain"); Edmund Berkeley and Dorothy Smith Berkeley, eds., *The Correspondence of John Bartram, 1734–1777* (Gainesville, Fla., 1992), 392.

4. William Aiton, *Hortus Kewensis*, 3 vols. (London, 1789). For these plants, see, seriatim, III, 17, I, 148, II, 220, II, 346, III, 445, I, 170, III, 35. There are, of course, other plants that Aiton classifies as "Catesby introductions"—*Catesbaea spinosa* (I, 147), *Convolvus brasiliensis* (I, 215), *Rhamnus colubrinus* (I, 264), *Rhus elegans* (I, 366), *Sophora alba* (II, 46), *Cassia ligustrina* (II, 52), *Tilia pubescens* (II, 229), *Erythrina herbacea* (III, 8), and *Mimosa circinalis* (III, 439)—but these were never considered as candidates for cultivation outdoors and thus lie beyond discussion of planting design in the eighteenth-century pleasure ground.

The second edition by the younger Aiton followed in 1810–1813. For the background to the Aitons' research, see John H. Harvey, "Fritillary and Martagon—Wild or Garden?" *Garden History*, XXIV (1996), 30: "Over 200 years many more details have come to light but the fundamental reliability of the Aitons' dating remains." John Harvey pointed out to me in his letter of Aug. 26, 1996, that Philip Miller's 1736 list of plants growing at Lord Petre's Thorndon Hall, Essex, reveals that several trees were already growing in English soil before the dates given in *Hortus Kewensis*: *Carya glabra* (Miller) Sweet, *Fraxinus caroliniana* Miller, *Pinus echinata* Miller, *P. taeda* L., *P. virginiana* Miller, *Quercus virginiana* Miller.

foliata L. (reintroduced after the failure of John Banister's initial imports) and *Ceanothus americanus* L. There are also the herbaceous plants sent home or first discovered on his two visits to America: *Coreopsis lanceolata,* for example, or two species of sawwort, *Liatris spicata* and *L. squarrosa.*[5] Moreover, given the widespread circulation of *The Natural History,* Catesby's contribution to the planting of English gardens in the eighteenth century is incalculable. His publications must have engendered much activity on the estates and in the nurseries of England, as acquisitive plant lovers were animated to consumption by his seductive illustrations.

The "List of the Encouragers" at the front of the first volume (1731) is itself testimony to his influence. The subscribers include the following illustrious names: Richard Bateman, whose Grove House, Old Windsor, witnessed the development of the first picturesque flower garden; the earl of Burlington, who with William Kent's assistance created the embryonic landscape garden at Chiswick House; Peter Collinson, cloth merchant of Peckham and Mill Hill; John Bartram of Philadelphia, whose joint enterprise commercialized plant importation from North America; Robert Furber and Christopher Gray, who were among the first nurserymen to stock North American plants; Philip Miller, celebrated gardener at Chelsea Physic Garden and pioneer in growing "curious" plants; Lord Petre, who transformed the grounds of Thorndon Hall in Essex and Worksop in Nottinghamshire into "North American thickets"; and the duke of Richmond, whose estate of Goodwood in Sussex contained an "American Grove" and "the best Collection of Exotic hardy Trees" in England.[6]

The role that Mark Catesby played in the English horticultural revolution has been somewhat overshadowed by the story of Peter Collinson, John Bartram, and their many distinguished clients: Lord Petre and the

5. John Harvey in his appendixes to the two articles by Sandra Morris on Bishop Henry Compton's garden in Fulham has revised our information on two species: *Amorpha fruticosa* and *Ilex cassine.* Both appear to have been growing at Fulham before the bishop's death in 1713. See Sandra Morris, "Legacy of a Bishop: The Trees and Shrubs of Fulham Palace Gardens Introduced 1675–1713," *Garden History,* XIX (1991), 47–59; part 2, XXI (1993), 14–23.

On the herbaceous plants, see John Fisher, *The Origins of Garden Plants* (London, 1982), 116–118. *Coreopsis lanceolata* was introduced in 1724, and the two *Liatris* spp. by 1732, after Catesby's return to England. (Herbaceous plants are beyond the scope of this essay.)

6. For the background to these planters and the landscape garden, see Laird, *The Flowering of the Landscape Garden.*

37. The Dogwood Tree and the Mock-Bird. *Mark Catesby,* The Natural History of Carolina, Florida, and the Bahama Islands . . . *(London, 1731–1747), I, pl. 27. (Cf. Figure 29). Courtesy, Colonial Williamsburg Foundation*

duke of Richmond, Charles Hamilton and the duke of Argyll.[7] And yet the "mania" for collecting North American plants is unimaginable without the stimulus of Catesby's magnificent plates. Through *The Natural History,* Catesby's contemporaries became attuned to seeing plants with his eyes. As Peter Collinson recorded on May 17, 1761:

> I was invited by Mr. Sharp at South Lodge on Enfield Chace to dine and see the Virginian dogwood [*Cornus florida* L., Figure 37]. The calyx of the flowers is as large as figured by Catesby, and (what is remarkable) this is the only tree that bears these flowers amongst many hundreds that I have seen. It began to bear them in May 1759.[8]

7. See, for example, Chambers, *The Planters of the English Landscape Garden.* Chambers discusses the use of North American plants in the context of extensive woodland planting and the reafforestation of English estates.

8. Linnean Society, London: "Notes relating to Botany, collected from the manuscripts of the late Peter Collinson by A. B. Lambert 1809," MS SP 235A, 30–31.

The correspondence of image and actuality recorded by Collinson must have occurred on many occasions, as curious gardeners pored over the plates of *The Natural History,* finding themselves impelled to acquire a particular plant. After waiting for it to germinate and grow, they no doubt prayed for the reward of a display that rivaled Catesby's portrait. However, more often than not, they must have been disappointed by the discrepancy between the glorious image and the ailing plant. The dogwood, for example, was something of a nonstarter in English conditions. We know that it was readily available through the nursery trade from Robert Furber's catalog of 1727 onwards. It was also being supplied by Peter Collinson in the middle of the eighteenth century. And in 1751 a "Sweet Flowering Carolina Dog-wood" was among the plants delivered to Norborne Berkeley's estate of Stoke Gifford near Bristol, where Thomas Wright was creating "Wood Walks" embellished with flowers and flowering shrubs. But whether the dogwood ever bloomed remains unrecorded. Indeed, whether the pink form (*Cornus florida* f. *rubra* [West] Schelle) made an appearance in English gardens before the nineteenth century is also a matter of speculation. It is clear that Mark Catesby brought it into cultivation in Virginia, for he commented in *The Natural History* that he had found one "with Flowers of a rose-colour, which was luckily blown down, and many of its Branches had taken Root, which I transplanted into a Garden."[9] Philip Miller was certainly aware of it when he mentioned the variety with "a red involucrum" in *The Gardeners Dictionary* of 1768, but this might have been in allusion to Catesby's account. Indeed, back in 1731 in the first volume of *The Natural History,* Mark Catesby had emphasized that Thomas Fairchild stocked only the white-flowered dogwood.

Thus, evidence of the introduction of the dogwood to English gardens should not be equated with a picture of shrubberies resplendent with white and pink bloom. Of the many plants that Catesby introduced to England, some prospered while others failed. The impact of Mark Catesby's plant introductions on English gardens of the eighteenth century is a history of trial and error. Thus the rather inconsequential story of *Callicarpa americana* is offset by the momentous tale of *Catalpa bignonioides.*

9. Gloucestershire Record Office, QP4/5/1; W. J. Bean, *Trees and Shrubs Hardy in the British Isles,* 8th ed. (London, 1973), s.v. "Cornus florida" (which suggests that the pink form was probably only cultivated in the nineteenth and twentieth centuries); Mark Catesby, *The Natural History of Carolina, Florida, and the Bahama Islands . . . ,* 2 vols. (London, 1731–1743), I, 27.

Callicarpa americana *and* Amorpha fruticosa*:*
Failures and Successes in the Shrubbery

Mark Catesby was impressed by the *Callicarpa,* or "Frutex baccifer," which he saw growing in the woods around Charleston. He depicted it together with the "blueish green Snake" in volume II of *The Natural History* (Figure 38) and recorded the following observations:

> These Shrubs arise with several Stalks from the Ground, branching out on each Side, and in Height about four or five Feet; most of the Stalks are surrounded with Clusters of very small red Flowers, having four Petals each, with yellow *Stamina,* and growing at the Distance of about two Inches asunder, beginning to flower at the Bottom, and successively proceeding to flower to the Top of the Branch: From every Tuft of Flowers, grow opposite each other a Pair of serrated rough Leaves, the Berries which succeed the Flowers grow in Clusters, so closely connected, that none of their Foot-stalks can be perceived without separating them, which then discovers them to be held together by many small branching Stalks. These Berries are covered with a shining red Skin, containing many very small Seeds. They blossom in *April* and *May,* the Berries are ripe in *July.*[10]

In *The Gardeners Dictionary* of 1768, Philip Miller informed the reader that the *Callicarpa* (or "Johnsonia Americana," as he called it in defiance of Linnaeus's name) required a covering of straw or ferns to protect it from the English winters. This had come out of bitter experience:

> The seeds of this plant were sent me by Mr. Catesby, from Carolina, in 1724; and many of the plants were then raised in several curious gardens in England; most, if not all of them were afterward planted in the open air, where they flourished very well for some years, but these were not succeeded by fruit; and in the severe frost in 1740, they were most of them destroyed . . . so that until the Doctor [Dale] sent a fresh supply of seeds in 1744, there were scarce any of the plants living in the English gardens; but since then there has been quantities of the seeds brought to England.[11]

---

10. Catesby, *Natural History,* II, 47.

11. Philip Miller, *The Gardeners Dictionary* . . . 8th ed. (London, 1768), s.v. "Johnsonia Americana.

38. The Callicarpa *(Frutex Baccifer)*. Catesby, Natural History, *II, pl. 47. Courtesy, Colonial Williamsburg Foundation*

Collinson was clearly one of the suppliers of seed, for we find the name "Johnsonia" itemized as number 79 on his list of plants in the manuscript of circa 1767 in the Botany Library of the Natural History Museum in London. This corresponds to number 74 in a specific order supplied to Charles Polhill in Kent in 1760. Yet the *Callicarpa* was not recorded at the duke of Argyll's great garden of Whitton, at Charles Hamilton's Painshill, or indeed in any of the "curious" collections visited by Dr. John Hope on his tour of England in the summer of 1766. Thomas Mawe and John Abercrombie might have claimed in the *Universal Gardener and Botanist* of 1778 that it was hardy and "proper for the shrubbery," but the nurserymen Kennedy and Lee as well as Loddiges listed it as a greenhouse plant in their catalogs of 1774 and 1777. Indeed, in the one record where it crops up—John Blackburne's garden at Orford Hall in Lancashire—it was part of the greenhouse collection.[12] Not until the oriental callicarpas (*Callicarpa bodinieri* Levl., *C. dichotoma* K. Koch, and *C. japonica* Thunb.) reached England in the Victorian period did English gardens benefit from the promise of Catesby's clustering berries.

Difficulties in getting *Cornus florida* to flower and *Callicarpa americana* to fruit and flourish were part of the gamble of ordering seeds from North America. The adventurous and patient planter was, however, rewarded by regular successes. Bastard indigo (*Amorpha fruticosa*) was surely one of the better bets. In *The Gardeners Dictionary* of 1768, Philip Miller wrote of this shrub:

> The seeds of this plant were sent to England from Carolina, by Mr. Mark Catesby, F.R.S. in 1724, from which many plants were raised in the gardens near London; these were of quick growth, and many of the plants produced flowers in three years. At present it is become very common in all the gardens and nurseries, where it is propagated as a flowering shrub, for the ornament of the shrubbery. It is generally propagated by seeds which are annually sent to England from different parts of America.[13]

It would seem that Catesby's batch of seeds was not the first consignment to reach England, for *Amorpha fruticosa* is now known to have been growing at Bishop Henry Compton's garden at Fulham before his death in 1713. Interestingly too, the bastard indigo fails to make an appearance in *The Natural History*. However, Catesby included it in his *Hortus Britanno-Americanus* of 1763 and *Hortus Europae Americanus* of 1767 (Figure 39), suggesting that it "will stand our sharpest winters in a warm aspect." We can trace the course of the *Amorpha*'s dispersal throughout England. We know, for

12. "Collinson's notebook ca. 1767," MSS COL., Botany Library, Natural History Museum, London; MS 528/5, 92–94, Archives Division, University of London Library, Senate House, London; Thomas Mawe and John Abercrombie, *The Universal Gardener and Botanist* (London, 1778); Adam Neal, *A Catalogue of the Plants in the Garden of John Blackburne, Esq. at Orford, Lancashire* (Warrington, 1779).

13. Miller, *Gardeners Dictionary* (1768), s.v. "Amorpha Fruticosa."

39. Three Types of Smilax and Bastard Indigo. *Mark Catesby,* Hortus Britanno-
Americanus . . . *(London, 1763), figs. 31, 32, 33, 34. Courtesy, Colonial Williamsburg Foundation*

example, that Charles Polhill was receiving seeds in 1760 through the
agency of Peter Collinson. In his memorandum book for the estate of Polhill in Kent, he recorded: "In January 1760 I Received a Box of Seeds from
Mr. Bartram of Philadelphia which cost me Box and freight [left blank] the
seeds were Collected from all Parts of North America." Polhill itemized
106 different woody plants, and entry 92 reads: "Amorpha, from S. Carolina—a Bastard Indigo."[14] The seeds appear not to have come up, for entry

14. Morris, "Legacy of a Bishop," part 2, *Garden History,* XXI (1993), 22; *Hortus Siccus* in
Sloane Herbarium 175 f 90; Mark Catesby, *Hortus Britanno-Americanus* . . . (London, 1763), 19;
and *Hortus Europae Americanus* . . . (London, 1767); MS 528/5, 92–94, Archives Division,
Senate House.University of London Library. Although the price of shipment is left blank in

92 is missing from the list of thirty-odd successful germinations. *Amorpha* does not seem to have been a regular part of Collinson's shipments from John Bartram, presumably because it was only marginally hardy north of the Carolinas. We can conclude, therefore, that, like many species collected in the wild and shipped to England, seeds of *Amorpha fruticosa* were sent annually from collectors or gardeners in Charleston and its environs.

Amorpha fruticosa: *Plant Introductions and the Nursery Trade*

The bastard indigo was, however, also available in England through the nursery trade. It was first stocked in Christopher Gray's catalog of 1739. Thus, in 1759, we find that Christopher Gray—Mark Catesby's close friend —was supplying William Constable of Burton Constable in East Yorkshire with one "Bastard Indigo" for 1s. 6d. The same year, Sir William Lee of Hartwell in Buckinghamshire received two plants for 4s. through his landscape gardener, Richard Woods.[15] At 2s. per plant, Woods's stock was slightly more expensive than Christopher Gray's (perhaps being larger plants), and twice the price of Polhill's failed package of seeds. This was the equation behind the gamble: if Bartram's seeds germinated and grew well, the bet paid off; if they did not, the investment at the nursery proved the better deal. In some cases, the nurseryman seems to have been able to cover most of the initial costs of importation, selling a plant for the 1s. price of the seed package. Thus, for example, in December 1762, Samuel Driver was supplying James Leigh of Adlestrop with two bastard indigos for a total of 2s. In 1752, James Gordon was able to offer it for 10d., and, from 1764 to 1787, it averaged between 9d. and 1s.[16] Thus, what had begun as a collector's curiosity was transformed by the nursery trade into an affordable commodity. It was still more costly than a standard shrub of 2d. or 3d., but well below the top-priced magnolias, kalmias, and rhododendrons, which could sometimes fetch 15s. or even 2 guineas a specimen.

---

the Polhill memorandum, we know from other complementary documentation that the 105 or 106 packages of seeds cost the standard five guineas ($£5$ 5s). The entry for 11 was missing, so Polhill's total was in fact 105.

15. Elisabeth Hall, "The Plant Collections of an Eighteenth-Century Virtuoso," *Garden History,* XIV (1986), app. B by John Harvey, 29; Harvey, *Early Nurserymen,* 204–206. One of Richard Woods's other clients, Sir Robert Throckmorton of Buckland, was also receiving 2 bastard indigos in 1758 (Warwickshire Record Office, CR 1998/box 57).

16. The Shakespeare Birthplace Trust Records Office, Stratford-upon-Avon, DR 18/8/7/5; figures taken from Michael Symes, Alison Hodges, and John Harvey, "The Plantings at Whitton," *Garden History,* XIV (1986), 138–172.

The way in which a nurseryman brought plants such as the bastard indigo or Virginia dogwood into the trade is revealed in a letter from Christopher Gray to John Bartram, dated August 16, 1753. Peter Collinson acted as an intermediary, commenting on the list where the nurseryman was muddled or imprecise or where he misspelled a name. (Collinson's annotations are in brackets, and I have added modern botanical names in the right-hand column to assist identification.) Gray wrote out the following order:

Mr Battarm—

I Desire you will Send me as Maney as you Can of those Sorts of Seeds for Me and put My Name upon the box—a goode Maney of the other Sorts as you Sent before—I do not like thorn   put Whole you Can of those Mention from
Sir Your very humble Servt
Christopher Gray
[I told Him I was in doubt if this order would come Soon enough   if it does it will make Nine Boxes—]

1 Virginia Tulip [Common Tulip poplar]	*Liriodendron tulipifera* L.
Ld way Mouth pine	*Pinus strobus* L.
3 Leaves pine	*Pinus taeda* L.
Jersey pine	*Pinus virginiana* Miller
Ditto pines 3 leaves	*Pinus rigida* Miller
[he might have said pine of all spcies—]	
2 Leaves Mountain pine	?*Pinus echinata* Miller
Mountain Red-Spurs	*Picea rubens* Sarg.
Black Spurs—	*Picea mariana* (Miller) Britt., Sterns and Pogg.
White Cedors	*Chamaecyparis thyoides* (L.) Britt., Sterns and Pogg.
Red Cedors—	*Juniperus virginiana* L.
Arbor Julia	*Cercis canadensis* L.
virg Dog Wood	*Cornus florida* L.
Benjamins	*Lindera benzoin* (L.) Blume
Tupelae 2 Sorts—	*Nyssa acquatica* L. and *N. sylvatica* Marsh.
Swamp Magnolia Minor	*Magnolia virginiana* L.
the ~~Larg Magnolia~~	*Magnolia grandiflora* L.
the New Sort Magnolia [Desseduius—]	*Magnolia acuminata* L. or *M. tripetala* L.
~~Swamp pine~~ [or Caroline]	?*Pinus elliottii* Engelm.
arbor vitia	*Thuya occidentalis* L.
Balm Gilard [Firr]	*Abies balsamea* Miller
Anona [papaw or]	*Asimina triloba* (L.) Dun.

Honey Succus—[Honeysuckles]   *Lonicera sempervirens* L.
Sassfaryos—[Sarsifrass]   *Sassifras albidum* Nees.
Scarlet Oakes—[Scarlet Oke acorns] *Quercus coccinea* Muenchh.[17]

A second letter from the nurseryman Nathaniel Powell completes the picture of North American exotics entering the nursery trade in the mid-eighteenth century—many of the same plants that Mark Catesby illustrated in *The Natural History*. Interestingly, Powell ordered a few flowers as well as flowering shrubs. Perhaps he simply wanted them for his own garden. However, from the evidence of stock in nursery catalogs, there must have been some consumer interest in herbaceous material from North America by the 1760s, even if the trade in lady's slippers and side-saddle flowers never reached the manic proportions of the trade in woody plants.[18] The letter was written on April 21, 1760, and shows how the nurseryman tried to get an edge on the estate owner by requesting large quantities and better-quality seed:

Mr. John Bartram
Sir

I write you last year for a Box of Seeds and plants but was disapointed I suppose my Letter miscaried or the Ship was taken. I have given Comisson to our good friend Mr. Collinson to send me Two Boxes of American seeds and Two boxes of Plants   if his miscarys this will be your Comisson   let them be fresh and good as many new sorts as posable   you know I trade in seeds   you will let me have larger boxes and more in quantity then you comonly send to Gentlemen for thare own youse. as below have sent a Catalogue of what plants wold have you send with any other sorts you think proper that are curious. let the seeds be all fresh and good   have named some sorts that I would have large quantitys of   wold have some of all the sorts as you send to others   your care in sending every thing good carfully packt and [as soon] as posable will oblige
    Sir
Your Old frind and Humble Servt
Nath: Powell

American Plants
Magnolias   Many plants   *Magnolia* spp.
Chamarodendren   Great and Small   *Rhododendron maximum* L. or *Kalmia latifolia* L.

---

17. Berkeley and Berkeley, eds., *Correspondence of Bartram*, 352–353.
18. See Laird, *The Flowering of the Landscape Garden*.

Kelmias all the sorts	*Kalmia latifolia* L. and *K. angustifolia* L.
Azalias all the sorts	*Rhododendron nudiflorum* Torr. and *R. viscosum* Torr.
Sweet Gale with Farn Leaves	*Comptonia peregrina* Coult.
Andromeda all the sorts	*Leucothoë racemosa* A. Gray and *Chamaedaphne calyculata* Moench.[19]
Papaw	*Asimina triloba* (L.) Dun.
Red flowring and Dwarfe Laurels	*Kalmia angustifolia* L. var. *rubra*
Stript Calcolus	*Cypripedium calceolus* var. *parviflorum* (Salisb.) Fern.
Sarasina	*Sarracenia purpurea* L. and *S. flava* L.
Chiononthus	*Chionanthus virginicus* L.
Ever green American Privet	*Forestiera acuminata* Poiret
Uva Ursi	*Arctostaphylos uva-ursi* (L.) Sprengel
Some others that are Curious	
Send Large quantitys of the following Seeds	
Magnolia	*Magnolia* spp.
Red and White Cedar	*Juniperus virginiana* L. and *Chamaecyparis thyoides* (L.) Britt., Sterns and Pogg.
Weymouth Pine	*Pinus strobus* L.
Bald Cypress	*Taxodium distichum* (L.) Rich.
all the sorts of Pines	*Pinus* spp.
Two thornd Acatia	?*Robinia pseudoacacia* L
Sasafras	*Sassafras albidum* Nees.
Benjamin Tree	*Lindera benzoin* (L.) Blume
Chionanthus	*Chionanthus virginicus* L
Maple all the sorts	*Acer* spp.
Myrtle	*Myrica cerifera* L. and *M. pensylvanica* Lois.
Red Cardional	*Lobelia cardinalis* L.
Great Chamorodendron	*Rhododendron maximum* L. or *Kalmia latifolia* L.
Chinqypins	*Castanea pumila* Miller

all sorts of Wall nuts [*Juglans* spp.] and Hecory [*Carya* spp.] with as many more new sorts as are to be got.

P.S. If you have my Comissons from Mr. Collinson you are only to send me two Boxes of Seeds and two Boxes of plants.

I want a Large quantity of Weymouth Pine   I believe the best way will be when the seed is Ripe to spred the Cones on a Cloth or Matt and lay them in the Sun   the seed

19. John Harvey has pointed out to me that under "Andromeda" many species could be intended: *Andromeda glaucophylla* Link, *A. rosmarinifolia* Pursh, *Chamaedaphne calyculata* Moench. and *C. calyculata* var. *angustifolia, Leucothoë racemosa* A. Gray, *Lyonia ligustrina* DC., *L. mariana* D. Don, and *Oxydendrum arboreum* DC.

will easley come out   you may send the seed without the Cones. I shall be pleas if you
will send me a large bag of the seed as much as you can get.[20]

The seeds were usually shipped loose, either separated by small dividers
in the box or layered with moss or straw. Occasionally the most valuable
seeds—or ones that were very small—were individually wrapped in paper.[21] The most successful way of transporting boxes of live plants was to
wrap sphagnum moss around dormant bare rootstock. This was done
over the winter months. Yet, however careful the packaging and however
skilled the nurseryman in taking care of the contents, the processes of
transportation and germination were fraught with difficulties. There was
no guarantee that a given plant would take. Thus the chinquapin requested
by Powell at the end of his order continued to defy the most practiced
horticulturists. In 1746, Collinson could write to Bartram:

> Is there no more Chinquapin to be Had, why Does thou not Raise a
> plantation in thy own Garden of Chinquapin Trees, to serve thy Corre-
> spondents   From the first Wee wanted them and and if they had been
> then Sown by this Time thou would have had plenty to serve us for it is
> a tree that is not to be had here for Money.[22]

In the eighth edition of *The Gardeners Dictionary* (1768), Philip Miller was
still describing it as very rare in England, adding that "not one seed in five
hundred sent over ever grew."[23]

In contrast to Powell's chinquapin, Catesby's *Amorpha* was not hard to
come by in the middle of the eighteenth century. Through annual importation from Carolina it was widely disseminated, and it pops up in records
of many gardens throughout the shires of England. It was recorded at the
duke of Argyll's Whitton in 1765 and at John Blackburne's Orford Hall in
1779. However, precisely how and where it was used remains a mystery. In
the *Universal Gardener and Botanist* of 1778, Mawe and Abercrombie suggested that, as it grew up to ten or twelve feet, it could be "employed to
good advantage in composing large shrubberies." We know that at Chelsea Physic Garden—a medicinal garden set up by the Society of Apothecaries in 1673—Philip Miller had been growing plants in his "shrubbery."

20. Berkeley and Berkeley, eds., *Correspondence of Bartram,* 483–485.

21. The processes of transportation are discussed in detail in Laird, *The Flowering of the
Landscape Garden.*

22. Berkeley and Berkeley, eds., *Correspondence of Bartram,* 276.

23. Miller, *Gardeners Dictionary* (1768), s.v. "Castanea."

However, additional plants were also located in the "swamp."[24] By 1772 or 1773, under the new direction of Stanesby Alchorne, the "swamp" had been converted from a rectangular pool on the central axis of the garden (Figures 40, 41). It became the collecting ground for many of the North American species. Here was some recognition of the need to create a moist and shady habitat that was suited to the requirements of the ericaceous species—kalmias and rhododendrons—or swamp plants such as *Clethra alnifolia*.[25] Botanical science and medicinal needs thus contributed to the process of acclimatizing exotics—to the benefit of nurserymen, who then knew how to manage them appropriately for sale to consumers.

Within the protective walls of Chelsea Physic Garden, the *Amorpha* would not have been especially prone to frost damage. However, in gardens in the north of England—Orford Hall, for example—the bastard indigo must frequently have been burned by winter frosts. In such cases, the gardener would have been obliged to cut the shrub to the ground, allowing it to sprout with fresh stems in the spring. Sometimes, no doubt, the *Amorpha* appeared permanently in a juvenile condition, far from its potential ten or twelve feet. In this sense, judging which was the appropriate row for a particular plant within the "theatrical" hierarchy of the shrubbery posed a problem for the garden designer. When James Meader illustrated the *Disposition of Deciduous Trees and Shrubs for a Plantation* in his manual *The Planter's Guide* of 1779 (Figure 42), he placed the bastard indigo in the fourth row, alongside tall shrubs such as the oleaster (*Elaeagnus angustifolia* Kuntze.) or low trees such as the judas tree (*Cercis siliquastrum* L.).[26] In front of it he placed a syringa (*Philadelphus coronarius* L.) and a maiden's-blush rose (*Rosa alba* var. *regalis* Thory.). It is debatable whether this location would have favored or hindered the *Amorpha*. Although

24. Whitton: Symes, Hodges, and Harvey, "The Plantings at Whitton," *Garden History,* XIV (1986), 138–172; Orford Hall: Neal, *A Catalogue of the Plants in the Garden of John Blackburne;* Mawe and Abercrombie, *Universal Gardener,* s.v. "Amorpha fruticosa"; MS H. IV 24 at Chelsea Physic Garden, "Index Horti Chelseiani," initialed "SA" (Stanesby Alchorne) and dated 1772, with additions of 1773: shrubbery no. 112; swamp no. 70.

25. This process is discussed in more detail in Mark Laird, "Approaches to Planting in the Late Eighteenth Century: Some Imperfect Ideas on the Origins of the American Garden," *Journal of Garden History,* XI (1991), 168. For a discussion of the scientific ramifications of plant collecting in botanic gardens, see Therese O'Malley, "Art and Science in the Design of Botanic Gardens, 1730–1830," in Hunt, ed., *Garden History: Issues, Approaches, Methods,* 279–302.

26. James Meader, *The Planter's Guide; or, Pleasure Gardener's Companion* (London, 1779), introduction entitled "On Planting and Plantations" (unpaginated).

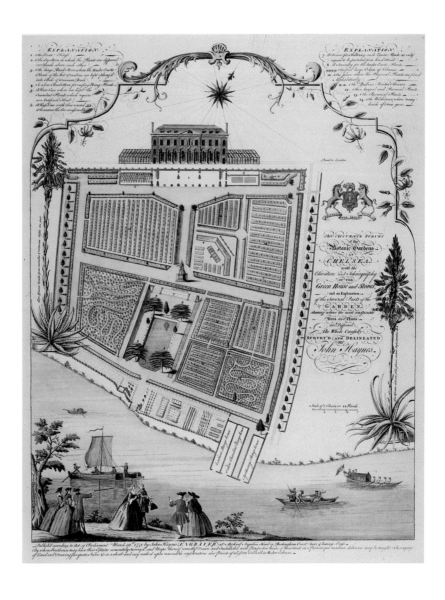

40. *An Accurate Survey of the Botanic Gardens at Chelsea.* John Haynes. 1751. Courtesy of the Royal Society

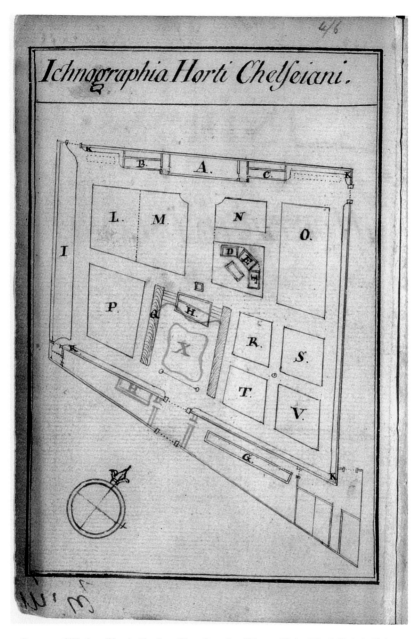

41. Layout of Chelsea Physic Garden. *From Stanesby Alchorne, "Index Horti Chelseiani" (1772–1773). From a manuscript in the Library of the Chelsea Physic Garden. By permission of the Chelsea Physic Garden Company*

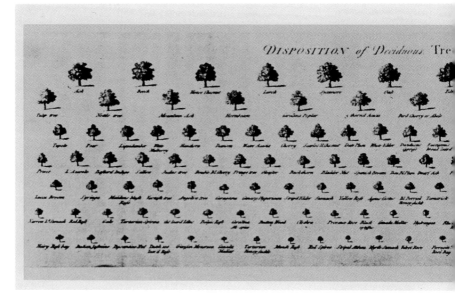

42. *Disposition of Deciduous Trees and Shrubs for a Plantation.* James Meader, *The Planter's Guide; or, Pleasure Gardener's Companion* (London, 1779). Dumbarton Oaks, Studies in Landscape Architecture, Garden Library

protected from frosts by the surrounding vegetation, it might have struggled to keep pace with the growth of its neighbors.

Gleditsia aquatica, Ptelea trifoliata, *and* Wisteria frutescens: *Stature in the Shrubbery*

Even when plants proved hardy, they did not necessarily grow as rapidly as in their home environment. The water acacia (*Gleditsia aquatica* Marsh.), for example, introduced by Mark Catesby in 1723, proved a slow-grower in English soil. It first appeared in the nursery trade in Robert Furber's catalog of 1727 and Christopher Gray's catalog of 1739. In 1752 James Gordon could charge 5s. per plant, but by 1764 John Whittingham of Coventry had brought the price down to 2s. 6d. In 1751, it was among the plants delivered to Norborne Berkeley at Stoke Gifford, and in 1758 Sir Robert Throckmorton had 2 plants growing at Buckland. Thus, the water acacia had been around in English gardens for several decades when Dr. John Hope visited Kew in 1766 and recorded with interest a "water acacia 8 feet high; not hurt by last year's frosts." The tree that grows up to fifty or sixty feet in North America would eventually succeed in reaching

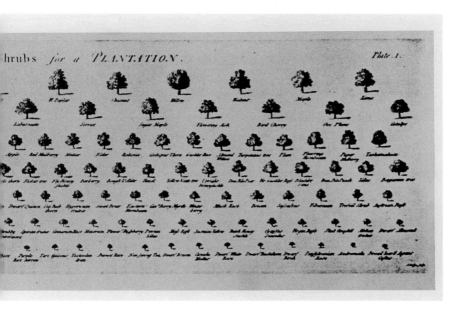

thirty feet in English soil.[27] But throughout the eighteenth century we should imagine it as a rather delicate specimen, struggling to justify its place in James Meader's fifth row.

William Marshall, while attempting to divide ornamental shrubs and trees into eight ranks, admitted as late as 1796:

> An accuracy of arrangement cannot reasonably be expected, in a *first attempt* of this nature; the heights to which many exotics rise, in this island, are imperfectly known: nor is a critical exactness, in this case, requisite. It is not an even surface of foliage, like what we see in Conservatories, we ask for in Grounds. Even if it were, it would be difficult to produce it. Soil, aspect, and the habits of individual plants, ever tend to occasion an inequality of growth, and a desirable variety of surface: a slight error in the Classification will only tend to increase this Variety.[28]

27. John Harvey, part 2, in Symes, Hodges, and Harvey, "The Plantings at Whitton," *Garden History,* XIV (1986), 151; Gloucestershire R.O., QP4/5/1; Warwickshire R.O., CR 1998/box 57; John H. Harvey, "A Scottish Botanist in London in 1766," *Garden History,* IX (1981), 50; Bean, *Trees and Shrubs* (thirty-five feet given as maximum height).

28. [William Marshall], *Planting and Rural Ornament,* 2 vols. (London, 1796), II, 437–438.

43. Ptelea, or Shrub Trefoil *(Frutex Virginianus Trifolius)*. Catesby, Natural History, *II, pl. 83.*
Courtesy, Colonial Williamsburg Foundation

James Meader demonstrated a further "error in the Classification" in
placing the "Trefoil Shrub" in the third row of his *Disposition*. This Carolina shrub trefoil *(Ptelea trifoliata)*—reintroduced by Mark Catesby in 1724
after the intial stock of 1693 failed—was claimed in the 1778 edition of
Mawe and Abercrombie's *Universal Gardener* to grow to about eight or ten
feet. Yet more than a decade before, Dr. John Hope had already recorded
one in the duke of Argyll's garden at Whitton that was eighteen or twenty

feet tall. At Cambridge he noted another specimen under the category "thriving plants."[29] Perhaps Meader assumed that the shrub trefoil was unlikely to attain the height that Catesby had documented in its native habitat. In the second volume of *The Natural History*, Catesby described the species as well over ten feet, and so might have led Meader to underestimate its potential in the cooler climatic conditions in England (Figure 43). A complicating factor, however, was that Catesby's plants were collected in the mountains, a less favorable growing environment. As he explained:

> These Trees usually grow to the Height of twelve or fifteen Feet, with a Trunk as big as one's Leg, having a pale greenish smooth Bark. Its Leaves are trifoliate, set on long Footstalks. The Flowers grow in spiked Bunches, many of them together, each Flower having four white Petals, and are succeeded by Bunches or Clusters of Seeds.
>
> These trees grow on the upper Parts of the *Savannah* River in *Carolina* and no where that ever I saw in the lower inhabited Parts of the Country.[30]

Their location in upland terrain may account for a relatively stunted stature when compared to the specimens of Whitton. Once in cultivation, it proved to reach twenty-five feet or more. Thus, Catesby's unfamiliarity with lowland *Ptelea,* compounded by Meader's underestimation of potential growth (whether through ignorance or second-guessing), resulted in an erroneous placement within the graduated "theater" of the shrubbery.

In *The Gardeners Dictionary* of 1768, Philip Miller explained how Catesby came to reintroduce the *Ptelea:*

> It was first discovered in Virginia by Mr. Banister, who sent the Seeds to England, from which some plants were raised at Fulham, and some other curious gardens, but . . . they were destroyed by a severe winter, so that there were scarce any of the plants left in England. In 1724, Mr. Catesby sent over a good quantity of the seeds from Carolina, which succeeded so well as to furnish many gardens with plants.[31]

By 1727 it was firmly established in the nursery trade, but it took a few years before its price made it affordable to any but the "curious" collectors. William Constable was prepared to pay 1s. 6d. for a single specimen

---

29. Harvey, "A Scottish Botanist," *Garden History,* IX (1981), 48, 61.

30. Catesby, *Natural History,* II, 83.

31. Miller, *Gardeners Dictionary* (1768), s.v. "Ptelea Trifoliata."

in 1759, but by 1764 William Burchell could sell it for 6d. Toward the end of the century, it averaged around 8d.–1s., the price no doubt depending on the quality or size of the plant.[32]

There were, of course, ways to control the height and spread of any particular shrub. The pruning regime was especially critical in the eighteenth century.[33] In some cases too the plant was a climbing species that could be attached to a stake or allowed to grow up the stems of adjacent trees. The Carolina kidney bean tree (*Wisteria frutescens* [L.] Poir.) was one such climber. Thus, in *The Gardeners Dictionary* of 1737, Philip Miller wrote:

> The Seeds of this Plant were sent from Carolina by Mr. Catesby, in the Year 1724 and distributed to several curious Persons in London, from which many Plants have been raised, which are very hardy. . . . This Plant is very proper to place among other climbing Shrubs in the small Wilderness Quarters, where, if it be supported with strong stakes, it will rise twelve or fourteen Feet high.[34]

By the 1752 edition, he was suggesting that it could be allowed to grow rampant, twining itself around tree stems. According to the Society of Gardeners' *Catalogus Plantarum* of 1730, it flowered first in the garden of the nurseryman Robert Furber, and by 1766 Dr. John Hope could record a "Glycine frutescens—beautiful" at Kew. By 1778, Mawe and Abercrombie described it as "an elegant shrubbery climber, ornamental both in foliage and flowers."[35] It would be nearly forty years later that the spectacular *Wisteria sinensis* Sweet would reach England from a garden in Canton, thereafter eclipsing the *Wisteria frutescens*. However, over the course of the eighteenth century, Catesby's climber remained one of the uncontested glories of the shrubbery.

Ilex cassine *and* Ceanothus americanus: *Foliage and Flowers in the Shrubbery*

An additional point that gardeners had to consider—beyond stature and speed of growth—was whether the exotic was evergreen or decid-

---

32. Hall, "The Plant Collections," *Garden History,* XIV (1986), 28; Symes, Hodges, and Harvey, "The Plantings at Whitton," *Garden History,* XIV (1986), 165.

33. Discussed in Laird, *The Flowering of the Landscape Garden.*

34. Miller, *Gardeners Dictionary* (1737), s.v. "Phaseoloides Carolinianum."

35. *Catalogus Plantarum . . . A Catalogue of Trees, Shrubs, Plants, and Flowers . . . By a Society of Gardeners* (London, 1730); Harvey, "A Scottish Botanist," *Garden History,* IX (1981), 50.

uous. Since the seventeenth century, it had been customary to segregate the evergreens to create what John Evelyn called a *Ver Perpetuum* of perennial greens. Philip Miller upheld the tradition—for visual as well as cultural reasons—by supporting the idea of segregated evergreen and deciduous wilderness quarters. Thus in the first edition of *The Gardeners Dictionary* of 1731, he wrote: "This manner of separating the Evergreens from the deciduous Trees, will not only make a much better Appearance, but also cause them to thrive far beyond what they usually do when intermix'd; therefore I should never advise any Person to plant them promiscuously together." When James Meader published his *Planter's Guide* in 1779, it was still customary to think of separate deciduous and evergreen plantations. Hence he illustrated, in addition to the *Deciduous Plantation,* a second diagram entitled the *Disposition of Trees and Shrubs for an Evergreen Plantation* (Figure 44). In this shrubbery, he incorporated the pines, spruce, red and white cedars, arborvitae, bald cypress, and others that Christopher Gray and Nathaniel Powell had ordered in 1753 and 1760.

We might thus expect to find Mark Catesby's introduction of 1726—the evergreen dahoon holly *(Ilex cassine* L.)—placed in its appropriate row within the graduated *Evergreen Plantation.*[36] Yet it was absent. In volume I of *The Natural History,* Catesby, illustrating the "Agrifolium Carolinense" with the "Little Thrush" (Figure 45), had described it as a tall shrub or small tree but without specifying that it was evergreen:

> This Holly usually grows erect, sixteen Feet high; the Branches shooting straighter, and being of quicker Growth than the common Kind. The Leaves are longer, of a brighter green, and more pliant; not prickly, but serrated only. The Berries are red, growing in large Clusters. This is a very uncommon Plant in *Carolina,* I having never seen it but at Col. *Bull*'s Plantation on *Ashley* River, where it grows in a Bog.[37]

In England it would prove to be an equally uncommon sight. Like the *Callicarpa,* this holly was only borderline hardy in English soil, and by 1768

---

36. Mark Laird, "Parterre, Grove, and Flower Garden: European Horticulture and Planting Design in John Evelyn's Time," in Therese O'Malley and Joachim Wolschke-Bulmahn, eds., *John Evelyn's "Elysium Britannicum" and European Gardening,* Dumbarton Oaks Colloquium on the History of Landscape Architecture, XVII (Washington, D.C., 1997), 196–200; Miller, *Gardeners Dictionary* (1731), s.v. "Wilderness"; John H. Harvey's appendix to Morris, "Legacy of a Bishop" *Garden History,* XIX (1991), 57–59, where *Ilex cassine* L. is identified tentatively as the plant introduced in 1700 to Bishop Compton's garden in Fulham.

37. Catesby, *Natural History,* I, 31.

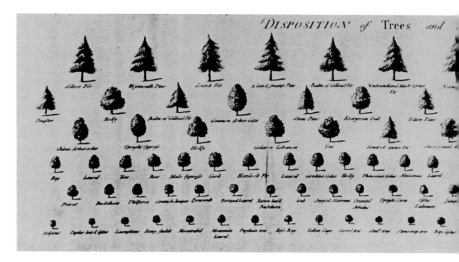

44. *Disposition of Trees and Shrubs for an Evergreen Plantation.* Meader, *The Planter's Guide.*
Dumbarton Oaks, Studies in Landscape Architecture, Garden Library

Philip Miller was already warning that it needed protection in severe
frosts. Loddiges classified it as a "greenhouse" plant in the catalog of
1777, and in 1779 at Orford Hall in Lancashire it was recorded in the
greenhouse collection. This explains its absence in Meader's evergreen
plantation. Indeed, in general the North American hollies turned out to be
a flop in English conditions, nothing to rival the handsome native—*Ilex
aquifolium*—and its many cultivars. Thus, when William Constable paid
Christopher Gray the high price of 4s. for a single specimen of the dahoon
holly in 1759, we might wonder whether he was forced to keep it under
glass in winter or whether it languished outdoors in his pleasure ground at
Burton Constable.

Perhaps the most important quality of an exotic in both the evergreen
and deciduous plantations was whether it produced flowers, and whether
these flowers were enjoyable at a distance or close to. The flowering of
the New Jersey tea, for example—the *Ceanothus americanus* L. that Mark
Catesby might have sent to Bishop Compton in Fulham before 1713—was
only discernible at close quarters.[38] Its dullish white flowers could easily be
overlooked. In any case, growing to only three or four feet, it was naturally

38. Aiton, *Hortus Kewensis,* I, 270: "Cult. before 1713, by Bishop Compton." However, in
John Harvey's appendix to Morris, "Legacy of a Bishop," *Garden History,* XIX (1991), there is
no evidence to confirm this claim. John Fisher, in *The Origins of Garden Plants,* 116, suggests
that *Ceanothus americanus* was one of Catesby's discoveries.

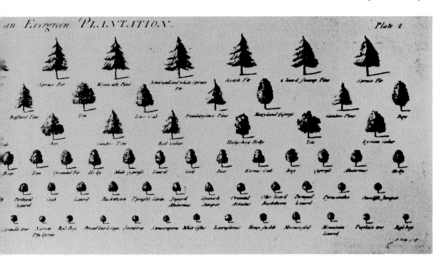

suited to the front row of James Meader's deciduous plantation. There it was placed between the "Burnet Rose" (*Rosa pimpinellifolia* L.) and a "Dwarf Broom" (perhaps *Genista sagittalis* L.). Mawe and Abercrombie described it as "a most elegant little flowering shrub, as when it flowers it appears wholly covered with bloom, and therefore is well calculated for the most conspicuous compartments of the shrubbery plantations."[39] Eventually it would be eclipsed by the strikingly beautiful blue *Ceanothus* species of California and Mexico and their many hybrids, but for the whole of the eighteenth century it preserved its appeal as a front-row flowering shrub.

Calycanthus floridus *and* Robinia hispida *and the Development of the "American Garden"*

The blooms of the Carolina allspice (*Calycanthus floridus* L.)—the plant that Mark Catesby introduced to England in 1726—also represent a subtle beauty. They were portrayed in plate 46 of the first volume of *The Natural History,* along with the handsome "Chatterer" (Figure 46). In his account, Catesby referred to the flowers as resembling in form "those of the *Star-Anemony,* compos'd of many stiff copper-colour'd Petals, enclosing a Tuft of short yellow *Stamina.*" He added that "the Bark is very aromatic, and as odoriferous as Cinnamon." This must have been enough to promote the

39. Mawe and Abercrombie, *Universal Gardener.*

45. *Agrifolium Carolinense* and the Little Thrush. *Catesby,* Natural History, *I, pl. 31. Courtesy,*
Colonial Williamsburg Foundation

shrub to many collectors in England. Yet, in *The Gardeners Dictionary* of
1768 under the name "Basteria," Philip Miller wrote that the flowers were
of "a sullen purple colour, and have a disagreeable scent. . . . This plant
was very scarce in England, till within a few years past, that many of them
have been brought from Carolina."[40]

40. Catesby, *Natural History,* I, 46; Miller, *Gardeners Dictionary* (1768), s.v. "Basteria."

46. Carolina Allspice *(Frutex Corni Foliis Conjugatis).* Catesby, Natural History, *I, pl. 46. Courtesy, Colonial Williamsburg Foundation*

It seems that it took some years before the allspice received the acclaim it deserved. In James Meader's scheme for a deciduous plantation of 1779, however, it already took up a prominent position in the second row, and in Mawe and Abercrombie's *Universal Gardener* of 1778 its "aromatic bark" was noted. They suggested that it needed "a warm situation and dry soil, in the fronts of the principal shrubbery compartments." By the early nineteenth century it had become an essential part of the "American garden"—an area specially devoted to plants from the New World.[41] Thus, when John Rutter described the "American Plantations" at Fonthill in his *Delineations of Fonthill and Its Abbey* of 1823, he highlighted the *Calycanthus floridus* for its "exquisite perfume":

> It was our good fortune to behold this extraordinary shrubbery at the season of its greatest beauty. Its winding paths led us through groves of the loftiest rhododendrons, whose deep pink flowers shed an universal glow over an extensive declivity—here and there the beautiful magnolia displayed the exquisite whiteness of its large blossoms—while clusters of azaleas mingled with these loftier exotics in the richest harmony of colour and fragrance; the Carolina rose profusely studded the walks with its gorgeous blossoms—the allspice of the same region shed its exquisite perfume over the whole extent of these gardens—and the arbutus luxuriated in groups as lofty and as branching as the Portugal laurel.[42]

Back in 1772–1773 it had been recorded by Stanesby Alchorne in the newly created "swamp" at Chelsea Physic Garden (Figures 40, 41), and we may speculate that this ordering of American plants into a "habitat garden" was one impetus behind the development of the American garden in the eighteenth century.[43]

At the earl of Egremont's Petworth in Sussex, one such American garden evolved out of the wilderness that Capability Brown had embellished with exotics in the 1750s.[44] It was described by a French visitor in 1810 on his return from several years' stay in America. He wrote that the pleasure grounds were

41. Mawe and Abercrombie, *Universal Gardener;* Laird, "Approaches to Planting," *Journal of Garden History,* XI (1991), 159–172.

42. John Rutter, *Delineations of Fonthill and Its Abbey* (London, 1823), 90. John Harvey has pointed out to me that the name "Early Carolina Allspice" was applied to an unrelated (but also heavily scented) species from China, *Chimonanthus praecox,* introduced in 1766. We can be certain, however, that Rutter meant the true allspice of North America, since this flowers in early to middle summer, along with the rhododendrons and magnolias. The Chinese shrub flowers from December to February.

43. "Swamp" no. 35.

44. See Laird, *The Flowering of the Landscape Garden.*

planted with the largest trees, close together, something like a heavy-
timbered American forest, of which they suggest the idea. Many of the
trees were indeed American. We found here our old acquaintances the
hemlock, the black spruce, the tulip tree, the occidental plane, the
acacia, and several kinds of oaks. All these trees seem to accommodate
themselves extremely well with the climate of England and not to feel,
while growing within the inclosed grounds of a peer or monarchy, the
loss of American liberty. Under their shade we observed the rhododendron, the fragrant and the common azalia, and other American
plants, finer and more luxuriant than in their native soil. In some places
the trees, having sufficient space, grow in the English Taste; and the
spruce, thus civilised, extends its mighty limbs over the green lawn with
the grace and majesty of a park oak.[45]

The third earl of Egremont's plantings in the 1780s, 1790s, and early 1800s
transformed the pleasure ground. Nurserymen's bills survive for the years
1773, 1774, 1783, 1794, 1803, 1805, 1807, and 1812, and, in one bill from
Matthew Burchell, "12 Rose Acacia" were itemized along with magnolias
and trumpet flowers (*Campsis radicans* Seem.).[46]

This acacia was the *Robinia hispida* L. (Figure 47) that Mark Catesby had
first encountered in the Carolinas in the 1720s. His account in the appendix at the end of volume II of *The Natural History* is as follows:

The flowers and leaves differ little in their shape from the *Pseudo Acacia
flore albo*. The stalks and larger branches are thick set with prickly hairs,
and with sharp spines placed alternately. The flowers, which are pa-
pilionaceous are of a faint purple colour or rose-colour, and of a fragrant smell, I never saw any of these trees but at one place near the
Apalatchian mountains, where Buffellos had left their dung; and some of
the trees had their branches pulled down, from which I conjecture they
had been browsing on the leaves. What with the bright verdure of the
leaves, and the beauty of its flowers, few trees make a more elegant
appearance. I visited them again at the proper time to get some seeds,
but the ravaging *Indians* had burn'd the woods many miles round, and
totally destroyed them, to my great disappointment; so that all I was
able to procure of this specious tree was some specimens of it which

45. Louis Simond, *Journal of a Tour . . . 1810 and 1811,* 2d ed. (Edinburgh 1817), 323.
46. Petworth Household Accounts, seriatim, 8685, 8115, 8057, 8065, 5953, 8084, 9272,
8705, 9212. The Burchell account is under 8057.

47. *Bison Americanus* and Rose Acacia. *Catesby,* Natural History, *II, Appendix, pl. 20. Courtesy, Colonial Williamsburg Foundation*

remain in the *Hortus siccus* of Sir *H. Sloane* and that of Professor *Dillenius* at *Oxford*. But since I am informed that a plant of this tree had been introduced from *America* by Sir *John Colliton,* Bart. to his Gardens at *Exmouth* in *Devonshire*.[47]

In *The Gardeners Dictionary* of 1768, Philip Miller seemed to confirm Catesby's suggestion that Sir John Colleton—the man who had grown the *Magnolia grandiflora* "Exmouth" with great success—had brought the Rose Acacia to Devon. He commented:

> In England at present it seems to be of low growth . . . not as yet produced any pods in England . . . at present scarce in the gardens about London, but in Devonshire it is in greater plenty.[48]

It appears to have arrived in England by 1743, two decades after Catesby had first sighted it in the Carolinas. Soon after this, Devon was not the only place where the *Robinia hispida* was in demand. In the nurseryman's bill from Samuel Driver to James Leigh of Adlestrop, dated December 8 and 9, 1762, for example, one "Red Rose Acacia" was itemized for the very high price of 5s. By 1766, Dr. John Hope saw it growing at several sites around London: at Kew, where it was "cut like a willow shortend autumn and spring"; at Ravensworth House on the Fulham Road; and at James Gordon's Mile End Nursery, where it was in flower. At Chelsea Physic Garden in 1772, it was grown in the "3rd large perennial quarter" (no. 106), and even at Orford Hall it was recorded out of doors in 1779. By the end of the century, it crops up in Richard Twiss's proposed plan for the town garden of his friend Francis Douce, who lived on Upper Gower Street. Sketched in 1791, the planting plan shows the "Robinia hispida" in a middle-ranked location, prominently displayed opposite a garden seat between an azalea and a kalmia. In a small, walled enclosure, this was an enormous tribute to the attractive pink-flowered shrub, whose cost had dropped to 2s. 6d. From 1770 onwards it could be obtained for between 1s. 6d. and 2s. 6d. The more affordable price may account for its widespread use in the early nineteenth century. For the planting up of the shrubberies at the Brighton Pavilion, for example, a batch of twelve was ordered in 1820, and six in 1824.[49]

47. Catesby, *Natural History*, II, Appendix, 20.

48. Miller, *Gardeners Dictionary* (1768), s.v. "Robinia Hispida."

49. Shakespeare B.P.T.R.O., Stratford, DR 18/8/7/5; Harvey, "A Scottish Botanist," *Garden History*, IX (1981), 54, 58, 67; Mark Laird, "Ein Gartenplan für Upper Gower St. 13,

Catesby as Promoter of Stuartia malacodendron *and* Kalmia latifolia

Mark Catesby also played an indirect role in promoting the introduction of a number of other striking North American shrubs, notably *Kalmia latifolia* L. and *Stuartia malacodendron* L. In the appendix to volume II of *The Natural History,* he noted in his account of the "Steuartia" (Figure 48):

> For this elegant Plant I am obliged to my good friend Mr. *Clayton,* who sent it me from *Virginia,* and three months after its arrival it blossom'd in my garden at *Fulham,* in May 1742. . . . The right honourable and ingenious Earl of *Bute* will, I hope, excuse my Calling this new genus of Plants after his name.[50]

John Clayton of Virginia (1694–1773), author of the *Flora Virginica* of 1739–1743, is thus given the the credit for its introduction, and John Stuart, third earl of Bute (1713–1792)—the adviser to Kew—lends his name to its beautiful form. Yet Catesby was clearly growing the plant ten years before Philip Miller recorded in *The Gardeners Dictionary* (1752 edition) that it flowered at Christopher Gray's nursery. It seems to have been slow to gain a foothold in English gardens. In 1766 Dr. Hope spotted it at Kew, where it had flowered, and in James Gordon's nursery at Mile End. By 1772 or 1773 it was growing in the "swamp" at Chelsea Physic Garden (no. 78). However, in the eighth edition of *The Gardeners Dictionary* (1768), Miller could still report: "The seeds are seldom brought to England, and those frequently fail"; and, even in 1778, Mawe and Abercrombie pointed out that it was "not as yet near so plentiful here as many other American shrubs."[51] Not until the mid-1770s did it become readily available through the nursery trade. In the long term, nonetheless, it proved one of the most glorious North American imports.

The *Kalmia latifolia* (Figure 49) also took a while to get established but

---

London: Mustmassungen über Anlage, Pflege, und Entwicklung eines Bürgergartens im ausgehenden 18. Jahrhundert," in Erika Schmidt, Wilfried Hansmann, and Jörg Gamer, eds., *Garten, Kunst, Geschichte: Festschrift für Dieter Hennebo zum 70. Geburtstag* (Worms am Rhein, 1994), 82–94; Public Record Office LSII/I/XC000480. See Virginia Hinze, "The Recreation of John Nash's Regency Gardens at the Royal Pavilion, Brighton," *Garden History,* XXIV (1996), 45–53.

50. Catesby, *Natural History,* II, Appendix, 13.

51. Harvey, "A Scottish Botanist," *Garden History,* IX (1981), 50, 58; Miller, *Gardeners Dictionary* (1768), s.v. "Stuartia."

48. *Stuartia*. Catesby, *Natural History*, II, Appendix, pl. 13. Courtesy, Colonial Williamsburg
Foundation

49. *Kalmia (Chamaedaphne Foliis)*. Catesby, *Natural History*, II, pl. 98. Courtesy, Colonial Williamsburg Foundation

was more widespread by the middle of the eighteenth century. Mark Catesby explained in the second volume of *The Natural History* why there was an initial difficulty with imports:

> After several unsuccesful Attempts to propagate it from Seeds, I procured Plants of it at several Times from *America,* but with little better Success, for they gradually diminished, and produced no Blossoms; 'till my curious Friend Mr. *Peter Collinson,* excited by a View of its dried Specimens, and Description of it, procured some Plants of it from *Pensilvania,* which Climate being nearer to that of *England,* than from whence mine came, some Bunches of Blossoms were produced in *July* 1740, and in 1741, in my Garden at *Fulham.*[52]

Unlike the dahoon holly then, the kalmias (*K. latifolia* L. and *K. angustifolia* L.) proved hardy in English conditions and joined the evergreen magnolia (*M. grandiflora* L.) as one of the successes of the Collinson/Bartram enterprise. In James Meader's diagram of an evergreen plantation, the *Kalmia,* or mountain laurel, takes up a front-row position, and from this arrangement it is possible to visualize the *Kalmia*'s role in Cobbett's mile-deep shrubbery.

The Triumph of Catalpa bignonioides

The *Catalpa* that formed the rear of Cobbett's ideal shrubbery was placed at the back of James Meader's diagram of a deciduous plantation. (Cobbett had clearly abandoned the segregated disposition.) However, Meader did not locate it in the seventh and final row, just in the penultimate row. Here was a case where the horticulturist must have found himself in danger of committing Marshall's "slight error in the Classification." After all, in the first volume of *The Natural History,* this was how Mark Catesby described the tree that he had seen in the Carolinas, the *Catalpa bignonioides* Walt. (Figure 50): "usually a small Tree, seldom rising above 23 Foot in Height." Furthermore, Mawe and Abercrombie were still following this measurement in their *Universal Gardener and Botanist* of 1778. Yet, as early as 1766 the observant Dr. Hope had already recorded a *Catalpa* at the duke of Argyll's Whitton that was more than thirty feet in height with a spread of forty feet. Eventually the tree known as the "Trumpet Flower" would prove that it could exceed forty feet and justify

52. Catesby, *Natural History,* II, 98.

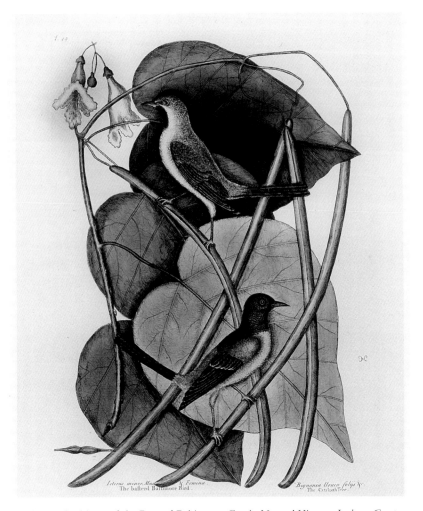

50. The Catalpa Tree and the Bastard Baltimore. *Catesby,* Natural History, *I, pl. 49. Courtesy, Colonial Williamsburg Foundation*

its place at the rear of Cobbett's fictional shrubbery.[53] That place of honor was also accorded to a species of extraordinary beauty. Mark Catesby's plate 49, while underplaying the opulence of the flowers, captures something of the tropical feel of the *Catalpa*—gigantic leaves and huge pods, set off by the yellow plumage of the male and female "Bastard Baltimore." His description elaborated on that image:

53. Ibid., I, 49; Mawe and Abercrombie, *Universal Gardener;* Harvey, "A Scottish Botanist," *Garden History,* IX (1981), 61. It has been recorded up to eighteen meters, or sixty feet.

The Bark smooth; The Wood soft and spongy; the Leaves shaped like those of the *Lilax,* but much larger, some being ten Inches over. In May it produces spreading Bunches of tubulous Flowers, like the common Fox-glove, white, only variegated with a few redish purple Spots and yellow Streaks on the Inside. The *Calix* is of a Copper-Colour. These Flowers are succeeded by round Pods, about the thickness of one Finger, fourteen Inches in Length; which, when ripe, opens and displays its Seeds, which are winged, and lie over each other like the Scales of Fish. This Tree was unknown to the inhabited Parts of *Carolina* till I brought the Seeds from the remoter Parts of the Country. And tho' the Inhabitants are little curious in Gard'ning, yet the uncommon Beauty of the Tree has induc'd them to propogate it; and 'tis become an Ornament to many of their Gardens, and probably will be the Same to ours in *England,* it being as hardy as most of our American Plants; many of them now at Mr. *Christopher Grays,* at *Fulham,* having stood ou[r] several Winters, and produced plentifully their beautiful Flowers, without any Protection, except the first Year.[54]

Catesby's words proved auspicious. The tree with the tropical appearance turned out to be much hardier than the *Callicarpa,* the dahoon holly, or the *Stuartia.* However, after its initial introduction in 1726, it took a few years to spread across the country. In the Society of Gardeners' *Catalogus Plantarum* of 1730 it was described as "at present very little known in England." And in *The Gardeners Dictionary* of 1733, Philip Miller wrote that it had been "brought from the Bahama Islands by Mr. Catesby a few Years since." He continued, "It hath not, as yet, produc'd any Flowers in England, but is very hardy, and grows to be a handsome upright Tree." Nevertheless, by the 1752 edition (still, as in 1733, under the name "Bignonia"), Miller commented, "Now it is propagated pretty commonly in the Nurseries near London, and sold as a flowering Tree to adorn Pleasure-gardens." And in the 1768 edition: "It is now very plenty in the English gardens, especially near London, where there are some of them near twenty feet high, with large stems, and have the appearance of trees."[55]

The moment when it first bloomed in England must have been a festive occasion. Indeed, Catesby recorded in his *Hortus Britanno-Americanus* of 1763 that the *Catalpa* "did in August 1748 produce, at Mr. GRAY's, such

---

54. Catesby, *Natural History,* I, 49.
55. *Catalogus Plantarum;* Miller, *Gardeners Dictionary* (1733), (1752), (1768), s.v. "Bignonia."

51. Catalpa etc. *Catesby*, Hortus Britanno-Americanus, *figs. 47, 48, 49, 50. Courtesy, Colonial Williamsburg Foundation*

numbers of blossoms, that the leaves were almost hid thereby," adding, "It delights in a rich moist soil, not exposed to winds." At Chelsea Physic Garden it was growing in both the "shrubbery" and the "wood" in 1772, and its presence is documented in gardens from Painshill to Ravensworth House, Fulham Road. It entered the nursery trade in the 1730s, and in the following decades nurserymen were busy delivering it to gardens in the north as well as the south. In 1755 John Williamson, for example, sent three plants to Petworth, where Capability Brown was busy planting up the outskirts of the wilderness for the earl of Egremont. He charged a total of 4s. 6d., or 1s. 6d. a plant (Figure 51). In 1759 Richard Woods was able to command 2s. per plant for two *Catalpas* supplied to Sir William Lee at Hartwell, yet in the same year Christopher Gray had brought his prices down to 1s. for the single specimen ordered by William Constable for his curious collection at Burton Constable in East Yorkshire. The price of 2s. was still obtained by Samuel Driver from James Leigh of Adlestrop in 1762. In John and George Telford's York catalog of 1775, and in William and John Perfect's catalog, published in Pontefract in 1777, 2s. was the going rate. Clearly the relatively high price did not reduce its appeal to the consumer. In 1751 John Proudfoot procured a plant from London for the garden of Norborne Berkeley at Stoke Gifford near Bristol. John Williamson supplied a *Catalpa* to the Earl Temple at Stowe on January 18, 1755, and, at Cannon Hall in Yorkshire, there were four trees in the early 1760s.[56]

The *Catalpa* is not especially long-lived, and there is no specimen that survives from the eighteenth century.[57] However, its prodigious success in English soil has guaranteed it a place beyond the pleasure grounds of the landscape park—in many suburban gardens and provincial parks up and down the country. Each season, along the streets of London and by the Houses of Parliament, it comes late into leaf and flower. Around July,

---

56. Catesby, *Hortus Britanno-Americanus,* 25; Symes, "Charles Hamilton's Plantings at Painshill," *Garden History,* XI (1983); Harvey, "A Scottish Botanist," *Garden History,* IX (1981), 67; Petworth House Archives, 6623; Harvey, *Early Nurserymen,* 204–206; Hall, "The Plant Collections," *Garden History,* XIV (1986), 29; Shakespeare B.P.T.R.O., DR 18/8/7/5; Harvey, *Early Gardening Catalogues,* 92, 110; Gloucestershire R.O., QP4/5/1; Huntington Collection; Sheffield Central Library, City Archive, Sp. St. 60673/6.

57. Alan F. Mitchell, *A Field Guide to the Trees of Britain and Northern Europe* (London, 1974), 386–387: "Large trees only where hot summers can occur, notably in London, Bath and Cambridge areas. 18 × 3.4 m. . . . Rapid but short-lived. . . . Decay and breakage set in when the girth exceeds about 3m which may take less than 100 years."

when most of the blossom trees are over, the *Catalpas* are covered in a mass of frothy white blooms as magnificent as the inflorescences of the horse chestnut in late April. By November the huge leaves have already dropped, and in December and January the silhouette of the *Catalpa*—twisting branches and dangling pods—stands out black against the grey sky. Thus each time cabinet ministers are driven from the Commons to 10 Downing Street, they take stock (whether they realize it or not) of the superb "Indian Bean Trees" that beautify the metropolis. They pay tribute thereby to the work of Mark Catesby in the early import trade.

The Final Reckoning

During the eighteenth century, the introduction of North American plants to English gardens was beset with difficulties. Back in 1728 Collinson had already observed: "Hitherto the laudable design of improving and cultivating exotic trees in this country meets with a number of discouragements too tedious to enumerate except one, which I think is hereditary to America, this is—great promise but slender performance."[58] In one sense, this remark was still valid fifty years later when Catesby's plants—so carefully observed in American habitats and so temptingly illustrated in *The Natural History*—had been tried out in English soil. The *Callicarpa americana* and *Ilex cassine* were outright failures in the open. The *Amorpha fruticosa, Robinia hispida,* and *Calycanthus floridus* were best suited to mild, sheltered locations (and are rarely used today), and the *Ceanothus americanus, Cornus florida,* and *Wisteria frutescens* were quickly forgotten as superior species came in from the Orient or from western North America. In the course of the nineteenth century, for example, *Cornus nuttallii* Audub. arrived from the American West Coast, and *Cornus kousa* Hance. was introduced from Japan, transforming the appearance of English gardens. Of course, the *Kalmia latifolia* and *Stuartia malacodendron* that Catesby had helped promote were both notable success stories, yet even these were not widely grown because of their high price or limited availability. Only the *Catalpa bignonioides* was an immediate and lasting triumph.

During the 1770s a debate was conducted among horticultural theorists on the dangers of "excessive variety"—an embarrassment of riches that had resulted from the influx of exotics. For William Chambers this

58. Quoted from Gorer, *The Growth of Gardens,* 51.

had various repercussions: first, there was the confusion that ensued from too much diversity; and, second, there was the sickly appearance of many North American shrubs and trees. He dressed up his criticism in the voice of an outside observer, the Chinese artist:

> We are sensible . . . that no plant is possessed of all good qualities; but choose such as have the fewest faults; and avoid all the exotics, that vegetate with difficulty in our climate; for though they may be rare, they cannot be beautiful, being always in a sickly state: have, if you please, hot-houses and cool-houses, for plants of every region, to satisfy the curiosity of botanists; but they are mere infirmaries: the plants which they contain, are valetudinarians, divested of beauty and vigor; which only exist by the power of medicine, and by dint of good nursing.[59]

Thus, paradoxically, the "curious" exotic, which had generated the need for the "shrubbery," was gradually perceived by some as a liability, often failing in "beauty and vigor." The temptation to cram the shrubbery full of the exotics that Catesby had so lovingly illustrated also received the censure of Chambers's Chinese critic:

> The excessive variety of which some European Gardeners are so fond in their plantations, the Chinese artist blames, observing, that a great diversity of colours, foliage, and direction of branches, must create confusion, and destroy all the masses upon which effect and grandeur depend; they observe too, that it is unnatural; for, as in Nature most plants sow their own seed, whole forests are generally composed of the same sorts of trees. They admit, however, of moderate variety; but are by no means promiscuous in the choice of their plants; attending, with great care, to the colour, form, and foliage of each; and only mixing together such as harmonize and assemble agreeably.[60]

The shrubbery that James Meader illustrated in *The Planter's Guide* of 1779—a graduated arrangement of alternated specimens—was precisely what Chambers had in mind in denouncing the "unnatural" plantation. And when Richard Payne Knight attacked the fashion for "prim shrub-beries" in his poem *The Landscape* (1794), it was directed at the same "motley" collection of exotics:

---

59. William Chambers, *A Dissertation on Oriental Gardening* (London, 1772), 79–80.
60. Ibid., 80.

So the capricious planter often tries
By quaint variety to cause surpise:
Collects of various trees a motley host,
Natives of every clime and every coast;
Which, placed in chequer'd squares, alternate grow,
And forms and colours unconnected show:
Here blue Scotch firs with yellow plane trees join,
There meagre larches rise, and fringe the line;
While scatter'd oaks and beeches sculk unseen,
Nor dare expose their chaste and modest green.[61]

Chambers's critique was later used to support a new planting method that developed in the early nineteenth century. It was the system that Loudon called the "Select or Grouped Manner"—a way of massing shrubs in large irregular drifts.[62] Although still graduated, the "grouped" shrubbery produced a more ragged profile than the "mingled or mixed" system that Meader had illustrated. "Grouping" or "massing" was employed by John Nash in the 1820s and 1830s, when he planted up the shrubberies of the Royal Pavilion grounds in Brighton and Saint James's Park in London. The extensive lists of plants ordered for Brighton between 1817 and 1820 show how the new shrubs of the Orient—the *Aucuba japonica* Thunb. or the *Ligustrum lucidum* Ait.—were beginning to change the composition of the shrubbery. Of Catesby's plants, only the rose acacia (*Robinia hispida*) was still represented.

Thus, it could be argued that Mark Catesby's enduring legacy lies more in the perennial beauty of the plates of *The Natural History,* in that ubiquitous tree—the *Catalpa bignonioides*—and in the plant that carries his name, *Catesbaea spinosa* L., or the lily thorn of the Bahamas.[63] Even in the case of the *Catalpa,* it should be stressed that its true calling came as an individual specimen on lawns and along streets, away from the social hierarchy of the shrubbery. Yet, for all this, the trial and error of eighteenth-century plant-

61. Richard Payne Knight, *The Landscape: A Didactic Poem,* 2d ed. (London, 1795), 72, book 3, ll. 47–56.

62. John Claudius Loudon, *An Encylopaedia of Gardening* (London, 1822), 914. This new system of grouping or massing is discussed in some detail in Laird, "Ornamental Planting," in Hunt, ed., *Garden History: Issues, Approaches, Methods,* 268–271.

63. P.R.O., LSII/1/XC000480. The lily thorn is one of sixteen species in the genus *Catesbaea.*

ing, in which Catesby's plants played such a significant role, proved the testing ground for many subsequent developments in horticulture, planting design, and landscape theory.[64] In this respect, the landscape architect of today owes Mark Catesby and his "curious" friends a lasting debt of gratitude.

64. See Laird, "Ornamental Planting," in Hunt, ed., *Garden History: Issues, Approaches, Methods.*

Amy R. W. Meyers

PICTURING A WORLD IN FLUX: MARK CATESBY'S RESPONSE TO ENVIRONMENTAL INTERCHANGE AND COLONIAL EXPANSION

Mark Catesby's *Natural History of Carolina, Florida, and the Bahama Islands* has come to be recognized as the earliest and most important examination of environmental relationships in Britain's colonial possessions in the Americas during the first half of the eighteenth century. Discussions of Catesby's interest in the interplay between flora and fauna have been largely confined, however, to the naturalist's published etchings and the drawings upon which they were based, with little regard for the text of *The Natural History*—indeed, Catesby himself argued for the primacy of visual representation over verbal description in conveying empirical observations of the natural world.[1] Yet, an examination of the naturalist's prints

This essay marks a point of departure in my interpretation of Catesby's work—one that has resulted, in large part, from disucssions with David Brigham and Leo Mazow as well as from conversations with Chandos Brown, Robert C. Ritchie, Karen Kupperman, Shelley Bennett, Therese O'Malley, Laura Rigal, Margaret Pritchard, Christopher Brown, Jennifer Tucker, Kay Dian Kriz, and Michael Braddick. I am particularly indebted to Fredrika Teute, Carla Pestana, and Ian D'Aoust for their close readings of this manuscript and for their excellent suggestions for emendations. In addition, I am grateful to Edward Nygren, Director of the Art Division at The Huntington, for so generously allowing me time away from the office to rethink my stance toward Catesby. I would also like to thank my husband, Jack, for his patient and good-humored critique of this essay, and my daughter, Rachel, for a laugh the wry Mr. Catesby would have loved as much as I.

1. On Cateby's reputation, see George Frederick Frick and Raymond Phineas Stearns, *Mark Catesby: The Colonial Audubon* (Urbana, Ill., 1961), 60, 65, 73, 78; David Scofield Wilson, *In the Presence of Nature* (Amherst, Mass., 1978), 123–124; Raymond Phineas Stearns, *Science in the British Colonies of America* (Urbana, Ill., 1970), 321; Amy R. Weinstein Meyers, "Sketches from the Wilderness: Changing Conceptions of Nature in American Natural History Illustration, 1680–1880" (Ph.D. diss., Yale University, 1985), 46–47, 59; William H. Goetz-

and drawings in relation to his words—from his entries in *The Natural History* to his correspondence and other writings—discloses a much broader set of concerns regarding environmental relationships than his pictures alone reveal. One sees that Catesby was interested not only in characterizing the associations between species that he interpreted as native to American soil; he wished also to describe organic relationships recently introduced to the colonies through European settlement and global trade. He saw the integration of new animals and plants into the fabric of the natural world, as it existed in the Americas, as continual, promising to yield rich possibilities for human use—from agriculture and forestry to animal husbandry and ornamental gardens. He was also aware, however, of the problems that might result from this restructuring of organic relationships, and he occasionally expressed concern over the price that those who were responsible might have to pay.

Catesby's interest in shifting patterns of interchange extended beyond animals and plants to human beings. Reflections on the ways in which English colonists, enslaved peoples of African descent, and native Americans were coming together—by choice or by coercion—to forge a new social order occur only as brief passages in his texts and as subtle allusions in his images. Yet, when considered collectively, these suggestive intimations disclose Catesby's sophisticated understanding of the benefits and the costs that might accrue from this cultural amalgamation.

The full spectrum of Catesby's responses to the rapidly shifting environmental associations that he observed in the Americas can be discerned only through a detailed examination of his approach to the visual and verbal portrayal of organic interplay. Through close readings of Cates-

---

mann, *New Lands, New Men: America and the Second Great Age of Discovery* (New York, 1986), 84–90; Amy R. W. Meyers, "Imposing Order on the Wilderness: Natural History Illustration and Landscape Portrayal," in Edward J. Nygren, *Views and Visions: American Landscape before 1830* (Washington, D.C., 1986), 121; Thomas J. Lyon, ed., *This Incomperable Lande: A Book of American Nature Writing* (Boston, 1989), 31; Meyers, " 'The Perfecting of Natural History': Mark Catesby's Drawings of American Flora and Fauna in the Collection of the Royal Library, Windsor Castle," in Henrietta McBurney, *Mark Catesby's "Natural History" of America: The Watercolors from the Royal Library, Windsor Castle* (London, 1997), 20–23.

On Catesby's priorities: Mark Catesby, Preface, *The Natural History of Carolina, Florida, and the Bahama Islands . . .* (London, 1731–1743), I, xi–xii; Catesby, *Natural History,* II, Appendix (1747), 20; Catesby, "Proposals, for Printing an Essay towards a Natural History of Florida, Carolina, and the Bahama Islands . . ." (London, ca. 1729), n.p. See also Meyers, " 'The Perfecting of Natural History,' " in McBurney, *Mark Catesby's "Natural History" of America,* 13; Meyers, "Sketches from the Wilderness," 61–68.

by's images and texts, we can trace the critical steps by which he arrived at his methods of depiction and describe the larger picture of a world in flux that he was able to convey thereby.

Constructing a Visual Language to Depict Environmental Interchange

Sometime in the mid-1730s, while working on the plates that would constitute the eighth part of *The Natural History,* Catesby composed an etching of a snake he called "The Brown Viper" and a plant he identified as *"Arum maximum Aegyptiacum"* (Figure 52). As plate 45 of the second volume of his publication, this print exemplifies with particular clarity the compositional approach devised by Catesby to portray the characteristic relationships that link animals and plants from the same environment.[2] Thrusting up from a small island of matted vegetation so that the entirety of its form can be discerned against the blank page, the viper loops over itself as it moves to strike a newt escaping into the water below. The coiling form of the snake is echoed both in the bend of the newt's body to the left and in the shape of the large leaf that curls into the scene from the right. The mirrored curves of these organisms appear again in the twisting form of the flower (or, more properly, efflorescence) that presses into the scene from the left. The blossom's arched opening corresponds to a bulge in the snake's body, above and to the right, which seems to contain a recently ingested animal, and the flower's long, protruding spadix resembles in color and roughly in form the snake's flicking tongue. Tightly compressed within the rectangular outline of the plate mark, these carefully arranged compositional associations describe a set of physical and behavioral relationships that seem to bind these organisms to one another within a shared habitat.

Indeed, the text that accompanies the print amplifies these relationships, stressing the fact that Catesby had actually observed these organisms interacting in the wild, and paralleling the poisonous bite of the snake with the "acrimonious" taste of the plant.[3] The basic associations are first made evident, however, through the etching itself, which immediately establishes, through a visual language of reflected form, the naturalist's

2. For a discussion of Catesby's interest in the portrayal of environmental relationships and his development of a visual language to depict organic interplay, see Meyers, " 'The Perfecting of Natural History,' " in McBurney, *Mark Catesby's "Natural History" of America,* 20–23; Meyers, "Sketches from the Wilderness," 75–89, 110–112.

3. Catesby, *Natural History,* II, 45.

52. Brown Viper and Arum. *Mark Catesby,* The Natural History of Carolina, Florida, and the
Bahama Islands . . . *(London, 1731–1747), II, pl. 45. Courtesy, Colonial Williamsburg Foundation*

essential argument about the way in which the snake, the plant, and the newt interrelate environmentally.

Catesby's employment of this visual language of association to suggest environmental relationships in this plate (as well as in many others throughout *The Natural History*) stemmed at least in part from his work as an experimental horticulturist with an unusual amount of field experience. Catesby claimed that over the course of his first venture, in Virginia from 1712 to 1719, he transplanted hundreds of trees from the frontier regions of the colony to the gardens of wealthy Virginia planters, such as William Byrd II and John Custis IV.[4] He also sent seeds home to his mentor and colleague, Samuel Dale, and to the nurseryman Thomas Fairchild for cultivation in English gardens. Since his second venture, to Carolina from 1722 to 1726, was endorsed by the Royal Society and sponsored by a group of professional naturalists and gentlemen collectors as well as by the new governor of Carolina, Francis Nicholson, Catesby experimented even more intensively and systematically with the establishment of plants from the frontier in both English and American gardens.[5] Deeply con-

---

4. Catesby described his attempt to transplant trees from uninhabited regions of Virginia and Carolina into colonial gardens in a letter to the Oxford botanist John James (Johann Jakob) Dillenius (see Catesby to Dillenius, n.d., Sherard MSS, CCII, fol. 17, Dillenius Correspondence, Department of Plant Sciences Library, Oxford University). Catesby also discussed his experiments in moving plants from the Virginia frontier in several entries in *The Natural History* (see, for example, I, 27, 29, 39). For general discussions of Catesby's work as an experimental horticulturist in the Americas, see Frick and Stearns, *Mark Catesby*, 12, 91; Stearns, *Science in the British Colonies of America*, 287; Peter Martin, *The Pleasure Gardens of Virginia: From Jamestown to Jefferson* (Princeton, N.J., 1991), 54, 66, 178, 202; Margaret Beck Pritchard and Virginia Lascara Sites, *William Byrd II and His Lost History: Engravings of the Americas* (Williamsburg, Va., 1993), 106; and Therese O'Malley, "Mark Catesby and the Culture of Gardens," above.

5. On Catesby's services as a provider of Virginia seeds and plants for Dale during his expedition to the colony, see Catesby, *Natural History*, I, v; Frick and Stearns, *Mark Catesby*, 14, 15. On like services for Fairchild, see Frick and Stearns, *Mark Catesby*, 10; Stearns, *Science in the British Colonies of America*, 287.

For discussions of Catesby's transplantations from the Carolina frontier into gardens in and around Charleston, see Catesby, *Natural History*, I, 39, 49; Frick and Stearns, *Mark Catesby*, 31–32; O'Malley, "Mark Catesby and the Culture of Gardens," above. For similar discussions of his experiments with the introduction of Carolina plants into English gardens, see Catesby, *Natural History*, I, ix, 49, 53, 55, 56, 66, II, 59, 65, 78, 98, 100, and Appendix, 2, 4, 13, 15; Frick and Stearns, *Mark Catesby*, 23, 25–29, 31, 65–69, 90–94; Stearns, *Science in the British Colonies of America*, 316–317, 319, 323; Blanche Henrey, *No Ordinary Gardener:*

cerned about the success of these transplantations, Catesby closely examined the original environments in which he found the plants he sought to
collect, making careful notes on the animals that frequented them for
food and shelter. He also drew the subjects of his investigations, both for
himself and for his patrons, eventually combining depictions of individual
animals and plants into complex studies of organic interaction.[6]

Precisely when Catesby began to produce these more highly developed
portrayals of organic interchange cannot be determined with accuracy.
Since few visual prototypes existed for the creation of such images, he
began to formulate a new set of conventions almost entirely on his own—
a process of aesthetic and intellectual development that spanned the
whole of his career.[7] By the time he had begun to compose the first plates
for his *Natural History,* however, it is clear that he had fully committed

---

Thomas Knowlton, 1691–1781, ed. A. O. Chater (London, 1986), 26, 119, 167; Mark Laird,
"From Callicarpa to Catalpa: The Impact of Mark Catesby's Plant Introductions on English
Gardens of the Eighteenth Century," above; O'Malley, "Mark Catesby and the Culture of
Gardens," above.

6. Although Catesby's field notes have been lost, related descriptions of flora and fauna in
his letters to colleagues, *The Natural History,* and notations accompanying dried specimens
indicate that he must have kept a master set of written observations to which he repeatedly
referred as he wrote his various texts. It is clear that these notes often concerned the
interrelationships among species that he had observed in the field or described the physical
environments in which he had encountered the animals and plants that were the subjects of
his inquiry. For example, sections of the text of pl. 20 of the Appendix (which illustrates the
relationship between *"Bison Americanus"* and *"Pseudo Acacia"*) correspond to parts of Catesby's description of the animal and plant in "An Account of Carolina, and the Bahama
Islands." Certain portions of the text accompanying pl. 20 also relate to Catesby's captions
for the dried specimens of *"Pseudo Acacia"* that he sent to William Sherard and John James
Dillenius from Carolina. These correspondences suggest that Catesby used the same set of
notes as the basis for all of these texts. For the specimen captions, see nos. 1492, 1514, 1516,
Sherardian Herbarium, Department of Plant Sciences, Oxford University.

On Catesby's practice of combining individual studies of flora and fauna to formulate
more complex images of environmental interchange, see Meyers, " 'The Perfecting of Natural History,' " in McBurney, *Mark Catesby's "Natural History" of America,* 20–23. In the same
catalog, see also McBurney, "The Windsor Volumes," 29; section 3, "Crabs, Turtles, and
Corals," 89; section 4, "Snakes, Lizards, and Frogs," 99; section 6, "Insects," 125; catalog
entries 3, 7, 9, 10, 12, 13, 16, 17, 25, 27, 29, 30–40, 44, 45, 50, 52.

7. For discussions of how Catesby began to develop these conventions and the associa-
tions of his work with that of other naturalist artists, see Meyers, "Sketches from the
Wilderness," 46–48, 59, 65–89, 108–112; Meyers, " 'The Perfecting of Natural History,' " in
McBurney, *Mark Catesby's "Natural History" of America,* 20–26.

himself to the depiction of the ways in which he believed flora and fauna to be associated in their natural habitats and that he had determined his basic compositional approach to the creation of such pictures.

The complex steps by which Catesby arrived at a visual system to express environmental relationships can be seen, at least in part, through a comparison of his published etchings with an extensive set of preparatory drawings now owned by the Royal Library, at Windsor Castle. Contrasting the opening plate of his first volume with the drawing on which he based it demonstrates, for example, that Catesby occasionally experimented with the notion of contextualizing organic relationships in larger landscape settings, but that he ultimately rejected the idea when he began to etch his published prints in the late 1720s.[8] As its central subject, the preparatory drawing (Figure 53) depicts a "Bald Eagle" soaring down to retrieve a fish that has fallen from the grasp of another bird of prey (a bird identified later in *The Natural History* as a "Fishing Hawk").[9] The action takes place above a wide, rushing river, strewn with boulders and overhung with pines—an environment closely resembling the one described in the text for plate 1 as the eagle's characteristic breeding place. The dramatic contest between the birds is portrayed as specific not only to a particular location but also to a particular time, marked by the moment when the single occupant of a lone canoe turns back to observe the interchange. This specificity of time and place is sacrificed, however, in Catesby's translation of the image into his print (Figure 54). In the etching, the landscape, along with most of the narrative elements of the scene, is lost in order to highlight the eagle's physical attributes. This simplification of the image also focuses attention directly on the raptor's relationship with the fish as

8. For an extensive set of detailed comparisons, see McBurney, *Mark Catesby's "Natural History" of America*, catalog entries 1–52. On Catesby's experimentation with landscape settings, see catalog entries 1, 6.

9. The "Fishing Hawk" is the subject of pl. 2 of vol. I of *Natural History*. In the text accompanying this etching, Catesby describes the characteristic relationship between the hawk and the bald eagle portrayed in his drawing for pl. 1:

> Their manner of fishing is (after hovering a while over the water) to precipitate into it with a prodigious swiftness; where it remains for some minutes, and seldom rises without a fish: which the Bald Eagle (which is generally on the watch) no sooner spies, but at him furiously he flies: the Hawk mounts, screaming out, but the Eagle always soares above him, and compels the Hawk to let it fall; which the eagle seldom fails of catching, before it reaches the water. It is remarkable, that whenever the Hawk catches a Fish, he calls, as it were, for the Eagle; who always obeys the call, if within hearing.

its prey rather than with the fishing hawk, who now seems to watch the scene below as a distanced party.[10]

Catesby's decision to reduce the image from a fully developed narrative within a landscape to a more schematic portrayal of the way in which several organisms from the same habitat interact reflects the condensed approach he would take in composing the majority of his final studies for *The Natural History* and the plates based upon them. At an early stage in the preparation of his etchings, Catesby began to refine his basic technique for accentuating these environmental relationships by mirroring the form of one organism in the form of another. This mirroring of form served essentially as a shorthand for depicting organic interactions, freeing Catesby from the time-consuming task of writing a full narrative for every plate in his extensive publication. In composing his drawing of "The Blew Jay" and "The Bay-leaved *Smilax*" for plate 15 of volume I, for example, he probably combined separate field studies of the bird and plant (now lost) into the single, finished composition (Figures 55, 56)—a method he would employ to create many of the final studies for his etchings.[11] To meld the two images, he paralleled the sharply bent body of the screaming jay with the *L*-shaped form of the branch on which the bird stands. He also mirrored the shape and position of the jay's wing in the form and placement of the plant's lowest leaf on the right. The smilax and the jay pierce the empty space of the sheet on which they are drawn in unison: the shrill cry of the bird, implied by his sharp, widely opened beak and taut, outstretched tongue, seems to electrify the plant's tendrils, which twine actively into space.

Through the text that accompanies this image in *The Natural History*, Catesby augmented the parallels that he wished to draw between the bird and the plant. The penetrating cry of the jay, as conveyed by the picture, is reflected in the physical spread of the plant as described in the text:

> This Plant . . . sends forth from its root many green Stems, whose Branches overspread whatsoever stands near it, to a very considerable distance; and it frequently climbs above sixteen foot in height, growing

10. In his etching, Catesby included a schematic profile of the bird's head in place of the landscape to show a second aspect of the bird's physical appearance. Such a diagrammatic image could not have been integrated into the original drawing, which was more narrative in its emphasis.

11. See note 6, above.

53. Drawing of Bald Eagle. *Catesby, for* The Natural History, *I, pl. 1. RL.24828, The Royal Collection © Her Majesty Queen Elizabeth II*

54. Bald Eagle. *Catesby, Natural History, I, pl. 1. Courtesy, Colonial Williamsburg Foundation*

55. Drawing of Blew Jay and Smilax. *Catesby, for* The Natural History, *I, pl. 15. RL24828, The Royal Collection © Her Majesty Queen Elizabeth II*

so very thick, that in Summer it makes an impenetrable Shade, and in Winter a warm Shelter for Cattle.

Assuming an identity of image with verbal narration and description, Catesby analogizes the jay and smilax on the grounds of shared characteristics: the bird and plant overspread their environment in both sound and form. He also notes that they are linked through the food chain, since the smilax produces a berry that serves "particularly" to nourish the bird.[12] Analogous form thus argues for and narrates environmental interdependence.

Changing Patterns of Organic Interaction

Intimate organic interconnections such as those illustrated by Catesby's "Blew Jay" and *"Smilax"* are explicated through a comparison of his preparatory drawings with his prints and accompanying texts for many of

12. Catesby, *Natural History,* I, 15.

Smilax lævis lauri folio non serrat. baccis nigris.

Pica cristata cærulea.
The crested Jay.

56. Blew Jay and Smilax. *Catesby,* Natural History, *I, pl. 15. Courtesy, Colonial Williamsburg Foundation*

the entries throughout *The Natural History*—from those in volume I, associating birds and plants, to those in volume II, relating fishes, crustaceans, reptiles, amphibians, and mammals to a broad range of organisms from the same habitats.[13] In certain entries, however, Catesby's pictures and words focus not only on animals and plants the naturalist considered native to the southern colonies or to the Caribbean but on organisms introduced to the Americas through European settlement and trade. Catesby's interest in the ways in which newly introduced organisms from around the globe were changing existing patterns of organic interaction is reflected, for example, in his plate of the "Brown Viper" and *"Arum maximum Aegyptiacum"* (Figure 52). As we have seen, the image relies upon Catesby's language of reflected form to unite a small group of animals and plants interacting in a shared habitat. And, yet, the dramatic way in which the arum leaf and blossom press into the image from outside the bounds of the plate mark subtly counters the coherence of the scene. While partially enmeshed in the world of the newt and the viper, the plant remains rooted in another realm.

Catesby amplifies the alien nature of the arum in his text, explaining that it is a "Tropick Plant, not caring to encrease much in *Carolina,* and will grow no where North of that Colony." He goes on to state that only the extraordinary efforts of the "Negro's," who relish the arum as a food, cause the plant to multiply in an environment so unconducive to its natural propagation. Whether the kind of arum depicted by Catesby was actually native to the region explored by the naturalist is difficult to determine, since modern scholars have not been able to identify the plant with certainty. Catesby, however, clearly considered the plant to be somewhat out of place, associating it with the many kinds of arum found in warmer climates (including Africa, the Caribbean, and the Middle East) and referring his reader to a description of them published by his mentor, Sir Hans Sloane, in the first volume of his *Voyage to the Islands Madera, Barbados, Nieves, S. Christophers, and Jamaica* (1707).[14]

13. See notes 2, 6, 7, above.

14. Catesby, *The Natural History,* II, 45; Hans Sloane, *A Voyage to the Islands Madera, Barbados, Nieves, S. Christophers, and Jamaica* ... (London, 1707–1725), I, 166–167. Richard A. Howard and George W. Staples note that the plant illustrated might be *Alocacia* or *Xanthosoma;* see "The Modern Names for Catesby's Plants," *Journal of the Arnold Arboretum,* LXIV (1983), 514. The plant is identified as *Colocasia esculenta* (L.) Schott, in McBurney, *Mark Catesby's "Natural History" of America,* catalog entry 27.

Indeed, Catesby used the arum in his etching as the point of departure from which to discuss the recent introduction of a truly foreign type of arum to Carolina—a plant from Africa that was far more palatable than the one portrayed:

> A little before I left *Carolina,* there was introduced a new Kind, wholly without that bad Quality, and requiring no more than common Time to boil them, and may be eat raw, without offending the Throat or Palate; this was a welcome Improvement among the Negro's, and was esteemed a Blessing; they being delighted with all their *African* Food, particularly this, which a great part of *Africa* subsists much on.[15]

Observations of this kind, reflecting Catesby's interest in the introduction of new species of flora and fauna to the Americas through the recent establishment of human populations from Europe and Africa, appear throughout the naturalist's publications and his correspondence. And in certain cases, these observations extend to the impact of such introductions on established patterns of interaction among native species as well as on human patterns of consumption.[16]

15. Catesby, *Natural History,* II, 45.

16. Although Catesby's discussions of plant and animal introductions to the Americas are too numerous to list in full, important examples pertaining particularly to plants should be mentioned. In his "Account of Carolina," Catesby notes that "Bunched Guinea Corn" and "Spiked Indian Corn" had been transported to the New World by enslaved Africans, who continued to cultivate the crops in their own gardens (*Natural History,* II, xviii). In his letters to his patron, William Sherard, Catesby also made mention of experiments by Carolina planters to introduce coffee trees from Surinam (Catesby to Sherard, June 20, 1722, Sherard Letters, CCLIII, 164, Royal Society) and indigo (Nov. 13, 1723, 170). He himself speculated on the success of various crops, including ginger (June 20, 1722, 64), opium, rhubarb, wormseed (Aug. 16, 1724, 178), scammony and coloquintida (Nov. 26, 1724, 182). And in letters to various patrons, he requested, on behalf of his Carolina friends, plants common to European gardens, and then reported on the success of these introductions (June 20, 1722, 164, Apr. 6, 1724, 176; Catesby to Peter Collinson, from Alexander Skene's, Jan. 5, 1722/3, Botany Library, Autograph Collection, Natural History Museum, London).

Among his many discussions of interactions, Catesby noted that, over a twenty-year period, cattle and hogs introduced from Europe had probably caused the disappearance of many American flowering bulbs that might have been transplanted into colonial gardens, since these animals rooted them up for food (Catesby to Sherard, Jan. 16, 1723/4, Sherard Letters, CCLIII, 174). He pursued a similar argument concerning "The Laurel-tree of Carolina," remarking that cattle and hogs were so fond of the seedlings that the plant had "become almost extinct in many parts of the Country, where they abounded before the

That Catesby interpreted the organic relationships he observed as undergoing dramatic reformulation brought on by the movement of peoples around the globe is expressed metaphorically in a note to the text on the brown viper and arum. The scene Catesby intended his print to portray resulted from "a great Inundation" that "dislodged" a large variety of animals from their characteristic "Holes, etc.," casting them together in new relationships on "Heaps of Vegetable Refuse." Although the passage characterizes the resulting interactions as confusing, and even somewhat disturbing, with "the voracious and larger Serpents . . . continually preying upon the smaller, as well those of their own Kind," Catesby did not usually interpret the interaction of species introduced through the relocation of human populations in such a negative light.[17] He was, however, keenly aware that these importations were stimulating complex patterns of interaction, which, in some cases, might not prove entirely beneficial to the European settlers who had introduced the foreign species in the first place.

An Increasingly Intricate Matrix of Associations

In issuing the first part of his *Natural History* in 1729, Catesby immediately articulated his awareness of the complex and sometimes problematic patterns of interchange that might arise as the consequence of foreign introductions. His fourteenth entry, "Rice-Bird," consists of an image and a text that are both structured to convey the intimate relationship observed by the naturalist between the bird and the plant from which it received its name. In the plate, which closely replicates the preparatory drawing from the Windsor set, the female of the species is shown perched on an arching stem of rice with a seed in her mouth (Figures 57, 58). She

Introduction of cattle" (see Mark Catesby, *Hortus Britanno-Americanus . . .* [London, 1763], 1). Catesby also reported that the harvesting of brasiletto trees for the production of a valuable dye had caused a "Scarcity of it on the *Bahama* Islands" (*Natural History,* II, 51).

17. Catesby, *Natural History,* II, 45. In the image and text that constitute this entry, Catesby's allusions to the biblical flood and to the serpent of the Garden of Eden are amplified by his overtly sexual portrayal of the arum's efflorescence. The naturalist's interest in equating a biblical sense of human evil with the coming together of species that do not characteristically interact in the same environment might have derived from the discomfort that he felt with greed as the primary factor motivating people to transport natural productions from one part of the globe to another (for further discussion, see below). By extension, Catesby might also have meant to imply, through his image and his text, that the Americas were once a natural paradise that had been tainted by the human mixing of animals and plants (and, perhaps, peoples) that were not naturally intended to share the same habitat.

stretches forward to the right, following the elegant bend in the plant and reflecting its warm, gold color. The cock, who is labeled as such, stands directly below her, pecking for grains that have fallen to the ground. Corresponding with equal grace to the form of the plant, he is protectively contained within the arch of the stem and is held firmly in place on the little piece of turf from which the plant grows by a leaf sweeping elegantly down before his mate.

The textual entry does not describe the relationship between the "Rice-Bird" and rice plant as new to Carolina. Yet, as Catesby composed his etching and its accompanying text, he was surely cognizant that this association between the bird and plant had developed in the colony only over the last half-century. After many years spent in Carolina, the naturalist was undoubtedly aware that rice had just recently been brought to the colony through English settlement—as he would relate in "An Account of Carolina and the Bahama Islands," issued with the last part of *The Natural History,* in 1743.[18] In addition, by the time he was preparing the entry to his plate, he was probably already formulating the thesis that migrating birds, such as the "Rice-Bird," were altering their flight patterns to seek out new sources of their favorite foods as these were introduced to different parts of the Americas from distant regions of the globe. In his entry, he recognized specifically that it was rice that was attracting the "Rice-Bird" to Carolina from Cuba:

18. Catesby, *Natural History,* II, "Account," xvii. In his brief discussion of rice in the "Account," Catesby attributed the introduction of the grain to Carolina to the colonial governor Sir Nathaniel Johnson. He noted how, about 1688, Johnson had planted "a small unprofitable Kind" that, in 1696, was augmented by "a much fairer and larger Kind," brought by a ship from Madagascar that had accidentally landed in the colony. Daniel C. Littlefield, however, has argued that Catesby had only limited knowledge of the history and practice of rice cultivation in the colony (see his *Rice and Slaves: Ethnicity and the Slave Trade in Colonial South Carolina* [Baton Rouge, La., 1981], 101–102). Littlefield and other historians contend that the beginning of rice cultivation in Carolina can actually be credited to the agricultural knowledge of enslaved Africans (see, for example, Littlefield, *Rice and Slaves,* esp. 77–86, 98–114; Peter H. Wood, *Black Majority: Negroes in Colonial South Carolina from 1670 through the Stono Rebellion* [New York, 1974], 34–62). Considering Catesby's awareness of the role of enslaved Africans in the transplantation of other crops, such as "Bunched Guinea Corn" and "Spiked Indian Corn" (see note 16, above, and note 27, below), he might actually have recognized that a larger and more detailed narrative concerning the introduction of rice would, in fact, have included the participation of peoples of African descent. Given the importance of the crop to the economy of Carolina, he might have chosen, in his published synopsis, to place the credit solely with the English governor.

57. Rice-Bird (Male and Female). *Catesby,* Natural History, *I, pl. 14. Courtesy, Colonial Williamsburg Foundation*

58. Drawing of Rice-Bird (Male and Female). *Catesby, for* The Natural History, *I, 14.*
RL.24827, The Royal Collection © Her Majesty Queen Elizabeth II

In *September* 1725. lying upon the deck of a Sloop in a Bay at *Andros* Island, I and the Company with me heard, three nights successively, Flights of these Birds (their Note being plainly distinguishable from others) passing over our heads northerly, which is their direct way from *Cuba* to *Carolina;* from which I conceive, after partaking of the earlier crop of Rice at *Cuba,* they travel over sea to *Carolina,* for the same intent, the Rice there being at that time fit for them.[19]

In this early passage, in the first part of *The Natural History,* Catesby did not yet attempt to postulate a broader theory concerning the way in which the transplantation of crops might, in turn, alter the migratory patterns of birds. However, as he reflected on his own empirical observations in the course of producing his publication, he developed precisely this thesis as the conclusion to a paper entitled "Of Birds of Passage," delivered to the Royal Society on March 5, 1746/7:

Since the Discovery of *America* there have been introduced from *Europe* several Sorts of Grain, which were never before known in that Part of the World, and which not before some Length of Time were found out, and coveted by some of these migratory Birds. No wonder this Grain should not be immediately known to Birds of distant Regions; for above half a Century passed from the Time of cultivating Wheat, Rice, and Barley, in *Virginia* and *Carolina,* before those Grains were found out and frequented by these foreign Birds.

According to Catesby, when exotic plants were sown, exotic birds would eventually follow, infinitely enriching—and complicating—the matrix of organic relationships Catesby wished to describe and portray as characteristic of the Americas. He ended his address on migratory birds describing the latest report he had received on the sighting of a new species in Virginia:

One [bird] has but lately made its first Appearance in *Virginia* as my ingenious Friend Dr. Mitchel informs me, that he being in his Garden a Bird flew over his Head which appeared with uncommon Lustre, and surprised him the more, not having seen the like Bird before. Mentioning this to some of his Neighbours, he was told by them, what afterwards was confirmed to him by his own Observation; *viz.* that these

19. Catesby, *Natural History,* I, 14.

exotic Birds had but within these few years appeared in *Virginia,* and had never been observed there before.

They arrive annually at the time that Wheat (the Fields of which they most frequent) is at a certain Degree of Maturity; and have constantly every Year from their first Appearance arrived about the same time in numerous Flights. They have attain'd the Name of *Wheat-Birds*.[20]

The immediacy of this report seems to imply that new sightings of foreign birds such as the "Wheat-Bird" were continual—that the natural world of the Americas was a world in the making. To Catesby, this world was, not one with given limits, but one of endless possibility, brought about by the introduction of new species through European settlement. These species did not come one by one, but in complex associations, offering dynamic new relationships to a world of organic interchange that was, itself, just beginning to be understood.

The Costs and Benefits of New Associations

While Catesby was fully cognizant that European settlement contributed significantly to the flux that characterized the organic relationships he observed, he was also aware that not all facets of these shifting relationships would be advantageous to the settlers who were attempting to establish themselves in the Americas. In the case of the ricebird, for example, Catesby noted that its pursuit of the grain upon which it desired to feed created dire problems for the Carolina planters who had introduced the crop to the colony. Catesby began the text with the following observation:

In the beginning of *September,* while the Grain of Rice is yet soft and milky, innumerable Flights of these Birds arrive from some remote Parts, to the great detriment of the inhabitants. *Anno* 1724. an Inhabitant near *Ashley* river had forty acres of Rice so devoured by them, that he was in doubt, whether what they had left, was worth the expense of gathering in.[21]

20. Mark Catesby, "Of Birds of Passage," Royal Society, *Philosophical Transactions,* XLIV (1747), 443–444.

21. Catesby, *Natural History,* I, 14. As Alan Feduccia points out, the ricebird (reedbird or bobolink) actually migrates from southern Canada to South America annually and does most damage to crops on its return migration. Feduccia notes: "For a long period the

In this passage, Catesby implies that, while the bringing of rice to Carolina had been a controlled choice made by planters who sought economic advantage from its cultivation, the consequences, at times, obviated the benefits. Catesby, however, seems to have been reluctant to push his argument further. He immediately balanced the deleterious effect of the birds' eating habits against the fact that their rapid consumption of rice fattened them considerably, rendering them the "greatest delicacy" to the very planters whose crops they destroyed. Although he was unable to grant that the annual visits of the ricebird had only damaging consequences for the Carolina planters, Catesby was, at least, willing to entertain the idea that, from a human vantage point, the birds' migrations were more problematic than beneficial. Indeed, as a horticulturist directly involved in the business of transplanting species, Catesby seems to have been surprisingly open-minded about such considerations, moving beyond the obvious desire to promote the commercial interest of the plant trade to reflect on shifts in organic relationships that might affect European settlers adversely as well as on those that might enrich their lives.

Catesby was, in fact, highly conscious of the active role that he himself had taken in trafficking organic materials around the globe and in testing the efficacy of cultivating exotic species in England as well as in America. He was proud of these achievements, describing his successes both in his correspondence and in his publications.[22] He devoted the last period of his life to the production of *Hortus Britanno-Americanus,* a work that he hoped would publicly attest to his years of experience as an experimental horticulturist responsible for the importation of a large number of the North American plants that reached English gardens during the first half of the eighteenth century. In the preface, he explicitly stated the impor-

---

bobolink caused tremendous problems for planters from about the region of the Cape Fear River south through southern Georgia, where rice was cultivated on a large scale. During the migration entire farm families would take to the rice fields and remain from sunrise to sunset, firing shots into the air every few minutes to keep the crop from being destroyed." Alan Feduccia, ed., *Catesby's Birds of Colonia America* (Chapel Hill, N.C., 1985), 126–127.

22. See, for example, Catesby, *Natural History,* I, ix, 27, 29, 39, 49, 53, II, 65, 98, 100, Appendix, 2, 4, 13, 15. Much of Catesby's correspondence to colleagues concerns his role as a supplier of American seeds to colonial and English gardens and his experimentation with foreign introductions. See, for example, Catesby to Johann Jakob Dillenius, Dec. 10, 1737, fol. 16, n.d., fol. 17, n.d., fol. 17a, Sherard MSS, CCII, Dillenius Correspondence, Oxford; Catesby to Sherard, June 20, 1722, Jan. 10, 1724/5, Sherard Letters, CCLIII, 164, 184; Catesby to Peter Collinson, Jan. 5, 1722/3, Botany Library, Autograph Collection, Natural History Museum.

tance of the knowledge he had gained through this endeavor and suggested that his expertise might be put to further use through the employment of his book as a guide to planting:

> By a long acquaintance with the trees and shrubs of America, and a constant attention since for several years to their cultivation here, I have been enabled to make such observations on their constitution, growth, and culture, as may render the management of them easy to those who shall be desirous to inrich their country, and give pleasure to themselves, by planting and increasing these beautiful exotics; and I shall think myself very happy, if this little work may excite any to what in my opinion is evidently a public good.

Forgoing direct reference to himself as a prime purveyor of North American plants, he added, perhaps with some false modesty:

> I shall conclude with one observation, which of however little consequence is nevertheless remarkable, which is, that a small spot of land in America has, within less than half a century, furnished England with a greater variety of trees than has been procured from all the other parts of the world for more than a thousand years past.[23]

Catesby undoubtedly considered himself a key promoter of these many plant introductions to English soil, and he hoped to be recognized for his efforts.

In publishing his *Natural History*, however, Catesby had slightly different objectives in mind. Since he was producing an extensive scientific study of the animals and plants of colonial America rather than a horticultural treatise, he could distance himself from the obligation to focus primarily on the use and monetary value of the subjects he portrayed and described. Instead, through his illustrations and his text, he could offer not only a representation of the ways in which native American animals and plants interact but a close study of the movement of species to and from the Americas as well as from the colonial frontier to areas more densely populated by English settlers. He could also analyze, at times in moral terms, the human interests that set these organisms into motion.

And, yet, in producing his *Natural History*, Catesby would not neglect the practical advantages to be had from the cultivation of exotic species, both in the American colonies and in England. He would state, for example, in the preface to his *Natural History*, that he had concentrated his

23. Catesby, Preface, *Hortus Britanno-Americanus,* ii, iii.

botanical studies on trees and shrubs in order to show "their several Mechanical and other Uses, as in Building, Joynery, Agriculture, . . . Food and Medicine." His work, however, would go beyond issues "related to Commerce" (as he described them) to convey a picture of the organic world in a state of flux and to offer occasional reflections on the disturbing consequences as well as the exciting prospects that might result, for human beings, from such an unsettled state of nature. In his *Natural History* and in his essay "Of Birds of Passage," Catesby alluded to the motivations that drove human beings to explore and colonize beyond their known worlds, serving, by extension, as the catalysts that propelled other organisms to move. That Catesby understood material gain to be the primary object of these ventures is revealed most explicitly in a passage in which he compares the migration of birds in quest of food to "the lucrative Searches of Man thro' distant Regions."[24] Catesby clearly ranked these "lucrative Searches" in a moral hierarchy, judging, for example, the trade networks developed by "*Indian* inhabitants of the *North* and *West*" to procure the leaves of "*Casena*" from "maritim *Indians*" for the production of a medicinal drink in a more favorable light than those developed by Europeans to procure tea from China. The naturalist noted in his *Natural History*:

> By the sour Faces the *Indians* make in drinking this salubrious Liquor, it seems as little agreeable to an *Indian* as to a *European* Palate, and consequently that the Pains and Expenses they are at in procuring it from remote Distances does not proceed from Luxury (as Tea with us from *China*) but from its Virtue, and the Benefit they receive by it.[25]

Catesby's quiet disparagement of the enormous funds and labor expended to procure natural productions for luxurious rather than utilitarian purposes suggests a fuller critique of the activities involved in global exploration, trade, and settlement than might be expected from the naturalist's own work as a supplier of exotic plants as much to ornament gardens as to advance society in practical terms.[26]

24. Catesby, *Natural History*, I, vi, ix; "Of Birds of Passage," Royal Society, *Philosophical Transactions*, XLIV (1747), 443.

25. Catesby, *Natural History*, II, "Account," xv.

26. Catesby valued plants not only as sources for medicines, food, and building materials but as beautiful objects that might increase the aesthetic value of English and colonial

The Natural History *as an Ethical Assessment of English Empire Building*

A subtle but unmistakable moral critique can be discerned in Catesby's picture of human society as he understood its development in Britain's colonial possessions in the Americas—not so much in his visual images as in his verbal descriptions. Occasional passages in his *Natural History* and in his letters to English colleagues suggest that the colonization of the Americas and the trade networks that formed thereby were intermingling human populations as well as plant and animal species from different regions of the globe. When considered collectively, these scattered observations imply that the interactions of different peoples—indeed, their intimate interdependencies—were leading to unprecedented interweavings of cultural customs and patterns of behavior. Catesby's verbal picture of these interweavings parallels the formal analogues that he drew between flora and fauna in the plates of his *Natural History*.

Catesby expressed particular interest, for example, in the ways in which enslaved peoples of African descent were influencing patterns of plant cultivation and the consumption of foods and medicines on the part of their English masters. He articulated this interest most explicitly in his descriptions of crops, such as the arum, that were being introduced to the Americas by English planters who were forced to respond to the nutritional needs of their slaves in order to maintain a strong workforce.[27]

---

gardens. The plant he believed to be the most beautiful of all was one he identified as *"Chamaedaphne foliis Tini"* (commonly known today as mountain laurel), of which he wrote:

> As all Plants have their peculiar Beauties, 'tis difficult to assign to any one an Elegance excelling all others, yet considering the curious Structure of the Flower, and beautiful Appearance of this whole Plant; I know of no Shrub that has a better Claim to it. [*Natural History*, II, 98]

Catesby then described his own attempts as well as those of his colleagues to propagate *Chamaedaphne* in English gardens.

27. For an analysis of the crops brought from Africa to the Americas as a consequence of the slave trade, see Robert L. Hull, "Savoring Africa in the New World," in Herman J. Viola and Carolyn Margolis, eds., *Seeds of Change: A Quincentennial Commemoration* (Washington, D.C., 1991), 161–169. In certain cases, Catesby differentiated between African plants brought to America by Europeans and those brought by Africans, such as "Bunched Guinea Corn" and "Spiked Indian Corn" (*Natural History*, II, "Account," xviii). How Africans themselves transported plants is unclear. For further discussion, including a description of

However, Catesby also noted the importance of the agricultural knowledge of the slaves themselves, who, through cultivation in their own gardens and through the collection of wild plants, were bringing into use certain native American species to the benefit of Africans and Europeans alike. In February 1722/3, for example, he reported to the English botanist William Sherard on the use made of the root of the "Pellitory or Tooth-ach Tree" "by a famous Negro Dr who I have been credibly informed have done great good with the juice of the root boyled or infusion." Adding, "It is an excellent Stomacick and highly cryed up for other its virtues," Catesby sent Sherard live specimens of the plant, hoping to extend its medicinal benefits to England as well.[28]

Catesby repeated his respect for African expertise in the use of medicinal plants in his entry in *The Natural History* on "Snake-Root," which was generally understood in the period as an antidote for snake bites. Although Catesby discounted the efficacy of the plant's juice as a means for counteracting rattlesnake bites that pricked a vein or an artery, he hesitated to reject the powers of snakeroot entirely. Catesby noted that slaves provided the sole access to the plant:

> The usual price of the excellent Root, both in *Virginia* and *Carolina,* is about six pence a Pound when dryed, which is Money hardly earned. Yet the Negro Slaves (who only dig it) employ much of the little time allowed them by their Masters in search of it.[29]

In this entry and in several others relating to the collecting of American animals and plants by slaves, Catesby adopted a somewhat sympathetic tone, remarking, albeit in a small voice, on the restrictions and hardships imposed upon these peoples in their servitude. While pointing out the benefits brought to the lives of English settlers through the knowledge and industry of their African slaves, Catesby also suggested the moral cost involved in the terms of such an association. He wrote with concern of the limited availability of the foods that might nourish slaves adequately and that might be palatable to those from non-European backgrounds. In contrast to the empathy he expressed for Carolina slaves who received the introduction of the African arum as "a welcome Improvement" to their diet, esteeming it "a Blessing," Catesby lamented the fate of those in the

---

African agricultural techniques and practices relating specifically to the natural productions of Carolina, see Wood, *Black Majority,* 121–123; see also note 16, above.

28. Catesby to Sherard, Feb. 7, 1722/3, Sherard Letters, CCLIII, 167.

29. Catesby, *Natural History,* I, 29, II, 41.

"Sugar Island[s]," who, he believed, would "fare very hard" without the ability to hunt for "Land Crabs" to supplement the food provided by their masters. His compassion appears to have gone beyond that of his friend Colonel Byrd, who, Catesby reported, had consented to the demands of his weakened slaves for a diet of Indian corn instead of wheat because Byrd "found it in his Interest to comply with their Request."[30] The dryness of Catesby's remark about Byrd's motives may imply a modest censure of the planter's approach toward the care of his slaves—an approach Catesby had undoubtedly witnessed on his visits to Byrd's plantation during his first expedition to Virginia.

And, yet, Catesby's occasional sympathy for poorly nourished slaves and his scattered statements of admiration for the pharmacological expertise of slaves who provided the broader colonial population with medicinal plants do not constitute a condemnation of slavery in the Americas. Catesby clearly observed practices of English planters toward their slaves that he interpreted as morally reprehensible, and he wished to convey his feelings of pity toward those who suffered from these actions. In general, however, he seems to have applauded the knowledge that Africans, in their bondage, provided their English masters, and approved of the services they rendered as collectors—and even horticultural experimenters.

In fact, Catesby's text on the *"Anona,"* in volume II of *The Natural History,* implies that he considered black peoples of African descent to be lower on the scale of being than Caucasians from Europe. In this entry, he remarked, "All Parts of the Tree have a rank, if not a foetid Smell; nor is the Fruit relished but by very few, except *Negro's.*" The deprecating tenor of the observation that *"Negro's"* stood almost alone in relishing such a foul-smelling fruit diverges markedly from the comparatively compassionate tone of other passages in Catesby's work. Actually, the disparaging observation seems more closely in keeping with Catesby's early decision to purchase a "Negro Boy" to help him with his treks into the Carolina backcountry—a decision reported several times to Sherard without any moral compunction. As the reflection of a point of view that placed black Africans in the lowest rank of the human order, such a remark probably paralleled the views of a patron such as James Brydges, first duke of Chandos, who, as a major investor in the Royal African Company, had a financial interest in the promotion of slave labor in the Americas.[31] Brydges

30. Ibid., II, 33, "Account," xvii.
31. Ibid., II, 85; Catesby to Sherard, Dec. 9, 1722, Jan. 4, 1722/3, Mar. 19, 1723, Sherard

was intimately involved in Catesby's activities as a naturalist in the New World, serving as a principal patron for the Carolina venture and as a subscriber to *The Natural History*. Moreover, in 1721, he had attempted to send Catesby to Africa instead of Carolina—an attempt overridden by other backers of Catesby's Carolina expedition but one to which Catesby himself appears to have voiced no objection.[32] The chance to examine the natural productions of such an exotic continent must have outweighed any negative associations the naturalist might have drawn between his activities on behalf of the Royal African Company and the promotion of England's commercial interests in the slave trade.

In the end, as closely involved with the slave trade as Catesby might have been through patrons like Brydges and the colonial plantation owners on whose lands he examined American flora and fauna, the naturalist seems to have weighed the financial and intellectual benefits from transporting Africans to the New World as slaves against the moral costs. And while he did not decry the forced migration of Africans for the purposes of slave labor, he realized that, like the ricebird, ethical contradictions would follow in the wake of the spreading plantation economy.

Judging Patterns of Interaction between English Settlers and Native Americans

Catesby's unsettled conscience was not confined to his concerns about how Africans were brought to North America, but extended to his assessment of the impact of European settlement itself on native American

---

Letters, CCLIII, 165, 168, 169. On Chandos, see David Brigham, "Mark Catesby and the Patronage of Natural History in the First Half of the Eighteenth Century," above. Another of Catesby's subscribers, the founder of Georgia, James Oglethorpe, also served as a director of the Royal African Company (appointed 1731), and then as deputy governor (1732). However, Oglethorpe's attitudes toward slavery in the colonies appear to have changed over time. Although his original exclusion of black Africans from Georgia was not based on abolitionist sentiments, by the late 1730s he had come to adopt a moral argument against slavery, and he eventually became a firm supporter of abolitionism. See James Oglethorpe, "An Account of the Negroe Insurrection in South Carolina," in Rodney M. Baine, ed., *The Publications of James Edward Oglethorpe* (Athens, Ga., 1994), 252–253; Robert Wright, *A Memoir of General James Oglethorpe, One of the Earliest Reformers of Prison Discipline in England, and the Founder of Georgia, in America* (London, 1867), 81–84; Amos Aschbach Ettinger, *James Edward Oglethorpe, Imperial Idealist* (Oxford, 1936), 150, 179, 307–309, 319; Phinizy Spaulding, *Oglethorpe in America* (Chicago, 1977), 18–19, 49–50, 52, 61–75, 156–161; Betty Wood, *Slavery in Colonial Georgia, 1730–1775* (Athens, Ga., 1984), 5, 16–17, 30–31, 78.

32. Frick and Stearns, *Mark Catesby*, 19–20.

populations. His most detailed description of native American peoples, in his "Account of Carolina, and the Bahama Islands" at the end of *The Natural History,* was drawn largely from the 1714 edition of *A New Voyage to Carolina,* by the surveyor John Lawson—written for promotional ends, with the hope it would serve as the basis for a more general natural history, before Lawson died at the hands of the Tuscarora Indians, in 1711. Catesby justified his appropriation of Lawson's text on the grounds that he also had spent an extensive period of time living with Indian peoples native to Carolina during his venture to the colony and that his own impressions corroborated many of Lawson's views.[33]

Like Lawson, Catesby interpreted native Americans as "Savages" and "Barbarians," occupying, because of their cultural and religious differences, a lower station than Christian Englishmen. He seldom differentiated among the customs of individual Indian nations, choosing instead to generalize his remarks, both pejorative and laudatory, as if they applied equally to all of the native peoples he encountered.[34] Catesby's numerous criticisms included the judgment that native Americans were "indolent" in their approach to the use of natural resources. He expressed wonder over what seemed their persistent willingness to depend wholly on "Prov-

---

33. Catesby, *Natural History,* II, "Account," viii; John Lawson, *A New Voyage to Carolina, Containing the Exact Description and Natural History of That Country* . . . (London, 1709). Lawson's *New Voyage* was republished after his death as *The History of Carolina, Containing the Exact Description and Natural History of that Country* . . . (London, 1714). Catesby might well have been introduced to the work by the London apothecary James Petiver, who was an active member of the circle of naturalists known to Catesby and had served as Lawson's patron. For a discussion of Lawson's collecting activities and a synopsis of his work as an observer of the natural productions of Carolina, see Stearns, *Science in the British Colonies of America,* 305–314; Richard Beale Davis, *Intellectual Life in the Colonial South, 1585–1763,* 3 vols. (Knoxville, Tenn., 1978), I, 56–58, II, 840–844.

34. "Savage" and "Barbarian" are used throughout Catesby's "Account" in *The Natural History* (see, for example, II, viii, xii, xiii).

Concerning the similarities he perceived among Indian peoples, Catesby wrote:

Though the Difference between the Inhabitants of the various Parts of the Old World is such as would startle one's Faith, to consider them all as Descendants of *Adam,* in *America* it is otherwise. The Inhabitants there (at least of the northern Hemisphere, if not from Pole to Pole) seem to be the same People, or sprung from the same Stock; this Affinity in the *Aborigines* of *America* with one another, holds not only in regard to Resemblance, in Form and Features, but their Customs, and Knowledge of Arts are in a manner the same; some little Differences may be in the Industry of one Nation more than others, and a small mechanick Knowledge that some may have more than others. [vii]

idence" for food and raw materials, whereas following the example of English "Industry" and "Oeconomy" in cultivating crops and raising animals would, in his opinion, have made their lives more materially secure. In commenting on their intellectual powers, Catesby also noted with disdain that, while Indians were "generally allowed to have a good Capacity," it was "adapted and even confined to their savage Way of Life." He reported that, although "a great Number of them have been, and still continue to be educated at *Williamsburg*-College in *Virginia*" in order to "inculcate amongst their Brethren true Religion and Virtue," he had "never heard of an Instance conformable to that worthy Intention."[35]

Still, Catesby allowed that the Indian "Disesteem for Literature," or "their Incapacity of attaining it," was "in some measure compensated by a Sagacity or Instinct that *Europeans* are incapable of . . . which is particularly adapted to their Conveniency of Life."[36] He then described with great admiration the abilities of native Americans to navigate their way across vast tracts of unmapped terrain using a myriad of clues imperceptible to the European eye. This passage is, in fact, only one of many that counter the naturalist's more sweeping condemnations of native American character and culture. Throughout *The Natural History,* Catesby expressed his respect for the knowledge possessed by native Americans about the natural world and the ingenious means they devised for living comfortably within it. In his preface, he wrote, for example, of the importance of taking several journeys with a group of Indians toward the mountains above Fort Moore—a frontier outpost near the present site of Augusta, Georgia, used by Catesby as a base for his expeditions into the Carolina backcountry. He was careful to voice particular appreciation for the help and civility extended by his Indian companions:

> To the Hospitality and Assistance of these Friendly *Indians,* I am much indebted, for I not only subsisted on what they shot, but their First Care was to erect a Bark Hut, at the Approach of Rain to keep me and my Cargo from Wet.[37]

Although Catesby had paid one of these Indians to carry his box of paints and dried specimens, he offered his thanks to all who had traveled with him for acts of kindness that he believed approached comradeship.

35. Ibid., ix, xii.
36. Ibid., xii.
37. Ibid., I, viii–ix.

Catesby clearly hoped to convey how fully he had relied upon his traveling companions to show him "not only a Succession of new vegetable Appearances, but most delightful Prospects imaginable," and he even voiced his appreciation for the recreation they had offered him "in Hunting Buffello's, Bears, Panthers, and other wild Beasts."[38] From his opening words, Catesby wished to establish his indebtedness to a group of people who were culturally distinct and who, because of their very differences, had been able to provide him a new set of experiences vital to his understanding of the natural world that he sought to portray and describe.

Catesby's gratitude toward many of the native Americans he encountered was accompanied by a concern over the dramatic loss in population that many Indian nations had suffered since Europeans had arrived in the Americas. In part, he attributed this loss in numbers to the continual wars that had long been waged among Indian nations. However, he also held migrating Europeans responsible for the problem, since they had brought with them the "Vices and Distempers" that he thought "contributed even to extinguish the Race of these Savages, who it is generally believ'd were at first four, if not six times as numerous as they now are."[39] Catesby's particular consternation over smallpox and drunkenness derived not only from his own observations but from similar distress voiced by John Lawson in his *History of Carolina*. Both men lamented the way in which these afflictions were ravaging Indian populations, since they both believed that native American culture had contributed in important ways to the successful development of English society in the New World. Indeed, Lawson, in recognizing that it was English settlers who were dispossessing native Americans of their lands, claimed that native Americans "are really better to us, than we are to them." Not going so far as to suggest that the English incursions be stopped or contained, Lawson proposed that native peoples might be fully assimilated into English life to "become Members of the same Ecclesiastical and Civil Government."[40] Although the sur-

---

38. Ibid., I, viii.

39. Ibid., II, "Account," xv–xvi.

40. Ibid., xiii, xv, xvi; Lawson, *History of Carolina*, 235, 237. On Lawson's sympathetic view of native American peoples, see Davis, *Intellectual Life in the Colonial South*, I, 57; Homer D. Kemp, "John Lawson," in Emory Elliott, ed., *American Colonial Writers, 1606–1734* (Detroit, 1984), 192, vol. XXIV of *Dictionary of Literary Biography*. As a means to achieve assimilation, Lawson proposed intermarriage between native Americans and English colonists, an idea also voiced by William Byrd and Robert Beverley. See Gary B. Nash, "The Image of the Indian in the Southern Colonial Mind," *William and Mary Quarterly*, XXIX (1972), 227–228.

veyor believed that this assimilation would benefit native Americans, he also thought that it would prove advantageous to the English:

> By this Method . . . , we should have a true Knowledge of all the *Indians* Skill in Medicine and Surgery; they would inform us of the Situation of Our Rivers, Lakes, and Tracts of Land in the Lords Dominions, where by their Assistance, greater Discoveries may be made than has been hitherto found out, and by their Accompanying us in our Expeditions, we might civilize a great many other Nations of the Savages, and daily add to our Strength in Trade, and Interest; so that we might be sufficiently enabled to conquer, or maintain our Ground, against all the Enemies to the Crown of *England* in *America,* both Christian and Savage.[41]

For Lawson, a "Reasonable" and "Christian" approach to the treatment of native American peoples that included "Tenderness," "Mildness," and "Clemency" would ensure the protection of English interests on American soil.[42]

Such a programmatic projection of all the benefits that might accrue to the English from the absorption of native Americans into their culture was not voiced as explicitly by Catesby. In fact, the naturalist's somewhat more skeptical view toward the potential success of assimilation was probably conditioned by his knowledge of Lawson's own murder by the very Indians the surveyor purportedly sought to help.[43] Yet Catesby clearly believed that by coming in contact with native Americans through colonization, English settlers had gained enormously in their understanding of the natural resources that could be exploited in the New World.[44]

41. Lawson, *History of Carolina,* 238.

42. Lawson contrasted his recommended approach to conversion and assimilation with that of the Spaniards, who, he believed, had set up their "Christian Banner in a Field of Blood," baptizing "one hundred with the Sword for one at the Font" (ibid., 236–238).

43. Catesby reflected on Lawson's death, "I cannot but here lament the hard Fate of this inquisitive Traveller, who, though partial in his favourable Opinion of the *Barbarians,* died by their bloody Hands, for they roasted him alive in revenge for Injuries they pretended to have received from him" (*Natural History,* II, "Account," viii).

44. Much has been written on the dynamics in colonial Carolina between native Americans and the English colonists who ventured beyond the line of settlement, particularly English traders. For a sampling, see James H. Merrell, *The Indians' New World: Catawbas and Their Neighbors from European Contact through the Era of Removal* (Chapel Hill, N.C., 1989), esp. 30–32, 47–91, 169–170; Merrell, " 'Our Bond of Peace': Patterns of Intercultural Exchange in the Carolina Piedmont," in Peter H. Wood, Gregory A. Waselkov, and Thomas Hatley, eds., *Powhatan's Mantle: Indians in the Colonial Southeast* (Lincoln, Nebr., 1989), 198–222; and

He articulated this conviction quite explicitly in the preparatory drawing that he produced as the model for the first plate of *The Natural History* (Figure 53). In this image of competing raptors (discussed above), Catesby offers the viewer the privileged bird's-eye view of the English naturalist, suggesting that, when analytical thought is applied to empirical observation, the viewer is released from an earthbound perspective and given a wider view.[45] Still, by including the figure paddling in the canoe looking up at the contest between the two birds, Catesby does not allow the viewer to forget the vantage point from which the naturalist's empirical observations of the scene were originally made. The identity of the canoeist is left unclear—the figure might be either a native American or Catesby himself. This ambiguity is, however, central to the meaning of the image, since it suggests Catesby's belief that he had actually assumed the perspective of an Indian when he traveled beyond the bounds of the frontier into country made accessible only by native peoples.

The image is particularly poignant because the act observed by the man in the canoe (as well as by the viewer from above) is theft. Catesby might thus have intended his drawing to allude metaphorically to the recognition by native Americans and Englishmen alike that the appropriation of native American lands—and resources—by English settlers was morally suspect. That such a critique might have been Catesby's private purpose in composing the work is supported by the fact that he dropped almost all reference to thievery in the final composition that he etched for *The Natural History* (Figure 54). The landscape that contextualizes the narra-

---

James Axtell, *The Indians' New South: Cultural Change in the Colonial Southeast* (Baton Rouge, La., 1997), 38–69.

John Lawson's experiences as a surveyor have been considered in this light, but Mark Catesby's experiences as a naturalist have barely been noticed. Scholars have addressed how English colonists and native Americans accommodated each other's culture for financial and material objectives and mutual physical security and scrutinized the cultural misunderstandings that arose, but self-consciously articulated ethical concerns, such as Lawson's and Catesby's, have been slighted. Such an investigation in the spirit of Anthony Pagden's *European Encounters with the New World: From Renaissance to Romanticism* (New Haven, Conn., 1993), focused on Carolina specifically and the southern colonies more generally, would be welcome.

45. On the origins of the use of the bird's-eye view in depicting America's natural productions, see Meyers, "Imposing Order on the Wilderness," in Nygren, *Views and Visions*, 105–108. In conversation, Margaretta Lovell has observed that the dramatic tilt of the horizon line might have been intended to emphasize the marked shift in frame of reference that Catesby wished to offer the viewer of this New World landscape.

tive and renders it comprehensible in the drawing has been eliminated, and the canoeist who gazes at the interaction between the two birds has disappeared. The hawk becomes a simple observer rather than the eagle's victim, and the emotional impact of the scene is diffused.

Catesby probably believed it necessary to transform this morally charged image into a more straightforward specimen drawing for commercial purposes. He undoubtedly realized that potential subscribers to his *Natural History* would hold widely ranging points of view on colonization and that he would imperil the marketability of his work if he problematized established patterns of interaction between English settlers and native Americans in his opening plate.[46] Nonetheless, his subtle understanding of the consequences—both good and bad—that would result from the continued intermingling of these groups can be read in small turns of phrase throughout *The Natural History*. In many ways, the book, in both its plates and its text, constitutes an attempt to explore the outcome of the changing relationships among peoples as well as among animals and plants that were resulting from the highly complicated processes of colonial expansion. If his reflections on the nature of these newly formed associations remain somewhat tentative, it is, at least in part, because the interchanges he was examining so closely were evolving at such a rapid pace. Catesby also faced the difficult task of appealing to widely divergent points of view on these relationships while he formulated opinions of his own—points of view that ranged from those of his English patrons and colonial planter friends to those of the native Americans and the enslaved peoples of African descent whom he encountered on his travels. Nevertheless, Catesby's *Natural History*, along with his other writings, does give a sense of the brilliant techniques that he improvised, as an artist and writer, to represent the shifting scene before him. When considered together,

---

46. The self-conscious care with which Catesby crafted the language describing his own interactions with native Americans indicates his awareness of the varying points of view held by his subscribers toward these peoples. His own views probably corresponded most closely with those of James Oglethorpe, who realized that strong alliances with regional Indian nations, based on trust and mutual aid, would ensure the peaceful establishment of Georgia more effectively than confrontation. On Oglethorpe's Indian policy, see James Edward Oglethorpe, "A Description of the Indians in Georgia" (1733) and "An Account of Carolina and Georgia" (1739), in Baine, ed., *The Publications of James Edward Oglethorpe*, 241–245, 249–250; Wright, *A Memoir of General James Oglethorpe*, 62–71, 90, 94–95, 125–135, 190, 219, 223; Leslie F. Church, *Oglethorpe: A Study of Philanthropy in England and Georgia* (London, 1932), 110, 113–140; Spaulding, *Oglethorpe in America*, 49, 76–97, 156, 161–162.

Catesby's pictures and his words indicate that his own immersion in the building of English colonial society did not hinder him from pondering the practical and moral repercussions of moving people and natural productions around the globe. Indeed, this very immersion allowed him to consider these repercussions from a close vantage point and to draw his own at times unsettling conclusions about empire's nature.

Index

Italic folios indicate illustrations.

Notes on the Contributors

Amy R. W. Meyers, curator of American Art at the Huntington, is a contributor to *Mark Catesby's "Natural History" of America: The Watercolors from the Royal Library, Windsor Castle,* by Henrietta McBurney, and editor of *Art and Science in America: Issues of Representation.*

Margaret Beck Pritchard is curator of prints, maps, and wallpaper at the Colonial Williamsburg Foundation and the coauthor (with Virginia Lascara Sites) of *William Byrd II and His Lost History: Engravings of the Americas.*

David Brigham is curator of American Art at the Worcester Art Museum and author of *Public Culture in the Early Republic: Peale's Museum and Its Audience.*

Joyce E. Chaplin is associate professor of history at Vanderbilt University and the author of *An Anxious Pursuit: Agricultural Innovation and Modernity in the Lower South, 1730–1815.*

Mark Laird, a garden historian and international landscape consultant, is adjunct professor in the Faculty of Architecture, Landscape, and Design, University of Toronto, and author of *The Flowering of the Landscape Garden: English Pleasure Grounds, 1720–1800.*

Therese O'Malley is associate dean, Center for Advanced Study in the Visual Arts, National Gallery of Art, author of numerous essays on gardens, and coeditor (with Marc Treib) of *Regional Garden Design in the United States,* Dumbarton Oaks Colloquium on the History of Landscape Architecture.